MW01599625

Selections from Previous Works. With remarks on Mr. G. J. Romanes' "Mental Evolution in Animals," and a Psalm of Montreal.

Samuel Butler, George John Romanes

Selections from Previous Works. With remarks on Mr. G. J. Romanes' "Mental Evolution in Animals," and a Psalm of Montreal.

Butler, Samuel
British Library, Historical Print Editions
British Library
Romanes, George John
1884
viii. 325 p. ; 8°.
12272.bb.7.

The BiblioLife Network

This project was made possible in part by the BiblioLife Network (BLN), a project aimed at addressing some of the huge challenges facing book preservationists around the world. The BLN includes libraries, library networks, archives, subject matter experts, online communities and library service providers. We believe every book ever published should be available as a high-quality print reproduction; printed on- demand anywhere in the world. This insures the ongoing accessibility of the content and helps generate sustainable revenue for the libraries and organizations that work to preserve these important materials.

The following book is in the "public domain" and represents an authentic reproduction of the text as printed by the original publisher. While we have attempted to accurately maintain the integrity of the original work, there are sometimes problems with the original book or micro-film from which the books were digitized. This can result in minor errors in reproduction. Possible imperfections include missing and blurred pages, poor pictures, markings and other reproduction issues beyond our control. Because this work is culturally important, we have made it available as part of our commitment to protecting, preserving, and promoting the world's literature.

GUIDE TO FOLD-OUTS, MAPS and OVERSIZED IMAGES

In an online database, page images do not need to conform to the size restrictions found in a printed book. When converting these images back into a printed bound book, the page sizes are standardized in ways that maintain the detail of the original. For large images, such as fold-out maps, the original page image is split into two or more pages.

Guidelines used to determine the split of oversize pages:

• Some images are split vertically; large images require vertical and horizontal splits.
• For horizontal splits, the content is split left to right.
• For vertical splits, the content is split from top to bottom.
• For both vertical and horizontal splits, the image is processed from top left to bottom right.

12272 bb 7

SELECTIONS

FROM

PREVIOUS WORKS

*WITH REMARKS ON MR. G. J. ROMANES' "MENTAL
EVOLUTION IN ANIMALS"*

AND

A PSALM OF MONTREAL

BY

SAMUEL BUTLER

K

" The course of true science, like that of true love, never did run smooth."
PROFESSOR TYNDALL, *Pall Mall Gazette*, Oct. 30, 1883.

(OP. 7)

LONDON
TRÜBNER & CO., LUDGATE HILL
1884
[*All rights reserved*]

Ballantyne Press
BALLANTYNE, HANSON AND CO.
EDINBURGH AND LONDON

PREFACE.

—o—

I DELAYED these pages some weeks in order to give Mr. Romanes an opportunity of explaining his statement that Canon Kingsley wrote about instinct and inherited memory in *Nature*, Jan. 18, 1867.* I wrote to the *Athenæum* (Jan. 26, 1884) and pointed out that *Nature* did not begin to appear till nearly three years after the date given by Mr. Romanes, and that there was nothing from Canon Kingsley on the subject of instinct and inherited memory in any number of *Nature* up to the date of Canon Kingsley's death. I also asked for the correct reference.

This Mr. Romanes has not thought it incumbent upon him to give. I am told I ought not to have expected him to give it, inasmuch as it is no longer usual for men of any but the lowest scientific standing to correct their misstatements when they are brought to book. Science is made for Fellows of the Royal Society, and for no one else, not Fellows of the Royal Society for science; and if the having achieved a certain position should still involve being obliged to be as scrupulous and accurate as other people, what is the good of the position? This view of the matter is practical, but I

* See page 234 of this book.

regret that Mr. Romanes should have taken it, for his having done so has prevented my being able to tell the reader what Canon Kingsley said about memory and instinct, and this he might have been glad to know.

I suspect, however, that what Canon Kingsley said was after all not very important. If it had been, Mr. Romanes would have probably told us what it was in his own book. I should think it possible that Mr. Romanes—not finding Canon Kingsley's words important enough to be quoted, or even referred to correctly, or never having seen them himself and not knowing exactly what they were, yet being anxious to give every one, and more particularly Canon Kingsley, his due—felt that this was an occasion on which he might fairly take advantage of his position and say at large whatever he was in the humour for saying at the moment.

I should not have thought this possible if I had not ere now had reason to set Mr. Romanes down as one who was not likely to be squeamish about trifles. Nevertheless, on this present occasion I certainly did think that he had only made a slip such as we all make sometimes, and such as he would gladly take the earliest opportunity to correct. As it is, I do not know what to think, except that D.C.L.'s and F.R.S.'s seem to be made of much the same frail materials as we ordinary mortals are.

As regards the extracts from my previous books given in this volume, I should say that I have revised and corrected the original text throughout, and intro-

duced a sentence or two here and there, but have nowhere made any important alteration. I regret greatly
that want of space has prevented me from being able
to give the chapters from Life and Habit on "The
Abeyance of Memory," and "What we should expect
to find if Differentiations of Structure and Instinct are
mainly due to Memory;" it is in these chapters that an
explanation of many phenomena is given, of which, so
far as I know, no explanation of any kind had been
previously attempted, and in which phenomena having
apparently so little connection as the sterility of hybrids,
the principle underlying longevity, the resumption of
feral characteristics, the sterility of many animals under
confinement, are not only made intelligible but are
shown to be all part and parcel of the same story—
all being explicable as soon as Memory is made the
main factor of heredity.

Feb. 16, 1884.

CONTENTS.

——o——

+

SELECTIONS FROM EREWHON.*

——o——

CURRENT OPINIONS.

(CHAPTER X. OF EREWHON.)

THIS is what I gathered. That in that country if a
man falls into ill health, or catches any disorder,
or fails bodily in any way before he is seventy years
old, he is tried before a jury of his countrymen, and
if convicted is held up to public scorn and sentenced
more or less severely as the case may be. There are
subdivisions of illnesses into crimes and misdemean-
ours as with offences amongst ourselves—a man being
punished very heavily for serious illness, while failure
of eyes or hearing in one over sixty-five who has had
good health hitherto is dealt with by fine only, or imprisonment in default of payment.

But if a man forges a cheque, sets his house on fire,
robs with violence from the person, or does any other
such things as are criminal in our own country, he is
either taken to a hospital and most carefully tended at
the public expense, or if he is in good circumstances,
he lets it be known to all his friends that he is suffering
from a severe fit of immorality, just as we do when we
are ill, and they come and visit him with great solicitude, and inquire with interest how it all came about,

* The first edition of Erewhon was published in the spring of 1872.

A

what symptoms first showed themselves, and so forth, ·—questions which he will answer with perfect unreserve; for bad conduct, though considered no less deplorable than illness with ourselves, and as unquestionably indicating something wrong with the individual who misbehaves, is nevertheless held to be the result of either pre-natal or post-natal misfortune. I should add that under certain circumstances poverty and ill luck are also considered criminal.

Accordingly, there exists a class of men trained in soul-craft, whom they call straighteners, as nearly as I can translate a word which literally means " one who bendeth back the crooked." These men practise much as medical men in England, and receive a quasi-surreptitious fee on every visit. They are treated with the same unreserve and obeyed just as readily as our own doctors—that is to say, on the whole sufficiently —because people know that it is their interest to get well as soon as they can, and that they will not be scouted as they would be if their bodies were out of order, even though they may have to undergo a very painful course of treatment.

When I say that they will not be scouted, I do not mean that an Erewhonian offender will suffer no social inconvenience. Friends will fall away from him because of his being less pleasant company, just as we ourselves are disclined to make companions of those who are either poor or poorly. No one with a due sense of self-respect will place himself on an equality in the matter of affection with those who are less lucky than himself in birth, health, money, good looks, capacity, or anything else. Indeed, that dislike and even disgust should be felt by the fortunate for the unfortunate, or at any rate for those who have been discovered to have met with any of the more serious and less familiar misfortunes, is not only natural, but desirable for any society, whether of man or brute; what progress either of body or soul had been otherwise possible ? The fact therefore that the Erewhonians attach none of that guilt to crime which they do to physical ailments, does not prevent the more selfish among them from neglecting a friend who has robbed a bank, for instance, till he has fully recovered; but it does prevent them from even thinking of treating criminals with that contemptuous tone which would seem to say, "I, if I were you, should be a better man than you are," a tone which is held quite reasonable in regard to physical ailment.

Hence, though they conceal ill health by every kind of cunning, they are quite open about even the most flagrant mental diseases, should they happen to exist, which to do the people justice is not often. Indeed, there are some who, so to speak, are spiritual valetudinarians, and who make themselves exceedingly ridiculous by their nervous supposition that they are wicked, while they are very tolerable people all the time. This however is exceptional; and on the whole they use much the same reserve or unreserve about the state of their moral welfare as we do about our health.

It has followed that all the ordinary greetings among ourselves, such as, How do you do? and the like, are considered signs of gross ill-breeding; nor do the politer classes tolerate even such a common complimentary remark as telling a man that he was looking well. They salute each other with, "I hope you are good this morning;" or "I hope you have recovered from the snappishness from which you were suffering when I last saw you;" and if the person saluted has not been good, or is still snappish, he says so, and is condoled with accordingly. Nay, the straighteners have gone so far as to give names from the hypothetical language (as taught at the Colleges of Unreason) to all known forms of mental indisposition, and have classified them according to a system of their own, which, though I could not understand it, seemed to work well in practice, for they are always able to tell a man what is the matter with him as soon as they have heard his story, and their familiarity with the long names assures him that they thoroughly understand his case.

.   .   .   .   .   .

We in England rarely shrink from telling our doctor what is the matter with us merely through the fear that he will hurt us. We let him do his worst upon us, and stand it without a murmur, because we are not scouted for being ill, and because we know the doctor is doing his best to cure us, and can judge of our case better than we can; but we should conceal all illness if we were treated as the Erewhonians are when they have anything the matter with them; we should do as we do with our moral and intellectual diseases,—we should feign health with the most consummate art, till we were found out, and should hate a single flogging given by way of mere punishment more than the amputation of a limb, if it were kindly and courteously performed from a wish to help us out of our difficulty, and with the full consciousness on the part of the doctor that it was only by an accident of constitution that he was not in the like plight himself. So the Erewhonians take a flogging once a week, and a diet of bread and water for two or three months together, whenever their straightener recommends it.

I do not suppose that even my host, on having swindled a confiding widow out of the whole of her property, was put to more actual suffering than a man will readily undergo at the hands of an English doctor. And yet he must have had a very bad time of it. The sounds I heard were sufficient to show that his pain was exquisite, but he never shrank from undergoing it. He was quite sure that it did him good; and I think he was right. I cannot believe that that man will ever embezzle money again. He may—but it will be a long time before he does so.

During my confinement in prison, and on my journey, I had discovered much of the above; but it still seemed new and strange, and I was in constant fear of committing some rudeness from my inability to look at things from the same stand-point as my neighbours; but after a few weeks' stay with the Nosnibors I got to understand things better, especially on having heard all about my host's illness, of which he told me fully and repeatedly.

It seemed he had been on the Stock Exchange of the city for many years and had amassed enormous wealth, without exceeding the limits of what was generally considered justifiable or at any rate permissible dealing; but at length on several occasions he had become aware of a desire to make money by fraudulent representations, and had actually dealt with two or three sums in a way which had made him rather uncomfortable. He had unfortunately made light of it and pooh-poohed the ailment, until circumstances eventually presented themselves which enabled him to cheat upon a very considerable scale;—he told me what they were, and they were about as bad as anything could be, but I need not detail them;—he seized the opportunity, and became aware when it was too late that he must be seriously out of order. He had neglected himself too long.

He drove home at once, broke the news to his wife and daughters as gently as he could, and sent off for one of the most celebrated straighteners of the kingdom to a consultation with the family practitioner, for the case was plainly serious. On the arrival of the straightener he told his story, and expressed his fear that his morals must be permanently impaired.

The eminent man reassured him with a few cheering words, and then proceeded to make a more careful diagnosis of the case. He inquired concerning Mr. Nosnibor's parents—had their moral health been good? He was answered that there had not been anything seriously amiss with them, but that his maternal grandfather, whom he was supposed to resemble somewhat in person, had been a consummate scoundrel and had ended his days in a hospital,—while a brother of his father's, after having led a most flagitious life for many years, had been at last cured by a philosopher of a new school, which as far as I could understand it bore much the same relation to the old as homœopathy to allopathy. The straightener shook his head at this, and laughingly replied that the cure must have been due to nature. After a few more questions he wrote a prescription and departed.

I saw the prescription. It ordered a fine to the State of double the money embezzled; no food but bread and milk for six months, and a severe flogging once a month for twelve. He had received his eleventh flogging on the day of my arrival. I saw him later on the same afternoon, and he was still twinged; but even though he had been minded to do so (which he showed no sign of being), there would have been no escape from following out the straightener's prescription, for the so-called sanitary laws of Erewhon are very rigorous, and unless the straightener was satisfied that his orders had been obeyed, the patient would have been taken to a hospital (as the poor are), and would have been much worse off. Such at least is the law, but it is never necessary to enforce it.

On a subsequent occasion I was present at an interview between Mr. Nosnibor and the family straightener, who was considered competent to watch the completion of the cure. I was struck with the delicacy with which he avoided even the remotest semblance of inquiry after the physical well-being of his patient, though there was a certain yellowness about my host's eyes which argued a bilious habit of body. To have taken notice of this would have been a gross breach of professional etiquette. I am told that a straightener sometimes thinks it right to glance at the possibility of some slight physical disorder if he finds it important in order to assist him in his diagnosis; but the answers which he gets are generally untrue or evasive, and he forms his own conclusions upon the matter as well as he can.

Sensible men have been known to say that the straightener should in strict confidence be told of every physical ailment that is likely to bear upon the case; but people are naturally shy of doing this, for they do not like lowering themselves in the opinion of the straightener, and his ignorance of medical science is supreme. I heard of one lady however who had the hardihood to confess that a furious outbreak of ill-humour and extravagant fancies for which she was seeking advice was possibly the result of indisposition.

"You should resist that," said the straightener, in a kind, but grave voice; "we can do nothing for the bodies of our patients; such matters are beyond our province, and I desire that I may hear no further particulars." The lady burst into tears, promised faithfully that she would never be unwell again, and kept her word.

To return however to Mr. Nosnibor. As the afternoon wore on many carriages drove up with callers to inquire how he had stood his flogging. It had been very severe, but the kind inquiries upon every side gave him great pleasure, and he assured me that he felt almost tempted to do wrong again by the solicitude with which his friends had treated him during his recovery: in this I need hardly say that he was not serious.

During the remainder of my stay in the country Mr. Nosnibor was constantly attentive to his business, and largely increased his already great possessions; but I never heard a whisper to the effect of his having been indisposed a second time, or made money by other than the most strictly honourable means. I did hear afterwards in confidence that there had been reason to believe that his health had been not a little affected by the straightener's treatment, but his friends did not choose to be over curious upon the subject, and on his return to his affairs it was by common consent passed over as hardly criminal in one who was otherwise so much afflicted. For they regard bodily ailments as the more venial in proportion as they have been produced by causes independent of the constitution. Thus if a person ruin his health by excessive indulgence at the table, or by drinking, they count it to be almost a part of the mental disease which brought it about, and so it goes for little, but they have no mercy on such illnesses as fevers or catarrhs or lung diseases, which to us appear to be beyond the control of the individual. They are only more lenient towards the diseases of the young—such as measles, which they think to be like sowing one's wild oats—and look over them as pardonable indiscretions if they have not been too serious, and if they are atoned for by complete subsequent recovery.

AN EREWHONIAN TRIAL.

(CHAPTER XI. OF EREWHON.)

I SHALL best convey to the reader an idea of the entire perversion of thought which exists among this extraordinary people, by describing the public trial of a man who was accused of pulmonary consumption—an offence which was punished with death until quite recently. The trial did not take place till I had been some months in the country, and I am deviating from chronological order in giving an account of it here; but I had perhaps better do so in order to exhaust this subject before proceeding with others.

The prisoner was placed in the dock, and the jury were sworn much as in Europe; almost all our own modes of procedure were reproduced, even to the requiring the prisoner to plead guilty or not guity. He pleaded not guilty and the case proceeded. The evidence for the prosecution was very strong, but I must do the court the justice to observe that the trial was absolutely impartial. Counsel for the prisoner was allowed to urge everything that could be said in his defence.

The line taken was that the prisoner was simulating consumption in order to defraud an insurance company, from which he was about to buy an annuity, and that he hoped thus to obtain it on more advantageous terms.

If this could have been shown to be the case he would
have escaped criminal prosecution, and been sent to a
hospital as for moral ailment. The view however was
one which could not be reasonably sustained, in spite
of all the ingenuity and eloquence of one of the most
celebrated advocates of the country. The case was
only too clear, for the prisoner was almost at the point
of death, and it was astonishing that he had not been
tried and convicted long previously. His coughing
was incessant during the whole trial, and it was all that
the two jailers in charge of him could do to keep him
on his legs until it was over.

The summing up of the judge was admirable. He
dwelt upon every point that could be construed in
favour of the prisoner, but as he proceeded it became
clear that the evidence was too convincing to admit of
doubt, and there was but one opinion in the court as
to the impending verdict when the jury retired from
the box. They were absent for about ten minutes, and
on their return the foreman pronounced the prisoner
guilty. There was a faint murmur of applause but it
was instantly repressed. The judge then proceeded to
pronounce sentence in words which I can never forget,
and which I copied out into a note-book next day from
the report that was published in the leading newspaper.
I must condense it somewhat, and nothing which I
could say would give more than a faint idea of the
solemn, not to say majestic, severity with which it was
delivered. The sentence was as follows :—

"Prisoner at the bar, you have been accused of the
great crime of labouring under pulmonary consumption, and after an impartial trial before a jury of your
countrymen, you have been found guilty. Against
the justice of the verdict I can say nothing: the

evidence against you was conclusive, and it only remains for me to pass such a sentence upon you, as
shall satisfy the ends of the law.   That sentence must
be a very severe one.   It pains me much to see one
who is yet so young, and whose prospects in life were
otherwise so excellent, brought to this distressing condition by a constitution which I can only regard as
radically vicious ; but yours is no case for compassion :
this is not your first offence : you have led a career
of crime, and have only profited by the leniency shown
you upon past occasions, to offend yet more seriously
against the laws and institutions of your country.   You
were convicted of aggravated bronchitis last year : and
I find that though you are now only twenty-three years
old, you have been imprisoned on no less than fourteen
occasions for illnesses of a more or less hateful character ; in fact, it is not too much to say that you have
spent the greater part of your life in a jail.

" It is all very well for you to say that you came of
unhealthy parents, and had a severe accident in your
childhood which permanently undermined your constitution ; excuses such as these are the ordinary re-
fuge of the criminal ; but they cannot for one moment
be listened to by the ear of justice.   I am not here to
enter upon curious metaphysical questions as to the
origin of this or that—questions to which there would
be no end were their introduction once tolerated, and
which would result in throwing the only guilt on the
primordial cell, or perhaps even on the elementary gases.
There is no question of how you came to be wicked,
but only this—namely, are you wicked or not ?   This
has been decided in the affirmative, neither can I hesitate for a single moment to say that it has been decided
justly.   You are a bad and dangerous person, and stand

branded in the eyes of your fellow-countrymen with one of the most heinous known offences.

"It is not my business to justify the law: the law may in some cases have its inevitable hardships, and I may feel regret at times that I have not the option of passing a less severe sentence than I am compelled to do. But yours is no such case; on the contrary, had not the capital punishment for consumption been abolished, I should certainly inflict it now.

"It is intolerable that an example of such terrible enormity should be allowed to go at large unpunished. Your presence in the society of respectable people would lead the less able-bodied to think more lightly of all forms of illness; neither can it be permitted that you should have the chance of corrupting unborn beings who might hereafter pester you. The unborn must not be allowed to come near you: and this not so much for their protection (for they are our natural enemies), as for our own; for since they will not be utterly gainsaid, it must be seen to that they shall be quartered upon those who are least likely to corrupt them.

"But independently of this consideration, and independently of the physical guilt which attaches itself to a crime so great as yours, there is yet another reason why we should be unable to show you mercy, even if we are inclined to do so. I refer to the existence of a class of men who lie hidden among us, and who are called physicians. Were the severity of the law or the current feeling of the country to be relaxed never so slightly, these abandoned persons, who are now compelled to practise secretly, and who can be consulted only at the greatest risk, would become frequent visitors in every household; their organisation and

their intimate acquaintance with all family secrets
would give them a power, both social and political,
which nothing could resist. .The head of the household would become subordinate to the family doctor,
who would interfere between man and wife, between
master and servant, until the doctors should be the
only depositaries of power in the nation, and have all
that we hold precious at their mercy. A time of
universal dephysicalisation would ensue; medicine-
vendors of all kinds would abound in our streets and
advertise in all our newspapers. There is one remedy
for this, and one only. It is that which the laws of
this country have long received and acted upon, and
consists in the sternest repression of all diseases what-
soever, as soon as their existence is made manifest to
the eye of the law. Would that that eye were far
more piercing than it is.

"But I will enlarge no further upon things that are
themselves so obvious. You may say that it is not
your fault. The answer is ready enough at hand, and
it amounts to this—that if you had been born of
healthy and well-to-do parents, and been well taken
care of when you were a child, you would never have
offended against the laws of your country, nor found
yourself in your present disgraceful position. If you
tell me that you had no hand in your parentage and
education, and that it is therefore unjust to lay these
things to your charge, I answer that whether your
being in a consumption is your fault or no, it is a fault
in you, and it is my duty to see that against such faults
as this the commonwealth shall be protected. You
may say that it is your misfortune to be criminal; I
answer that it is your crime to be unfortunate.

"I do not hesitate therefore to sentence you to imprisonment, with hard labour, for the rest of your miserable existence. During that period I would earnestly entreat you to repent of these wrongs you have done already, and to entirely reform the constitution of your whole body. I entertain but little hope that you will pay attention to my advice; you are already far too abandoned. Did it rest with myself, I should add nothing in mitigation of the sentence which I have passed, but it is the merciful provision of the law that even the most hardened criminal shall be allowed some one of the three official remedies, which is to be prescribed at the time of his conviction. I shall therefore order that you receive two tablespoonfuls of castor-oil daily, until the pleasure of the court be further known."

When the sentence was concluded, the prisoner acknowledged in a few scarcely audible words that he was justly punished, and that he had had a fair trial. He was then removed to the prison from which he was never to return. There was a second attempt at applause when the judge had finished speaking, but as before it was at once repressed; and though the feeling of the court was strongly against the prisoner, there was no show of any violence against him, if one may except a little hooting from the bystanders when he was being removed in the prisoners' van. Indeed, nothing struck me more during my whole sojourn in the country, than the general respect for law and order.

MALCONTENTS.

(PART OF CHAPTER XII. OF EREWHON.)

I WRITE with great diffidence, but it seems to me
that there is no unfairness in punishing people
for their misfortunes, or rewarding them for their
sheer good luck: it is the normal condition of human
life that this should be done, and no right-minded
person will complain at being subjected to the common
treatment. There is no alternative open to us. It
is idle to say that men are not responsible for their
misfortunes. What is responsibility? Surely to be
responsible means to be liable to have to give an
answer should it be demanded, and all things which
live are responsible for their lives and actions should
society see fit to question them through the mouth of
its authorised agent.

What is the offence of a lamb that we should rear
it, and tend it, and lull it into security, for the express
purpose of killing it? Its offence is the misfortune
of being something which society wants to eat, and
which cannot defend itself. This is ample. Who
shall limit the right of society except society itself?
And what consideration for the individual is tolerable
unless society be the gainer thereby? Wherefore
should a man be so richly rewarded for having been
son to a millionaire, were it not clearly provable that

the common welfare is thus better furthered? We cannot seriously detract from a man's merit in having been the son of a rich father without imperilling our own tenure of things which we do not wish to jeopardise; if this were otherwise we should not let him keep his money for a single hour; we would have it ourselves at once. For property *is* robbery, but then we are all robbers or would-be robbers together, and have found it expedient to organise our thieving, as we have found it to organise our lust and our revenge. Property, marriage, the law; as the bed to the river, so rule and convention to the instinct.

But to return. Even in England a man on board a ship with yellow fever is held responsible for his mischance, no matter what his being kept in quarantine may cost him. He may catch the fever and die; we cannot help it; he must take his chance as other people do; but surely it would be desperate unkindness to add contumely to our self-protection, unless, indeed, we believe that contumely is one of our best means of self-protection. Again, take the case of maniacs. We say that they are irresponsible for their actions, but we take good care, or ought to take good care, that they shall answer to us for their insanity, and we imprison them in what we call an asylum (that modern sanctuary!) if we do not like their answers. This is a strange kind of irresponsibility. What we ought to say is that we can afford to be satisfied with a less satisfactory answer from a lunatic than from one who is not mad, because lunacy is less infectious than crime.

We kill a serpent if we go in danger by it, simply for being such and such a serpent in such and such a place; but we never say that the serpent has only

B

itself to blame for not having been a harmless creature. Its crime is that of being the thing which it
is: but this is a capital offence, and we are right in
killing it out of the way, unless we think it more
dangerous to do so than to let it escape; nevertheless
we pity the creature, even though we kill it.

But in the case of him whose trial I have described
above, it was impossible that any one in the court
should not have known that it was but by an accident
of birth and circumstances that he was not himself
also in a consumption; and yet none thought that it
disgraced them to hear the judge give vent to the
most cruel truisms about him. The judge himself
was a kind and thoughtful person. He was a man of
magnificent and benign presence. He was evidently
of an iron constitution, and his face wore an expression
of the maturest wisdom and experience; yet for all
this, old and learned as he was, he could not see things
which one would have thought would have been
apparent even to a child. He could not emancipate
himself from, nay, it did not even occur to him to feel,
the bondage of the ideas in which he had been born
and bred. So was it with the jury and bystanders;
and—most wonderful of all—so was it even with the
prisoner. Throughout he seemed fully impressed with
the notion that he was being dealt with justly: he
saw nothing wanton in his being told by the judge
that he was to be punished, not so much as a necessary protection to society (although this was not
entirely lost sight of), as because he had not been
better born and bred than he was. But this led me
to hope that he suffered less than he would have done
if he had seen the matter in the same light that I did.
And, after all, justice is relative.

I may here mention that only a few years before my arrival in the country, the treatment of all convicted invalids had been much more barbarous than now; for no physical remedy was provided, and prisoners were put to the severest labour in all sorts of weather, so that most of them soon succumbed to the extreme hardships which they suffered; this was supposed to be beneficial in some ways, inasmuch as it put the country to less expense for the maintenance of its criminal class; but the growth of luxury had induced a relaxation of the old severity, and a sensitive age would no longer tolerate what appeared to be an excess of rigour, even towards the most guilty; moreover, it was found that juries were less willing to convict, and justice was often cheated because there was no alternative between virtually condemning a man to death and letting him go free; it was also held that the country paid in recommittals for its overseverity; for those who had been imprisoned even for trifling ailments were often permanently disabled by their imprisonment; and when a man has been once convicted, it was probable he would never afterwards be long off the hands of the country.

These evils had long been apparent and recognised; yet people were too indolent, and too indifferent to suffering not their own, to bestir themselves about putting an end to them, until at last a benevolent reformer devoted his whole life to effecting the necessary changes. He divided illnesses into three classes—those affecting the head, the trunk, and the lower limbs —and obtained an enactment that all diseases of the head, whether internal or external, should be treated with laudanum, those of the body with castor-oil, and those of the lower limbs with an embrocation of strong sulphuric acid and water. It may be said that the classification was not sufficiently careful, and that the remedies were ill chosen; but it is a hard thing to initiate any reform, and it was necessary to familiarise the public mind with the principle, by inserting the thin end of the wedge first: it is not therefore to be wondered at that among so practical a people there should still be some room for improvement. The mass of the nation are well pleased with existing arrangements, and believe that their treatment of criminals leaves little or nothing to be desired; but there is an energetic minority who hold what are considered to be extreme opinions, and who are not at all disposed to rest contented until the principle lately admitted has been carried further.

THE MUSICAL BANKS.

(CHAPTER XIV. OF EREWHON.)

ON my return to the drawing-room, I found the ladies were just putting away their work and preparing to go out. I asked them where they were going. They answered with a certain air of reserve that they were going to the bank to get some money.

Now I had already collected that the mercantile affairs of the Erewhonians were conducted on a totally different system from our own; I had however gathered little hitherto, except that they had two distinct commercial systems, of which the one appealed more strongly to the imagination than anything to which we are accustomed in Europe, inasmuch as the banks conducted upon this system were decorated in the most profuse fashion, and all mercantile transactions were accompanied with music, so that they were called musical banks though the music was hideous to a European ear.

As for the system itself I never understood it, neither can I do so now: they have a code in connection with it, which I have no doubt they themselves understand, but no foreigner can hope to do so. One rule runs into and against another as in a most complicated grammar, or as in Chinese pronunciation, wherein I am told the slightest change in accentuation or tone of voice alters the meaning of a whole sentence.

Whatever is incoherent in my description must be referred to the fact of my never having attained to a full comprehension of the subject.

So far however as I could collect anything certain, they appeared to have two entirely distinct currencies, each under the control of its own banks and mercantile codes. The one of them (the one with the musical banks) was supposed to be *the* system, and to give out the currency in which all monetary transactions should be carried on. As far as I could see, all who wished to be considered respectable, did keep a certain amount of this currency at these banks; nevertheless, if there is one thing of which I am more sure than another it is that the amount so kept was but a very small part of their possessions. I think they took the money, put it into the bank, and then drew it out again, repeating the process day by day, and keeping a certain amount of currency for this purpose and no other, while they paid the expenses of the bank with the other coinage. I am sure the managers and cashiers of the musical banks were not paid in their own currency. Mr. Nosnibor used to go to these musical banks, or rather to the great mother bank of the city, sometimes but not very often. He was a pillar of one of the other kind of banks, though he held some minor office also in these. The ladies generally went alone; as indeed was the case in most families, except on some few great annual occasions.

I had long wanted to know more of this strange system, and had the greatest desire to accompany my hostess and her daughters. I had seen them go out almost every morning since my arrival, and had noticed that they carried their purses in their hands, not exactly ostentatiously, yet just so as that those who met them should see whither they were going.   I had never yet been asked to go with them myself.

It is not easy to convey a person's manner by words, and I can hardly give any idea of the peculiar feeling which came upon me whenever I saw the ladies in the hall, with their purses in their hands, and on the point of starting for the bank.   There was a something of regret, a something as though they would wish to take me with them, but did not like to ask me, and yet as though I were hardly to ask to be taken. I was determined however to bring matters to an issue with my hostess about my going with them, and after a little parleying and many inquiries as to whether I was perfectly sure that I myself wished to go, it was decided that I might do so.

We passed through several streets of more or less considerable houses, and at last turning round a corner we came upon a large piazza, at the end of which was a magnificent building, of a strange but noble architecture and of great antiquity.   It did not open directly on to the piazza, there being a screen, through which was an archway, between the piazza and the actual precincts of the bank.   On passing under the archway we found ourselves upon a green sward, round which there ran an arcade or cloister, while in front of us uprose the majestic towers of the bank and its venerable front, which was divided into three deep recesses and adorned with all sorts of marbles and many sculptures.   On either side there were beautiful old trees wherein the birds were busy by the hundred, and a number of quaint but substantial houses of singularly comfortable appearance; they were situated in the midst of orchards and gardens, and gave me an impression of great peace and plenty.

Indeed it had been no error to say that this building was one which appealed to the imagination; it did more—it carried both imagination and judgment by storm. It was an epic in stone and marble; neither had I ever seen anything in the least comparable to it. I was completely charmed and melted. I felt more conscious of the existence of a remote past. One knows of this always, but the knowledge is never so living as in the actual presence of some witness to the life of bygone ages. I felt how short a space of human life was the period of our own existence. I was more impressed with my own littleness, and much more inclinable to believe that the people whose sense of the fitness of things was equal to the upraising of so serene a handiwork, were hardly likely to be wrong in the conclusions they might come to upon any subject. My feeling certainly was that the currency of this bank must be the right one.

We crossed the sward and entered the building. If the outside had been impressive the inside was even more so. It was very lofty and divided into several parts by walls which rested upon massive pillars; the windows were filled with glass, on which had been painted the principal commercial incidents of the bank for many ages. In a remote part of the building there were men and boys singing; this was the only disturbing feature, for as the gamut was still unknown, there was no music in the country which could be agreeable to a European ear. The singers seemed to have derived their inspirations from the songs of birds and the wailing of the wind, which last they tried to imitate in melancholy cadences which at times degenerated into a howl. To my thinking the noise was hideous, but it produced a great effect upon my companions, who professed themselves much moved. As soon as the singing was over the ladies requested me to stay where I was, while they went inside the place from which it had seemed to come.

During their absence certain reflections forced themselves upon me.

In the first place, it struck me as strange that the building should be so nearly empty; I was almost alone, and the few besides myself had been led by curiosity, and had no intention of doing business with the bank. But there might be more inside. I stole up to the curtain, and ventured to draw the extreme edge of it on one side. No, there was hardly any one there. I saw a large number of cashiers, all at their desks ready to pay cheques, and one or two who seemed to be the managing partners. I also saw my hostess and her daughters and two or three other ladies; also three or four old women and the boys from one of the neighbouring Colleges of Unreason; but there was no one else. This did not look as though the bank was doing a very large business; and yet I had always been told that every one in the city dealt with this establishment.

I cannot describe all that took place in these inner precincts, for a sinister-looking person in a black gown came and made unpleasant gestures at me for peeping. I happened to have in my pocket one of the musical bank pieces, which had been given me by Mrs. Nosnibor, so I tried to tip him with it; but having seen what it was, he became so angry that it was all I could do to pacify him. When he was gone I ventured to take a second look, and saw Zulora in the very act of giving a piece of paper which looked like a cheque to one of the cashiers. He did not

examine it, but putting his hand into an antique
coffer hard by, he pulled out a quantity of dull-looking
metal pieces apparently at random, and handed them
over without counting them; neither did Zulora count
them, but put them into her purse and departed.   It
seemed a very singular proceeding, but I supposed that
they knew their own business best, at any rate Zulora
seemed quite satisfied, thanked him for the money, and
began making towards the curtain: on this I let it
drop and retreated to a reasonable distance.

Mrs. Nosnibor and her daughters soon joined me.
For some few minutes we all kept silence, but at last I
ventured to remark that the bank was not so busy to-
day as it probably often was.   On this Mrs. Nosnibor
said that it was indeed melancholy to see what little
heed people paid to the most precious of all institutions.
I could say nothing in reply, but I have ever been of
opinion that the greater part of mankind do approxi-
mately know where they get that which does them
good.   Mrs. Nosnibor went on to say that I must not
imagine there was any want of confidence in the bank
because I had seen so few people there; the heart of
the country was thoroughly devoted to these establishments, and any sign of their being in danger would
bring in support from the most unexpected quarters.
It was only because people knew them to be so very
safe, that in some cases (as she lamented to say in Mr.
Nosnibor's) they felt that their support was unnecessary.
Moreover these institutions never departed from the
safest and most approved banking principles.   Thus
they never allowed interest on deposit, a thing now frequently done by certain bubble companies, which by
doing an illegitimate trade had drawn many customers
away; and even the shareholders were fewer than

formerly, owing to the innovations of these unscrupulous persons.

It came out by and by that the musical banks paid little or no dividend, but divided their profits by way of bonus on the original shares once in every three hundred and fifty years; and as it was now only two hundred years since there had been one of these distributions, people felt that they could not hope for another in their own time and preferred investments whereby they got some more tangible return; all which, she said, was very melancholy to think of.

Having made these last admissions, she returned to her original statement, namely, that every one in the country really supported the bank.. As to the fewness of the people, and the absence of the able-bodied, she pointed out to me with some justice that this was exactly what we ought to expect. The men who were most conversant about the stability of human institutions, such as the lawyers, men of science, doctors, statesmen, painters, and the like, were just those who were most likely to be misled by their own fancied accomplishments, and to be made unduly suspicious by their licentious desire for greater present return, which was at the root of nine-tenths of the opposition, by their vanity, which would prompt them to affect superiority to the prejudices of the vulgar, and by the stings of their own conscience, which was constantly upbraiding them in the most cruel manner on account of their bodies, which were generally diseased; let a person's intellect be never so sound, unless his body were in absolute health, he could form no judgment worth having on matters of this kind. The body was everything: it need not perhaps be such a *strong* body (she said this because she saw I was thinking of the old and infirm-looking folks whom I had seen in the bank), but it must be in perfect health; in this case, the less active strength it had the more free would be the working of the intellect, and therefore the sounder the conclusion. The people, then, whom I had seen at the bank were in reality the very ones whose opinions were most worth having; they declared its advantages to be incalculable, and even professed to consider the immediate return to be far larger than they were entitled to; and so she ran on, nor did she leave off till we had got back to the house.

She might say what she pleased, but her manner was not one that carried much conviction; and later on I saw signs of general indifference to these banks that were not to be mistaken. Their supporters often denied it, but the denial was generally so couched as to add another proof of its existence. In commercial panics, and in times of general distress, the people as a mass did not so much as even think of turning to these banks. A few individuals might do so, some from habit and early training, some from hope of gain, but few from a genuine belief that the money was good; the masses turned instinctively to the other currency. In a conversation with one of the musical bank managers I ventured to hint this as plainly as politeness would allow. He said that it had been more or less true till lately; but that now they had put fresh stained glass windows into all the banks in the country, and repaired the buildings, and enlarged the organs, and taken to talking nicely to the people in the streets, and to remembering the ages of their children and giving them things when they were ill, so that all would henceforth go smoothly.

"But haven't you done anything to the money itself?" said I timidly.

To this day I do not know exactly what the bank-manager said, but it came to this in the end—that I had better not meddle with things that I did not understand.

On reviewing the whole matter, I can be certain of this much only, that the money given out at the musical banks is not the current coin of the realm. It is not the money with which the people do as a general rule buy their bread, meat, and clothing. It is like it; some coins very like it; and it is not counterfeit. It is not, take it all round, a spurious article made of base metal in imitation of the money which is in daily use; but it is a distinct coinage which, though I do not suppose it ever actually superseded the ordinary gold, silver, and copper, was probably issued by authority, and was intended to supplant those metals. Some of the pieces were really of exquisite beauty; and some were, I do verily believe, nothing but the ordinary currency, only that there was another head and name in place of that of the commonwealth. And here was one of the great marvels; for those who were most strongly in favour of this coinage maintained, and even grew more excited if they were opposed here than on any other matter, that the very self-same coin with the head of the commonwealth upon it was of little if any value, while it became exceedingly precious if stamped with the other image.

Some of the coins were plainly bad; of these last there were not many; still there were enough for them to be not uncommon. These were entirely composed of alloy; they would bend easily, would melt away to

nothing with a little heat, and were quite unsuited for
a currency. Yet there were few of the wealthier
classes who did not maintain that even these coins
were genuine good money, though they were chary of
taking them. Every one knew this, so they were
seldom offered; but all thought it incumbent upon
them to retain a good many in their possession, and
to let them be seen from time to time in their hands
and purses. Of course people knew their real value
exceedingly well; but few, if any, dared to say what
that value was; or if they did, it would be only in
certain companies or in writing in the newspapers
anonymously. Strange! there was hardly any insinua-
tion against this coinage which they would not tolerate
and even applaud in their daily papers; and yet, if
the same thing were said without ambiguity to their
faces—-nominative case verb and accusative being all
in their right places, and doubt impossible—they
would consider themselves very seriously and justly
outraged, and accuse the speaker of being unwell.

I never could understand, neither can I do so now,
why a single currency should not suffice them; it
would seem to me as though all their dealings would
have been thus greatly simplified; but I was met with
a look of horror if ever I dared to hint at it   Even
those who to my certain knowledge kept only just
enough money at the musical banks to swear by,
would call the other banks (where their securities
really lay) cold, deadening, paralsying, and the like.
I noticed another thing moreover which struck me
greatly. I was taken to the opening of one of these
banks in a neighbouring town, and saw a large as-
semblage of cashiers and managers. I sat opposite
them and scanned their faces attentively. They did

not please me; they lacked, with a few exceptions, the true Erewhonian frankness; and an equal number from any other class would have looked happier and better men. When I met them in the streets they did not seem like other people, but had, as a general rule, a cramped expression upon their faces which pained and depressed me.

Those who came from the country were better; they seemed to have lived less as a separate class, and to be freer and healthier; but in spite of my seeing not a few whose looks were benign and noble, I could not help asking myself concerning the greater number of those whom I met, whether Erewhon would be a better country if their expression were to be transferred to the people in general. I answered myself emphatically, no. A man's expression is his sacrament; it is the outward and visible sign of his inward and spiritual grace, or want of grace; and as I looked at the majority of these men, I could not help feeling that there must be a something in their lives which had stunted their natural development, and that they would have been more healthily-minded in any other profession.

I was always sorry for them, for in nine cases out of ten they were well-meaning persons; they were in the main very poorly paid; their constitutions were as a rule above suspicion; and there were recorded numberless instances of their self-sacrifice and generosity; but they had had the misfortune to have been betrayed into a false position at an age for the most part when their judgment was not matured, and after having been kept in studied ignorance of the real difficulties of the system. But this did not make their position the less a false one, and its bad effects upon themselves were unmistakable.

Few people would speak quite openly and freely before them, which struck me as a very bad sign. When they were in the room every one would talk as though all currency save that of the musical banks should be abolished; and yet they knew perfectly well that even the cashiers themselves hardly used the musical bank money more than other people. It was expected of them that they should appear to do so, but this was all. The less thoughtful of them did not seem particularly unhappy, but many were plainly sick at heart, though perhaps they hardly knew it, and would not have owned to being so. Some few were opponents of the whole system; but these were liable to be dismissed from their employment at any moment, and this rendered them very careful, for a man who had once been cashier at a musical bank was out of the field for other employment, and was generally unfitted for it by reason of that course of treatment which was commonly called his education. In fact it was a career from which retreat was virtually impossible, and into which young men were generally induced to enter before they could be reasonably expected, considering their training, to have formed any opinions of their own. Few indeed were those who had the courage to insist on seeing both sides of the question before they committed themselves to either. One would have thought that this was an elementary principle,—one of the first things that an honourable man would teach his boy to do; but in practice it was not so.

I even saw cases in which parents bought the right of presenting to the office of cashier at one of these banks, with the fixed determination that some one of their sons (perhaps a mere child) should fill it. There was the lad himself—growing up with every promise of becoming a good and honourable man—but utterly without warning concerning the iron shoe which his natural protector was providing for him. Who could say that the whole thing would not end in a life-long lie, and vain chafing to escape?

I confess that there were few things in Erewhon which shocked me more than this.

BIRTH FORMULÆ.

(CHAPTER XVII. OF EREWHON.)

I HEARD what follows not from·Arowhena, but from
Mr. Nosnibor and some of the gentlemen who occasionally dined at the house : they told me that the
Erewhonians believe in pre-existence ; and not only
this (of which I will write more fully in the next
chapter), but they believe that it is of their own free
act and deed in a previous state that people come to
be born into this world at all.

They hold that the unborn are perpetually plaguing
and. tormenting the married (and sometimes even the
unmarried) of both sexes, fluttering about them incessantly, and giving them no peace either of mind or body
until they have consented to take them under their
protection.   If this were not so—this is at least what
they urge—it would be a monstrous freedom for one
man to take with another, to say that he should undergo the chances and changes of this mortal life without
any option in the matter.   No man would have any
right to get married at all, inasmuch as he can never
tell what misery his doing so may entail forcibly upon
his children who cannot be unhappy as long as they
remain unborn.   They feel this so strongly that they are
resolved to shift the blame on to other shoulders ; they
have therefore invented a long mythology as to the
world in which the unborn people live, what they do,

and the arts and machinations to which they have recourse in order to get themselves into our own world.

I cannot think they seriously believe in this mythology concerning pre-existence; they do and they do not; they do not know themselves what they believe; all they know is that it is a disease not to believe as they do. The only thing of which they are quite sure is that it is the pestering of the unborn, which causes them to be brought into this world, and that they would not be here if they would only let peaceable people alone.

It would be hard to disprove this position, and they might have a good case if they would only leave it as it stands. But this they will not do; they must have assurance doubly sure; they must have the written word of the child itself as soon as it is born, giving the parents indemnity from all responsibility on the score of its birth, and asserting its own pre-existence. They have therefore devised something which they call a birth formula—a document which varies in words according to the caution of parents, but is much the same practically in all cases; for it has been the business of the Erewhonian lawyers during many ages to exercise their skill in perfecting it and providing for every contingency.

These formulæ are printed on common paper at a moderate cost for the poor; but the rich have them written on parchment and handsomely bound, so that the getting up of a person's birth formula is a test of his social position. They commence by setting forth, That whereas A. B. was a member of the kingdom of the unborn, where he was well provided for in every way, and had no cause of discontent, &c. &c., he did of his own wanton restlessness conceive a desire to enter into this present world; that thereon having taken the necessary steps as set forth in laws of the unborn kingdom, he set himself with malice aforethought to plague and pester two unfortunate people who had never wronged him, and who were quite contented until he conceived this base design against their peace; for which wrong he now humbly entreats their pardon. He acknowledges that he is responsible for all physical blemishes and deficiencies which may render him answerable to the laws of his country; that his parents have nothing whatever to do with any of these things; and that they have a right to kill him at once if they be so minded, though he entreats them to show their marvellous goodness and clemency towards him by sparing his life. If they will do this he promises to be their most abject creature during his earlier years, and indeed unto his life's end, unless they should see fit in their abundant generosity to remit some portion of his service hereafter. And so the formula continues, going sometimes into very minute details, according to the fancies of family lawyers, who will not make it any shorter than they can help.

The deed being thus prepared, on the third or fourth day after the birth of the child, or as they call it, the "final importunity," the friends gather together, and there is a feast held, where they are all very melancholy—as a general rule, I believe quite truly so—and make presents to the father and mother of the child in order to console them for the injury which has just been done them by the unborn. By and by the child himself is brought down by his nurse, and the company begin to rail upon him, upbraiding him for his impertinence and asking him

what amends he proposes to make for the wrong that
he has committed, and how he can look for care and
nourishment from those who have perhaps already
been injured by the unborn on some ten or twelve
occasions; for they say of people with large families,
that they have suffered terrible injuries from the
unborn; till at last, when this has been carried far
enough, some one suggests the formula, which is
brought forth and solemnly read to the child by the
family straightener. This gentleman is always invited
on these occasions, for the very fact of intrusion into
a peaceful family shows a depravity on the part of the
child which requires his professional services.

On being teased by the reading and tweaked by
the nurse, the child will commonly fall a-crying,
which is reckoned a good sign as showing a consciousness of guilt. He is thereon asked, Does he assent to
the formula? on which, as he still continues crying
and can obviously make no answer, some one of the
friends comes forward and undertakes to sign the document on his behalf, feeling sure (so he says) that the
child would do it if he only knew how, and that he
will release the present signer from his engagement on
arriving at maturity. The friend then inscribes the
signature of the child at the foot of the parchment,
which is held to bind the child as much as though he
had signed it himself. Even this, however, does not
fully content them, for they feel a little uneasy until
they have got the child's own signature after all. So
when he is about fourteen these good people partly
bribe him by promises of greater liberty and good
things, and partly intimidate him through their great
power of making themselves passively unpleasant to
him, so that though there is a show of freedom made,

there is really none, and partly they use the offices of the teachers in the Colleges of Unreason, till at last, in one way or another, they take very good care that he shall sign the paper by which he professes to have been a free agent in coming into the world, and to take all the responsibility of having done so on to his own shoulders. And yet, though this document is in theory the most important which any one can sign in his whole life, they will have him commit himself to it at an age when neither they nor the law will for many a year allow any one else to bind him to the smallest obligation, no matter how righteously he may owe it, because they hold him too young to know what he is about.

I thought this seemed rather hard, and not of a piece with the many admirable institutions existing among them. I once ventured to say a part of what I thought about it to one of the Professors of Unreason. I asked him whether he did not think it would do serious harm to a lad's principles, and weaken his sense of the sanctity of his word, and of truth generally, that he should be led into entering upon an engagement which it was so plainly impossible he should keep even for a single day with tolerable integrity—whether, in fact, the teachers who so led him, or who taught anything as a certainty of which they were themselves uncertain, were not earning their living by impairing the truth-sense of their pupils. The professor, who was a delight-ful person, seemed surprised at the view I took, and gave me to understand, perhaps justly enough, that I ought not to make so much fuss about a trifle. No one, he said, expected that the boy either would or could do all that he undertook; but the world was full of compromises; and there was hardly any engagement which would bear being interpreted literally. Human language was too gross a vehicle of thought—thought being incapable of absolute translation. He added, that as there can be no translation from one language into another which shall not scant the meaning somewhat, or enlarge upon it, so there is no language which can render thought without a jarring and a harshness somewhere—and so forth; all of which seemed to come to this in the end, that it was the custom of the country, and that the Erewhonians were a conservative people; that the boy would have to begin compromising sooner or later, and this was part of his education in the art. It was perhaps to be regretted that compromise should be as necessary as it was; still it was necessary, and the sooner the boy got to understand it the better for himself. But they never tell this to the boy.

From the book of their mythology about the unborn I made the extracts which will form the following chapter.

THE WORLD OF THE UNBORN.

(PART OF CHAPTER XVIII. OF EREWHON.)

THE Erewhonians say it was by chance only that the earth and stars and all the heavenly worlds began to roll from east to west, and not from west to east, and in like manner they say it is by chance that man is drawn through life with his face to the past instead of to the future. For the future is there as much as the past, only that we may not see it. Is it not in the loins of the past, and must not the past alter before the future can do so ?

They have a fable that there was a race of men tried upon the earth once, who knew the future better than the past, but that they died in a twelvemonth from the misery which their knowledge caused them. They say that if any were to be born too prescient now, he would die miserably, before he had time to transmit so peace-destroying a faculty to descendants.

Strange fate for man ! He must perish if he get that, which he must perish if he strive not after. If he strive not after it he is no better than the brutes, if he get it he is more miserable than the devils.

Having waded through many chapters like the above, I came at last to the unborn themselves, and found that they were held to be souls pure and simple, having no actual bodies, but living in a sort of gaseous yet more or less anthropomorphic existence, like that of a ghost; they have thus neither flesh nor blood nor warmth. Nevertheless they are supposed to have local habitations and cities wherein they dwell, though these are as unsubstantial as their inhabitants; they are even thought to eat and drink some thin ambrosial sustenance, and generally to be capable of doing whatever mankind can do, only after a visionary ghostly fashion, as in a dream. On the other hand, as long as they remain where they are they never die—the only form of death in the unborn world being the leaving it for our own. They are believed to be extremely numerous, far more so than mankind. They arrive from unknown planets, full grown, in large batches at a time; but they can only leave the unborn world by taking the steps necessary for their arrival here—which is, in fact, by suicide.

They ought to be a happy people, for they have no extremes of good or ill fortune; never marrying, but living in a state much like that fabled by the poets as the primitive condition of mankind. In spite of this, however, they are incessantly complaining; they know that we in this world have bodies, and indeed they know everything else about us, for they move among us whithersoever they will, and can read our thoughts, as well as survey our actions at pleasure. One would think that this should be enough for them; and indeed most of them are alive to the desperate risk which they will run by indulging themselves in that body with "sensible warm motion" which they so much desire; nevertheless, there are some to whom the *ennui* of a disembodied existence is so intolerable that they will venture anything for a change; so they resolve to quit. The conditions which they must accept are

so uncertain, that none but the most foolish of the unborn will consent to take them; and it is from these
and these only that our own ranks are recruited.

When they have finally made up their minds to
leave, they must go before the magistrate of the
nearest town and sign an affidavit of their desire to
quit their then existence.   On their having done this,
the magistrate reads them the conditions which they
must accept, and which are so long that I can only
extract some of the principal points, which are mainly
the following :—

First, they must take a potion which will destroy
their memory and sense of identity; they must go
into the world helpless, and without a will of their
own; they must draw lots for their dispositions before
they go, and take it, such as it is, for better or worse—
neither are they to be allowed any choice in the matter
of the body which they so much desire; they are simply
allotted by chance, and without appeal, to two people
whom it is their business to find and pester until they
adopt them.   Who these are to be, whether rich or
poor, kind or unkind, healthy or diseased, there is no
knowing; they have, in fact, to entrust themselves for
many years to the care of those for whose good constitution and good sense they have no sort of guarantee.

It is curious to read the lectures which the wiser
heads give to those who are meditating a change.
They talk with them as we talk with a spendthrift,
and with about as much success.

" To be born," they say, " is a felony—it is a capital crime, for which sentence may be executed at any
moment after the commission of the offence. You
may perhaps happen to live for some seventy or eighty
years, but what is that, in comparison with the eter-

nity which you now enjoy? And even though the
sentence were commuted, and you were allowed to
live for ever, you would in time become so terribly
weary of life that execution would be the greatest
mercy to you.   Consider the infinite risk; to be born
of wicked parents and trained in vice! to be born of
silly parents, and trained to unrealities! of parents
who regard you as a sort of chattel or property, belonging more to them than to yourself!   Again, you
may draw utterly unsympathetic parents, who will
never be able to understand you, and who will thwart
you as long as they can to the utmost of their power
(as a hen when she has hatched a duckling), and then
call you ungrateful because you do not love them, or
parents who may look upon you as a thing to be cowed
while it is still young, lest it should give them trouble
hereafter by having wishes and feelings of its own.

"In later life, when you have been finally allowed
to pass muster as a full member of the world, you
will yourself become liable to the pesterings of the
unborn—and a very happy life you may be led in
consequence!   For we solicit so strongly that a few
only—nor these the best—can refuse us; and yet not
to refuse is much the same as going into partnership
with half a dozen different people about whom one
can know absolutely nothing beforehand—not even
whether one is going into partnership with men or
women, nor with how many of either.   Delude not
yourself with thinking that you will be wiser than
your parents.   You may be an age in advance of
them, but unless you are one of the great ones (and
if you are one of the great ones, woe betide you), you
will still be an age behind your children.

"Imagine what it must be to have an unborn

quartered upon you, who is of a different temperament to your own; nay, half a dozen such, who will not love you though you may tell them that you have stinted yourself in a thousand ways to provide for their well-being,—who will forget all that self-sacrifice of which you are yourself so conscious, and of whom you may never be sure that they are not bearing a grudge against you for errors of judgment into which you may have fallen, but which you had hoped had been long since atoned for. Ingratitude such as this is not un-common, yet fancy what it must be to bear! It is hard upon the duckling to have been hatched by a hen, but is it not also hard upon the hen to have hatched the duckling?

"Consider it again, we pray you, not for our sake but for your own. Your initial character you must draw by lot; but whatever it is, it can only come to a tolerably successful development after long training; remember that over that training you will have no control. It is possible, and even probable, that what-ever you may get in after life which is of real pleasure and service to you, will have to be won in spite of, rather than by the help of, those whom you are now about to pester, and that you will only win your freedom after years of a painful struggle, in which it will be hard to say whether you have suffered most injury, or inflicted it.

"Remember also, that if you go into the world you will have free will; that you will be obliged to have it, that there is no escaping it, that you will be fettered to it during your whole life, and must on every occasion do that which on the whole seems best to you at any given time, no matter whether you are right or wrong in choosing it. Your mind will be a balance for considerations, and your action will go with the heavier scale. How it shall fall will depend upon the kind of scales which you may have drawn at birth, the bias which they will have obtained by use, and the weight of the immediate considerations. If the scales were good to start with, and if they have not been outrageously tampered with in childhood, and if the combinations into which you enter are average ones, you may come off well; but there are too many " ifs " in this, and with the failure of any one of them your misery is assured. Reflect on this, and remember that should the ill come upon you, you will have yourself to thank, for it is your own choice to be born, and there is no compulsion in the matter.

" Not that we deny the existence of pleasures among mankind ; there is a certain show of sundry phases of contentment which may even amount to very considerable happiness ; but mark how they are distributed over a man's life, belonging, all the keenest of them, to the fore part, and few indeed to the after. Can there be any pleasure worth purchasing with the miseries of a decrepit age ? If you are good, strong, and handsome, you have a fine fortune indeed at twenty, but how much of it will be left at sixty ? For you must live on your capital ; there is no investing your powers so that you may get a small annuity of life for ever : you must eat up your principal bit by bit and be tortured by seeing it grow continually smaller and smaller, even though you happen to escape being rudely robbed of it by crime or casualty. Remember, too, that there never yet was a man of forty who would not come back into the world of the unborn if he could do so with decency and honour. Being in the world, he will as a general rule stay till he is forced to go ; but do you think that

he would consent to be born again, and re-live his life,
if he had the offer of doing so? Do not think it.
If he could so alter the past as that he should never
have come into being at all, do you not think that he
would do it very gladly? What was it that one of
their own poets meant, if it was not this, when he cried
out upon the day in which he was born, and the night
in which it was said there is a man child conceived?
'For now,' he says, 'I should have lain still and been
quiet, I should have slept; then had I been at rest
with kings and counsellors of the earth, which built
desolate places for themselves; or with princes that
had gold, who filled their houses with silver; or as an
hidden untimely birth, I had not been; as infants
which never saw light. There the wicked cease from
troubling, and the weary are at rest.' Be very sure
that the guilt of being born carries this punishment at
times to all men; but how can they ask for pity, or
complain of any mischief that may befall them, having
entered open-eyed into the snare?

"One word more and we have done. If any faint
remembrance, as of a dream, flit in some puzzled moment across your brain, and you shall feel that the
potion which is to be given you shall not have done
its work, and the memory of this existence which you
are leaving endeavours vainly to return; we say in
such a moment, when you clutch at the dream but it
eludes your grasp, and you watch it, as Orpheus
watched Eurydice, gliding back again into the twilight kingdom, fly—fly—if you can remember the
advice—to the haven of your present and immediate
duty, taking shelter incessantly in the work which
you have in hand. This much you may perhaps recall;
and this, if you will imprint it deeply upon your every

faculty, will be most likely to bring you safely and honourably home through the trials that are before you." *

This is the fashion in which they reason with those who would be for leaving them, but it is seldom that they do much good, for none but the unquiet and unreasonable ever think of being born, and those who are foolish enough to think of it are generally foolish enough to do it. Finding therefore that they can do no more, the friends follow weeping to the courthouse of the chief magistrate, where the one who wishes to be born declares solemnly and openly that he accepts the conditions attached to his decision. On this he is presented with the potion, which immediately destroys his memory and sense of identity, and dissipates the thin gaseous tenement which he has inhabited: he becomes a bare vital principle, not to be perceived by human senses, nor appreciated by any chemical test. He has but one instinct, which is that he is to go to such and such a place, where he will find two persons whom he is to importune till they consent to undertake him; but whether he is to find these persons among the race of Chowbok or the Erewhonians themselves is not for him to choose.

* The myth above alluded to exists in Erewhon with changed names and considerable modifications. I have taken the liberty of referring to the story as familiar to ourselves.

SELECTIONS FROM THE FAIR HAVEN.

——o——

MEMOIR OF THE LATE JOHN PICKARD OWEN.

(CHARTER I. OF THE FAIR HAVEN. [*])

THE subject of this memoir, and author of the work which follows it, was born in Goodge Street, Tottenham Court Road, London, on the 5th of February 1832. He was my elder brother by about eighteen months. Our father and mother had once been rich, but through a succession of unavoidable misfortunes they were left with but a slender income when my brother and myself were about three and four years old. My father died some five or six years afterwards, and we only recollected him as a singularly gentle and humorous playmate who doted upon us both and never spoke unkindly.

The charm of such a recollection can never be dispelled; both my brother and myself returned his love with interest, and cherished his memory with the most affectionate regret, from the day on which he left us till the time came that the one of us was again to see him face to face. So sweet and winning was his nature that his slightest wish was our law—and whenever we pleased him, no matter how little, he never failed to thank us as though we had done him

[*] The first edition of the Fair Haven was published April 1873.

a service which we should have had a perfect right to withhold. How proud were we upon any of these occasions, and how we courted the opportunity of being thanked! He did indeed well know the art of becoming idolised by his children, and dearly did he prize the results of his own proficiency; yet truly there was no art about it; all arose spontaneously from the well-spring of a sympathetic nature which was quick to feel as others felt, whether old or young, rich or poor, wise or foolish. On one point alone did he neglect us—I refer to our religious education. On all other matters he was the kindest and most careful teacher in the world. Love and gratitude be to his memory!.

My mother loved us no less ardently than my father, but she was of a quicker temper, and less adept at conciliating affection. She must have been exceedingly handsome when she was young, and was still comely when we first remembered her; she was also highly accomplished, but she felt my father's loss of fortune more keenly than my father himself, and it preyed upon her mind, though rather for our sake than for her own. Had we not known my father we should have loved her better than any one in the world, but affection goes by comparison, and my father spoiled us for any one but himself; indeed, in after life, I remember my mother's telling me, with many tears, how jealous she had often been of the love we bore him, and how mean she had thought it of him to entrust all scolding or repression to her, so that he might have more than his due share of our affection. Not that I believe my father did this consciously; still, he so greatly hated scolding that I dare say we might often have got off scot-free when we really deserved reproof

D

had not my mother undertaken the *onus* of scolding us herself. We therefore naturally feared her more than my father, and fearing more we loved less. For as love casteth out fear, so fear love.

This must have been hard to bear, and my mother scarcely knew the way to bear it. She tried to upbraid us, in little ways, into loving her as much as my father; the more she tried this, the less we could succeed in doing it; and so on and so on in a fashion which need not be detailed. Not but what we really loved her deeply, while her affection for us was insurpassable; still we loved her less than we loved my father, and this was the grievance.

My father entrusted our religious education entirely to my mother. He was himself, I am assured, of a deeply religious turn of mind, and a thoroughly consistent member of the Church of England; but he conceived, and perhaps rightly, that it is the mother who should first teach her children to lift their hands in prayer, and impart to them a knowledge of the One in whom we live and move and have our being. My mother accepted the task gladly, for in spite of a certain narrowness of view—the natural but deplorable result of her earlier surroundings—she was one of the most truly pious women whom I have ever known; unfortunately for herself and us she had been trained in the lowest school of Evangelical literalism—a school which in after life both my brother and myself came to regard as the main obstacle to the complete overthrow of unbelief; we therefore looked upon it with something stronger than aversion, and for my own part I still deem it perhaps the most insidious enemy which the cause of Christ has ever encountered. But of this more hereafter.

My mother, as I said, threw her whole soul into the work of our religious education. Whatever she believed she believed literally, and, if I may say so, with a harshness of realisation which left little scope for imagination or mystery. Her ideas concerning heaven and her solutions of life's enigmas were clear and simple, but they could only be reconciled with certain obvious facts—such as the omnipotence and all-goodness of God—by leaving many things absolutely out of sight. And this my mother succeeded effectually in doing. She never doubted that her opinions comprised the truth, the whole truth, and nothing but the truth; she therefore made haste to sow the good seed in our tender minds, and so far succeeded that when my brother was four years old he could repeat the Apostles' Creed, the general confession, and the Lord's Prayer without a blunder. My mother made herself believe that he delighted in them; but, alas! it was far otherwise; for strange as it may appear concerning one whose later life was a continual prayer, in childhood he detested nothing so much as being made to pray, and to learn his catechism. In this I am sorry to say we were both heartily of a mind. As for Sunday the less said the better.

I have already hinted (but as a warning to other parents had better, perhaps, express myself more plainly) that this aversion was probably the result of my mother's undue eagerness to reap an artificial fruit of lip-service, which could have little meaning to the heart of one so young. I believe that the severe check which the natural growth of faith experienced in my brother's case was due almost entirely to this cause, and to the school of literalism in which he had been trained; but, however this may be, we both of us hated being made to say our prayers. Morning and evening it was our one bugbear, and we would avoid it, as indeed children generally will, by every artifice which we could employ.

Thus we were in the habit of feigning to be asleep shortly before prayer time, and would gratefully hear my father tell my mother that it was a shame to wake us; whereon he would carry us up to bed in a state apparently of the profoundest slumber when we were really wide awake and in great fear of detection. For we knew how to pretend to be asleep, but we did not know how we ought to wake again; there was nothing for it therefore when we were once committed, but to go on sleeping till we were fairly undressed and put to bed, and could wake up safely in the dark. But deceit is never long successful, and we were at last ignominiously exposed.

It happened one evening that my mother suspected my brother John, and tried to open his little hands which were lying clasped in front of him. Now my brother was as yet very crude and inconsistent in his theories concerning sleep, and had no conception what a real sleeper would do under these circumstances. Fear deprived him of his powers of reflection, and he thus unfortunately concluded that because sleepers, so far as he had observed them, were always motionless, therefore they must be rigid and incapable of motion; and indeed that any movement, under any circumstances (for from his earliest childhood he liked to carry his theories to their legitimate conclusion), would be physically impossible for one who was really sleeping; forgetful, oh! unhappy one, of the flexibility of his own body on being carried up stairs, and, more unhappy still, ignorant of the art of waking. He therefore clenched his fingers harder and harder as he felt my mother trying to unfold them, while his head hung listless, and his eyes were closed as though he were sleeping sweetly. It is needless to detail the agony of shame that followed. My mother begged my father to box his ears, which my father flatly refused to do. Then she boxed them herself, and there followed a scene, and a day or two of disgrace for both of us.

Shortly after this there happened another misadventure. A lady came to stay with my mother, and was to sleep in a bed that had been brought into our nursery, for my father's fortunes had already failed, and we were living in a humble way. We were still but four and five years old, so the arrangement was not unnatural, and it was assumed that we should be asleep before the lady went to bed, and be down stairs before she would get up in the morning. But the arrival of this lady and her being put to sleep in the nursery were great events to us in those days, and being particularly wanted to go to sleep, we of course sat up in bed talking and keeping ourselves awake till she should come up stairs. Perhaps we had fancied that she would give us something, but if so we were disappointed. However, whether this was the case or not, we were wide awake when our visitor came to bed, and having no particular object to gain, we made no pretence of sleeping. The lady kissed us both, told us to lie still and go to sleep like good children, and then began doing her hair.

I remember this was the occasion on which my brother discovered a good many things in connection with the fair sex which had hitherto been beyond his ken; more especially that the mass of petticoats and clothes which envelop the female form were not, as he expressed it to me, "all solid woman," but that women were not in reality more substantially built than men, and had legs as much as he had—a fact which he had never yet realised. On this he for a long time considered them as impostors, who had wronged him by leading him to suppose that they had far more "body in them" (so he said) than he now found they had.

This was a sort of thing which he regarded with stern moral reprobation. If he had been old enough to have a solicitor I believe he would have put the matter into his hands, as well as certain other things which had lately troubled him. For but recently my mother had bought a fowl, and he had seen it plucked, and the inside taken out; his irritation had been extreme on discovering that fowls were not all solid flesh, but that their insides—and these formed, as it appeared to him, an enormous percentage of the bird— were perfectly useless. He was now beginning to understand that sheep and cows were also hollow as far as good meat was concerned; the flesh they had was only a mouthful in comparison with what they ought to have considering their apparent bulk; insignificant, mere skin and bone covering a cavern. What right had they, or anything else, to assert themselves as so big, and prove so empty? And now this discovery of woman's falsehood was quite too much for him. The world itself was hollow, made up of shams and delusions, full of sound and fury signifying nothing.

Truly a prosaic young gentleman enough. Everything with him was to be exactly in all its parts what it appeared on the face of it, and everything was to go on doing exactly what it had been doing hitherto.

If a thing looked solid, it was to be very solid; if hollow, very hollow; nothing was to be half and half, and nothing was to change unless he had himself already become accustomed to its times and manners of changing; there were to be no exceptions and no contradictions; all things were to be perfectly consistent, and all premisses to be carried with extremest rigour to their legitimate conclusions. Heaven was to be very neat (for he was always tidy himself), and free from sudden shocks to the nervous system, such as those caused by dogs barking at him, or cows driven in the streets. God was to resemble my father, and the Holy Spirit to bear some sort of indistinct analogy to my mother.

Such were the ideal theories of his childhood—unconsciously formed, but very firmly believed in. As he grew up he made such modifications as were forced upon him by enlarged perceptions, but every modification was an effort to him, in spite of a continual and successful resistance to what he recognised as his initial mental defect.

I may perhaps be allowed to say here, in reference to a remark in the preceding paragraph, that both my brother and myself used to notice it as an almost invariable rule that children's earliest ideas of God are modelled upon the character of their father—if they have one. Should the father be kind, considerate, full of the warmest love, fond of showing it, and reserved only about his displeasure, the child, having learned to look upon God as his Heavenly Father through the Lord's Prayer and our Church Services, will feel towards God as he does towards his own father; this conception will stick to a man for years and years after he has attained manhood—probably it will never leave him. On the other hand, if a man has found his earthly father harsh and uncongenial, his conception of his Heavenly Parent will be painful. He will begin by seeing God as an exaggerated likeness of his father. He will therefore shrink from Him. The rottenness of still-born love in the heart of a child poisons the blood of the soul, and hence, later, crime.

To return, however, to the lady. When she had put on her night-gown, she knelt down by her bed-side and, to our consternation, began to say her prayers. This was a cruel blow to both of us; we had always been under the impression that grown-up people were not made to say their prayers, and the idea of any one saying them of his or her own accord had never occurred to us as possible. Of course the lady would not say her prayers if she were not obliged; and yet she did say them; therefore she must be obliged to say them; therefore we should be obliged to say them, and this was a great disappointment. Awe-struck and open-mouthed we listened while the lady prayed aloud and with a good deal of pathos for many virtues and blessings which I do not now remember, and finally for my father and mother and for both of us—shortly afterwards she rose, blew out the light and got into bed. Every word that she said had confirmed our worst apprehensions: it was just what we had been taught to say ourselves.

Next morning we compared notes and drew some painful inferences; but in the course of the day our spirits rallied. We agreed that there were many mysteries in connection with life and things which it was high time to unravel, and that an opportunity was now afforded us which might not readily occur again.

All we had to do was to be true to ourselves and equal to the occasion. We laid our plans with great astuteness. We would be fast asleep when the lady came up to bed, but our heads should be turned in the direction of her bed, and covered with clothes, all but a single peep-hole. My brother, as the eldest, had clearly a right to be nearest the lady, but I could see sufficiently, and could depend on his reporting faithfully whatever should escape me.

There was no chance of her giving us anything— if she had meant to do so she would have done it sooner; she might, indeed, consider the moment of her departure as the most auspicious for this purpose, but then she was not going yet, and the interval was at our own disposal. We spent the afternoon in trying to learn to snore, but we were not certain about it, and in the end concluded that as snoring was not *de rigueur* we had better dispense with it.

We were put to bed; the light was taken away; we were told to go to sleep, and promised faithfully that we would do so; the tongue indeed swore, but the mind was unsworn. It was agreed that we should keep pinching one another to prevent our going to sleep. We did so at frequent intervals; at last our patience was rewarded with the heavy creak, as of a stout elderly lady labouring up the stairs, and presently our victim entered.

To cut a long story short, the lady on satisfying herself that we were asleep, never said her prayers at all; during the remainder of her visit whenever she found us awake she always said them, but when she thought we were asleep, she never prayed. I should perhaps say that we had the matter out with her before she left, and that the consequences were

unpleasant for all parties; they added to the troubles
in which we were already involved as to our prayers,
and were indirectly among the earliest causes which
led my brother to look with scepticism upon religion.

For awhile, however, all went on as though nothing
had happened.   An effect of distrust, indeed, remained
after the cause had been forgotten, but my brother was
still too young to oppose anything that my mother
told him, and to all outward appearance he grew in
grace no less rapidly than in stature.

For years we led a quiet and eventless life, broken
only by the one great sorrow of our father's death.
Shortly after this we were sent to a day school in
Bloomsbury.   We were neither of us very happy
there, but my brother, who always took kindly to
his books, picked up a fair knowledge of Latin and
Greek; he also learned to draw, and to exercise himself a little in English composition.   When I was
about fourteen my mother capitalised a part of her
income and started me off to America, where she had
friends who could give me a helping hand; by their
kindness I was enabled, after an absence of twenty
years, to return with a handsome income, but not, alas!
before the death of my mother.

Up to the time of my departure my mother continued to read the Bible with us and explain it.   She
had become enamoured of those millenarian opinions
which laid hold of so many some twenty-five or thirty
years ago.   The Apocalypse was perhaps her favourite
book in the Bible, and she was imbued with a conviction that all the many and varied horrors with which
it teems were upon the eve of their accomplishment.
The year eighteen hundred and forty-eight was to be
(as indeed it was) a time of general bloodshed and con-

fusion, while in eighteen hundred and sixty-six, should it please God to spare her, her eyes would be gladdened by the visible descent of the Son of Man with a shout, with the voice of the Archangel, with the trump of God, and the dead in Christ should rise first; then she, as one of them that were alive, would be caught up with other saints into the air, and would possibly receive while rising some distinguishing token of confidence and approbation which should fall with due impressiveness upon the surrounding multitude; then would come the consummation of all things, and she would be ever with the Lord. She died peaceably in her bed before she could know that a commercial panic was the nearest approach to the fulfilment of prophecy which the year eighteen hundred and sixty-six brought forth.

These opinions of my mother's injured her naturally healthy and vigorous mind by leading her to indulge in all manner of dreamy and fanciful interpretations of Scripture, which any but the most narrow literalist would feel at once to be untenable. Thus several times she expressed to us her conviction that my brother and myself were to be the two witnesses mentioned in the eleventh chapter of the Book of Revelation, and dilated upon the gratification she should experience upon finding that we had indeed been reserved for a position of such distinction. We were as yet mere children, and naturally took all for granted that our mother told us; we therefore made a careful examination of the passage which threw light upon our future. On finding that the prospect was gloomy and full of bloodshed we protested against the honours which were intended for us, more especially when we reflected that the mother of the two witnesses was not menaced in

Scripture with any particular discomfort. If we were to be martyrs, my mother ought to wish to be a martyr too, whereas nothing was farther from her intention. Her notion clearly was that we were to be massacred somewhere in the streets of London, in consequence of the anti-Christian machinations of the Pope ; that after lying about unburied for three days and a half we were to come to life again ; and finally, that we should conspicuously ascend to heaven, in front, perhaps, of the Foundling Hospital.

She was not herself indeed to share either our martyrdom or our glorification, but was to survive us many years on earth, living in an odour of great sanctity and reflected splendour, as the central and most august figure in a select society. She would perhaps be able indirectly, through her sons' influence with the Almighty, to have a voice in most of the arrangements both of this world and of the next. If all this were to come true (and things seemed very like it), those friends who had neglected us in our adversity would not find it too easy to be restored to favour, however greatly they might desire it—that is to say, they would not have found it too easy in the case of one less magnanimous and spiritually-minded than herself. My mother said but little of the above directly, but the fragments which occasionally escaped her were pregnant, and on looking back it is easy to perceive that she must have been building one of the most stupendous aërial fabrics that have ever been reared.

I have given the above in its more amusing aspect, and am half afraid that I may appear to be making a jest of weakness on the part of one of the most devotedly unselfish mothers who have ever existed. But one can love while smiling, and the very wildness of

my mother's dream serves to show how entirely her
whole soul was occupied with the things which are
above. To her, religion was all in all; the earth was
but a place of pilgrimage—only so far important as it
was a possible road to heaven. She impressed this
upon both of us by every word and action—instant in
season and out of season, so that she might but fill us
more deeply with a sense of the things belonging to
our peace.

But the inevitable consequences happened; my
mother had aimed too high and had overshot her mark.
The influence indeed of her guileless and unworldly
nature remained impressed upon my brother even
during the time of his extremest unbelief (perhaps his
ultimate safety is in the main referable to this cause,
and to the happy memories of my father, which had
predisposed him to love God), but my mother had
insisted on the most minute verbal accuracy of every
part of the Bible; she had also dwelt upon the duty
of independent research, and on the necessity of
giving up everything rather than assent to things which
our conscience did not assent to. No one could have
more effectually taught us to try *to think* the truth,
and we had taken her at her word because our hearts
told us that she was right. But she required three
incompatible things. When my brother grew older he
came to feel that independent and unflinching examination, with a determination to abide by the results,
would lead him to reject the point which to my mother
was more important than any other—I mean the
absolute accuracy of the Gospel records. My mother
was inexpressibly shocked at hearing my brother doubt
the authenticity of the Epistle to the Hebrews; and
then, as it appeared to him, she tried to make him

violate the duties of examination and candour which he had learnt too thoroughly to unlearn. Thereon came pain and an estrangement which was none the less profound for being mutually concealed. It seemed to my mother that he would not give up the wilfulness of his own opinions for her and for his Redeemer's sake. To him it seemed that he was ready to give up not only his mother but Christ Himself for Christ's sake.

This estrangement was the gradual work of some five or six years, during which my brother was between eleven and seventeen years old. At seventeen, I am told that he was remarkably well informed and clever. His manners were, like my father's, singularly genial, and his appearance very prepossessing. He had as yet no doubt concerning the soundness of any fundamental Christian doctrine, but his mind was already too active to allow of his being contented with my mother's childlike faith. There were points on which he did not indeed doubt, but which it would none the less be interesting to consider; such for example as the perfectibility of the regenerate Christian, and the meaning of the mysterious central chapters of the Epistle to the Romans. He was engaged in these researches though still only a boy, when an event occurred which gave the first real shock to his faith.

. He was accustomed to teach in a school for the poorest children every Sunday afternoon, a task for which his patience and good temper well fitted him. On one occasion, however, while he was explaining the effect of baptism to one of his favourite pupils, he discovered to his great surprise that the boy had never been baptized. He pushed his inquiries further, and found that out of the fifteen boys in his class only five had been baptized, and, not only so, but that no differ-

ence in disposition or conduct could be discovered between the regenerate boys and the unregenerate. The
good and bad boys were distributed in proportions equal
to the respective numbers of the baptized and unbaptized. In spite of a certain impetuosity of natural
character, he was also of a matter-of-fact and experi-
mental turn of mind; he therefore went through the
whole school, which numbered about a hundred boys,
and found out who had been baptized and who had
not. The same results appeared. The majority had
not been baptized; yet the good and bad dispositions
were so distributed as to preclude all possibility of
maintaining that the baptized boys were better than
the unbaptized.

The reader may smile at the idea of any one's faith
being troubled by a fact of which the explanation is so
obvious, but as a matter of fact my brother was seriously and painfully shocked. The teacher to whom he
applied for a solution of the difficulty was not a man
of any real power, and reported my brother to the
rector for having disturbed the school by his inquiries.
The rector was old and self-opinionated; the difficulty,
indeed, was plainly as new to him as it had been to
my brother, but instead of saying so at once, and
referring to any recognised theological authority, he
tried to put him off with words which seemed intended
to silence him rather than to satisfy him; finally he
lost his temper, and my brother fell under suspicion of
unorthodoxy.

This kind of treatment did not answer with my
brother. He alludes to it resentfully in the introduc-
tory chapter of his book. He became suspicious that
a preconceived opinion was being defended at the expense of honest scrutiny, and was thus driven upon

his own unaided investigation. The result may be guessed: he began to go astray, and strayed further and further. The children of God, he reasoned, the members of Christ and inheritors of the kingdom of heaven, were no more spiritually minded than the children of the world and the devil. Was then the grace of God a gift which left no trace whatever upon those who were possessed of it? A thing the presence or absence of which might be ascertained by consulting the parish registry, but was not discernible in conduct? The grace of man was more clearly perceptible than this. Assuredly there must be a screw loose somewhere, which, for aught he knew, might be jeopardising the salvation of all Christendom. Where then was this loose screw to be found?

He concluded after some months of reflection that the mischief was caused by the system of sponsors and by infant baptism. He, therefore, to my mother's inexpressible grief, joined the Baptists, and was immersed in a pond near Dorking. With the Baptists he remained quiet about three months, and then began to quarrel with his instructors as to their doctrine of predestination. Shortly afterwards he came accidentally upon a fascinating stranger who was no less struck with my brother than my brother with him, and this gentleman, who turned out to be a Roman Catholic missionary, landed him in the Church of Rome, where he felt sure that he had now found rest for his soul. But here, too, he was mistaken; after about two years he rebelled against the stifling of all free inquiry; on this rebellion the flood-gates of scepticism were opened, and he was soon battling with unbelief. He then fell in with one who was a pure Deist, and was shorn of every shred of dogma which he had ever held, except a belief in the personality and providence of the Creator.

On reviewing his letters written to me about this time, I am painfully struck with the manner in which they show that all these pitiable vagaries were to be traced to a single cause—a cause which still exists to the misleading of hundreds of thousands, and which, I fear, seems likely to continue in full force for many a year to come—I mean, to a false system of training which teaches people to regard Christianity as a thing one and indivisible, to be accepted entirely in the strictest reading of the letter, or to be rejected as absolutely untrue. The fact is, that all permanent truth is as one of those coal measures, a seam of which lies near the surface, and even crops up above the ground, but which is generally of an inferior quality and soon worked out; beneath it there comes a labour of sand and clay, and then at last the true seam of precious quality, and in virtually inexhaustible supply. The truth which is on the surface is rarely the whole truth. It is seldom until this has been worked out and done with—as in the case of the apparent flatness of the earth—that unchangeable truth is discovered. It is the glory of the Lord to conceal a matter: it is the glory of the king to find it out. If my brother, from whom I have taken the above illustration, had had some judicious and wide-minded friend, to correct and supplement the mainly admirable principles which had been instilled into him by my mother, he would have been saved years of spiritual wandering; but, as it was, he fell in with one after another, each in his own way as literal and unspiritual as the other—each impressed with one aspect of religious truth, and with one only. In the end he became perhaps the widest-

E

minded and most original thinker whom I have ever met; but no one from his early manhood could have augured this result; on the contrary, he showed every sign of being likely to develop into one of those who can never see more than one side of a question at a time, in spite of their seeing that side with singular clearness of mental vision.   In after life, he often met with mere lads who seemed to him to be years and years in advance of what he had been at their age, and would say, smiling, " With a great sum obtained I this freedom; but thou wast free-born."

Yet when one comes to think of it, a late development and laborious growth are generally more fruitful than those which are over early luxuriant.   Drawing an illustration from the art of painting, with which he was well acquainted, my brother used to say that all the greatest painters had begun with a hard and precise manner, from which they had only broken after several years of effort; and that in like manner all the early schools were founded upon definiteness of outline to the exclusion of truth of effect.   This may be true; but in my brother's case there was something even more unpromising than this; there was a commonness, so to speak, of mental execution, from which no one could have foreseen his after-emancipation. Yet in the course of time he was indeed emancipated to the very uttermost, while his bonds will, I firmly trust, be found to have been of inestimable service to the whole human race.

For although it was so many years before he was enabled to see the Christian scheme *as a whole,* or even to conceive the idea that there was any whole at all, other than each one of the stages of opinion through which he was at the time passing; yet when the idea was at length presented to him by one whom I must not name, the discarded fragments of his faith assumed shape, and formed themselves into a consistently organised scheme. Then became apparent the value of his knowledge of the details of so many different sides of Christian verity. Buried in the details, he had hitherto ignored the fact that they were only the unessential developments of certain component parts. Awakening to the perception of the whole after an intimate acquaintance with the details, he was able to realise the position and meaning of all that he had hitherto experienced in a way which has been vouchsafed to few, if any others.

Thus he became truly a broad Churchman. Not broad in the ordinary and ill-considered use of the term (for the broad Churchman is as little able to sympathise with Romanists, extreme High Churchmen and Dissenters, as these are with himself—he is only one of a sect which is called by the name of broad, though it is no broader than its own base), but in the true sense of being able to believe in the naturalness, legitimacy, and truth *quâ* Christianity even of those doctrines which seem to stand most widely and irreconcilably asunder.

SELECTIONS FROM LIFE AND HABIT.

————o————

ON CERTAIN ACQUIRED HABITS.

(FROM CHAPTER I. OF LIFE AND HABIT.[*])

IT will be our business in the following chapters to consider whether the unconsciousness, or quasi-unconsciousness, with which we perform certain acquired actions, throws any light upon Embryology and inherited instincts, and otherwise to follow the train of thought which the class of actions above mentioned may suggest. More especially I propose to consider them in so far as they bear upon the origin of species and the continuation of life by successive generations, whether in the animal or vegetable kingdoms.

Taking then, the art of playing the piano as an example of the kind of action we are in search of, we observe that a practised player will perform very difficult pieces apparently without effort, often, indeed, while thinking and talking of something quite other than his music; yet he will play accurately and, possibly, with much expression. If he has been playing a fugue, say in four parts, he will have kept each part well distinct, in such a manner as to prove that his mind was not prevented, by its other occupations, from consciously or unconsciously following four distinct trains of musical thought at the same time, nor

[*] The first edition of Life and Habit was published in December, 1877.

from making his fingers act in exactly the required manner as regards each note of each part.

It commonly happens that in the course of four or five minutes a player may have struck four or five thousand notes. If we take into consideration the rests, dotted notes, accidentals, variations of time, &c., we shall find his attention must have been exercised on many more occasions than when he was actually striking notes: so that it may not be too much to say that the attention of a first-rate player has been exercised—to an infinitesimally small extent—but still truly exercised—on as many as ten thousand occasions within the space of five minutes, for no note can be struck nor point attended to without a certain amount of attention, no matter how rapidly or unconsciously given.

Moreover, each act of attention has been followed by an act of volition, and each act of volition by a muscular action, which is composed of many minor actions; some so small that we can no more follow them than the player himself can perceive them; nevertheless, it may have been perfectly plain that the player was not attending to what he was doing, but was listening to conversation on some other subject, not to say joining in it himself. If he has been playing the violin, he may have done all the above, and may also have been walking about. Herr Joachim would unquestionably be able to do all that has here been described.

So complete may be the player's unconsciousness of the attention he is giving, and the brain power he is exerting, that we may find it difficult to awaken his attention to any particular part of his performance without putting him out. Indeed we cannot do so.

We observe that he finds it hardly less difficult to compass a voluntary consciousness of what he has once learnt so thoroughly that it has passed, so to speak, into the domain of unconsciousness, than he found it to learn the note or passage in the first instance. The effort after a second consciousness of detail baffles him—compels him to turn to his music or play slowly. In fact it seems as though he knows the piece too well to be able to know that he knows it, and is only conscious of knowing those passages which he does not know so thoroughly.

At the end of his performance, his power of re-collecting appears to be no less annihilated than was his consciousness of attention and volition. For of the thousands of acts requiring the exercise of both the one and the other, which he has done during the five minutes, we will say, of his performance, he will remember hardly one when it is over. If he calls to mind anything beyond the main fact that he has played such and such a piece, it will probably be some passage which he has found more difficult than the others, and with the like of which he has not been so long familiar. All the rest he will forget as completely as the breath which he has drawn while playing.

He finds it difficult to remember even the difficulties he experienced in learning to play. A few may have so impressed him that they remain with him, but the greater part will have escaped him as completely as the remembrance of what he ate, or how he put on his clothes, this day ten years ago; nevertheless, it is plain he does in reality remember more than he re-members remembering, for he avoids mistakes which he made at one time, and his performance proves that

all the notes are in his memory, though if called upon
to play such and such a bar at random from the
middle of the piece, and neither more nor less, he will
probably say that he cannot remember it unless he
begins from the beginning of the phrase which leads
to it.

In spite, however, of the performer's present proficiency, our experience of the manner in which proficiency is usually acquired warrants us in assuming
that there must have been a time when what is now
so easy as to be done without conscious effort of the
brain was only done by means of brain work which
was very keenly perceived, even to fatigue and positive
distress. Even now, if the player is playing something
the like of which he has not met before, we observe he
pauses and becomes immediately conscious of attention.

We draw the inference, therefore, as regards piano-
forte or violin playing, that the more the familiarity or
knowledge of the art, the less is there consciousness of
such knowledge; even so far as that there should be
almost as much difficulty in awakening consciousness
which has become, so to speak, latent,—a consciousness
of that which is known too well to admit of recognised
self-analysis while the knowledge is being exercised—
as in creating a consciousness of that which is not yet
well enough known to be properly designated as known
at all. On the other hand, we observe that the less
the familiarity or knowledge, the greater the consciousness of whatever knowledge there is.

.   .   .   .   .   .

To sum up, then, briefly. It would appear as
though perfect knowledge and perfect ignorance were
extremes which meet and become indistinguishable
from one another; so also perfect volition and perfect

absence of volition, perfect memory and perfect forget-fulness; for we are unconscious of knowing, willing, or remembering, either from not yet having known or willed, or from knowing and willing so well and so intensely as to be no longer conscious of either. Conscious knowledge and volition are of attention; attention is of suspense; suspense is of doubt; doubt is of uncertainty; uncertainty is of ignorance; so that the mere fact of conscious knowing or willing implies the presence of more or less novelty and doubt.

It would also appear as a general principle on a superficial view of the foregoing instances (and the reader may readily supply himself with others which are perhaps more to the purpose), that unconscious knowledge and unconscious volition are never acquired otherwise than as the result of experience, familiarity, or habit; so that whenever we observe a person able to do any complicated action unconsciously, we may assume both that he must have done it very often before he could acquire so great proficiency, and also that there must have been a time when he did not know how to do it at all.

We may assume that there was a time when he was yet so nearly on the point of neither knowing nor willing perfectly, that he was quite alive to whatever knowledge or volition he could exert; going further back, we shall find him still more keenly alive to a less perfect knowledge; earlier still, we find him well aware that he does not know nor will correctly, but trying hard to do both the one and the other; and so on, back and back, till both difficulty and consciousness become little more than "a sound of going," as it were, in the brain, a flitting to and fro of something barely recognisable as the desire to will or know at all—much less as the desire to know or will definitely this or that. Finally they retreat beyond our ken into the repose—the inorganic kingdom—of as yet unawakened interest.

In either case—the repose of perfect ignorance or of perfect knowledge — disturbance is troublesome. When first starting on an Atlantic steamer, our rest is hindered by the screw; after a short time, it is hindered if the screw stops. A uniform impression is practically no impression. One cannot either learn or unlearn without pains or pain.

CONSCIOUS AND UNCONSCIOUS KNOWERS —THE LAW AND GRACE.

(FROM CHAPTER II. OF LIFE AND HABIT.)

CERTAIN it is that we know best what we are least conscious of knowing, or at any rate least able to prove ; as, for example, our own existence, or that there is a country England. If any one asks us for proof on matters of this sort, we have none ready, and are justly annoyed at being called to consider what we regard as settled questions. Again, there is hardly anything which so much affects our actions as the centre of the earth (unless, perhaps, it be that still hotter and more unprofitable spot the centre of the universe), for we are incessantly trying to get as near it as circumstances will allow, or to avoid getting nearer than is for the time being convenient. Walking, running, standing, sitting, lying, waking, or sleeping, from birth till death it is a paramount object with us ; even after death— if it be not fanciful to say so—it is one of the few things of which what is left of us can still feel the influence ; yet what can engross less of our attention than this dark and distant spot so many thousands of miles away ?

The air we breathe, so long as it is neither too hot nor cold, nor rough, nor full of smoke—that is to say, so long as it is in that state with which we are best

mode

acquainted—seldom enters into our thoughts; yet there is hardly anything with which we are more incessantly occupied night and day.

Indeed, it is not too much to say that we have no really profound knowledge upon any subject—no knowledge on the strength of which we are ready to act at moments unhesitatingly without either preparation or after-thought—till we have left off feeling conscious of the possession of such knowledge, and of the grounds on which it rests. A lesson thoroughly learned must be like the air which feels so light, though pressing so heavily against us, because every pore of our skin is saturated, so to speak, with it on all sides equally. This perfection of knowledge sometimes extends to positive disbelief in the thing known, so that the most thorough knower shall believe himself altogether ignorant. No thief, for example, is such an utter thief — so *good* a thief — as the kleptomaniac. Until he has become a kleptomaniac, and can steal a horse as it were by a reflex action, he is still but half a thief, with many unthievish notions still clinging to him. Yet the kleptomaniac is probably unaware that he can steal at all, much less that he can steal so well. He would be shocked if he were to know the truth. So again, no man is a great hypocrite until he has left off knowing that he is a hypocrite. The great hypocrites of the world are almost invariably under the impression that they are among the very few really honest people to be found; and, as we must all have observed, it is rare to find any one strongly under this impression without ourselves having good reason to differ from him.

Again, it has been often and very truly said that it is not the conscious and self-styled sceptic, as Shelley,

for example, who is the true unbeliever. Such a man
as Shelley will, as indeed his life abundantly proves,
have more in common than not with the true unself-
conscious believer. Gallio again, whose indifference to
religious animosities has won him the cheapest immortality which, so far as I can remember, was ever yet
won, was probably, if the truth were known, a person
of the sincerest piety. It is the unconscious unbeliever who is the true infidel, however greatly he
would be surprised to know the truth. Mr. Spurgeon
was reported as having asked God to remove Lord
Beaconsfield from office " *as soon as possible.*" There
lurks a more profound distrust of God's power in these
words than in almost any open denial of His existence.

In like manner, the most perfect humour and irony
is generally quite unconscious. Examples of both are
frequently given by men whom the world considers as
deficient in humour; it is more probably true that
these persons are unconscious of their own delightful
power through the very mastery and perfection with
which they hold it. There is a play, for instance, of
genuine fun in some of the more serious scientific and
theological journals which for some time past we have
looked for in vain in " ———."

The following extract, from a journal which I will
not advertise, may serve as an example:

" Lycurgus, when they had abandoned to his revenge
him who had put out his eyes, took him home, and
the punishment he inflicted upon him was sedulous in-
structions to virtue." Yet this truly comic paper does
not probably know that it is comic, any more than
the kleptomaniac knows that he steals, or than John
Milton knew he was a humorist when he wrote a
hymn upon the circumcision, and spent his honey-

moon in composing a treatise on divorce. No more again did Goethe know how exquisitely humorous he was when he wrote, in his Wilhelm Meister, that a beautiful tear glistened in Theresa's right eye, and then went on to explain that it glistened in her right eye and not in her left, because she had had a wart on her left which had been removed—and successfully. Goethe probably wrote this without a chuckle; he believed what a good many people who have never read Wilhelm Meister believe still, namely, that it was a work full of pathos—of fine and tender feeling; yet a less consummate humorist must have felt that there was scarcely a paragraph in it from first to last the chief merit of which did not lie in its absurdity.

But enough has perhaps been said. As the fish in the sea, or the bird in the air, so unreasoningly and inarticulately safe must a man feel before he can be said to know. It is only those who are ignorant and uncultivated who can know anything at all in a proper sense of the words. Cultivation will breed in any man a certainty of the uncertainty even of his most assured convictions. It is perhaps fortunate for our comfort that we can none of us be cultivated upon very many subjects, so that considerable scope for assurance will still remain to us; but however this may be, we certainly observe it as a fact that those are the greatest men who are most uncertain in spite of certainty, and at the same time most certain in spite of uncertainty, and who are thus best able to feel that there is nothing in such complete harmony with itself as a flat contradiction in terms. For nature hates that any principle should breed, so to speak, hermaphroditically, but will give to each an help meet for it which shall cross it and be the undoing of it; as in the case of descent with modification, of which the essence is that every offspring resembles its parents, and yet, at the same time, that no offspring resembles its parents. But for the slightly irritating stimulant of this perpetual crossing, we should pass our lives unconsciously as though in slumber.

Until we have got to understand that though black is not white, yet it may be whiter than white itself (and any painter will readily paint that which shall show obviously as black, yet it shall be whiter than that which shall show no less obviously as white), we may be good logicians, but we are still poor reasoners. Knowledge is in an inchoate state as long as it is capable of logical treatment; it must be transmuted into that sense or instinct which rises altogether above the sphere in which words can have being at all, otherwise it is not yet incarnate. For sense is to knowledge what conscience is to reasoning about right and wrong ; the reasoning must be so rapid as to defy conscious reference to first principles, and even at times to be apparently subversive of them altogether, or the action will halt. It must become automatic before we are safe with it. While we are fumbling for the grounds of our conviction, our conviction is prone to fall, as Peter for lack of faith sinking into the waves of Galilee ; so that the very power to prove at all is an *à priori* argument against the truth—or at any rate the practical importance to the vast majority of mankind—of all that is supported by demonstration. For the power to prove implies a sense of the need of proof, and things which the majority of mankind find practically important are in ninety-nine cases out of a hundred above proof. The need of proof becomes as obsolete in the case of assured knowledge, as the practice of fortifying towns in the middle of an old and long-settled country. Who builds defences for that which is impregnable or little likely to be assailed? The answer is ready, that unless the defences had been built in former times it would be impossible to do without them now; but this does not touch the argument, which is not that demonstration is unwise but that as long as a demonstration is still felt necessary, and therefore kept ready to hand, the subject of such demonstration is not yet securely known. *Qui s'excuse, s'accuse;* and unless a matter can hold its own without the brag and self-assertion of continual demonstration, it is still more or less of a parvenu, which we shall not lose much by neglecting till it has less occasion to blow its own trumpet. The only alternative is that it is an error in process of detection, for if evidence concerning any opinion has long been deemed superfluous, and ever after this comes to be again felt necessary, we know that the opinion is doomed.

If there is any truth in the above, it follows that our conception of the words " science " and " scientific " must undergo some modification. Not that we should speak slightingly of science, but that we should recognise more than we do, that there are two distinct classes of scientific people, corresponding not inaptly with the two main parties into which the political world is divided. The one class is deeply versed in those sciences which have already become the common property of mankind; enjoying, enforcing, perpetuating, and engraining still more deeply into the mind of man acquisitions already approved by common experience, but somewhat careless about extension of empire, or at any rate disinclined, for the most part, to active effort on their own part for the sake of such extension

—neither progressive, in fact, nor aggressive—but quiet, peaceable people, who wish to live and let live, as their fathers before them; while the other class is chiefly intent upon pushing forward the boundaries of science, and is comparatively indifferent to what is known already save in so far as necessary for purposes of extension. These last are called pioneers of science, and to them alone is the title "scientific" commonly accorded; but pioneers, important to an army as they are, are still not the army itself, which can get on better without the pioneers than the pioneers without the army. Surely the class which knows thoroughly well what it knows, and which adjudicates upon the value of the discoveries made by the pioneers—surely this class has as good a right or better to be called scientific than the pioneers themselves.

These two classes above described blend into one another with every shade of gradation. Some are admirably proficient in the well-known sciences—that is to say, they have good health, good looks, good temper, common sense, and energy, and they hold all these good things in such perfection as to be altogether without introspection—to be not under the law, but so entirely under grace that every one who sees them likes them. But such may, and perhaps more commonly will, have very little inclination to extend the boundaries of human knowledge; their aim is in another direction altogether. Of the pioneers, on the other hand, some are agreeable people, well versed in the older sciences, though still more eminent as pioneers, while others, whose services in this last capacity have been of inestimable value, are noticeably ignorant of the sciences which have already become current with the larger part of mankind—in other words, they are ugly, rude, and disagreeable people, very progressive, it may be, but very aggressive to boot.

The main difference between these two classes lies in the fact that the knowledge of the one, so far as it is new, is known consciously, while that of the other is unconscious, consisting of sense and instinct rather than of recognised knowledge. So long as a man has these, and of the same kind as the more powerful body of his fellow-countrymen, he is a man of science though he can hardly read or write. As my great namesake said so well, "He knows what's what, and that's as high as metaphysic wit can fly." As is usual in cases of great proficiency, these true and thorough knowers do not know that they are scientific, and can seldom give a reason for the faith that is in them. They believe themselves to be ignorant, uncultured men, nor can even the professors whom they sometimes outwit in their own professorial domain perceive that they have been outwitted by men of superior scientific attainments to their own. The following passage from Dr. Carpenter's "Mesmerism, Spiritualism," &c., may serve as an illustration :—

"It is well known that persons who are conversant with the geological structure of a district are often able to indicate with considerable certainty in what spot and at what depth water will be found; and men *of less scientific knowledge, but of considerable practical experience*"—(so that in Dr. Carpenter's mind there seems to be some sort of contrast or difference in kind between the knowledge which is derived from observation of facts and scientific knowledge)—"frequently arrive at a true conclusion upon this point without being able to assign reasons for their opinions."

"Exactly the same may be said in regard to the

F

mineral structure of a mining district; the course of a metallic vein being often correctly indicated by the shrewd guess of an *observant* workman, when *the scientific reasoning* of the mining engineer altogether fails."

Precisely. Here we have exactly the kind of thing we are in search of: the man who has observed and observed till the facts are so thoroughly in his head that through familiarity he has lost sight both of them and of the processes whereby he deduced his conclusions from them—is apparently not considered scientific, though he knows how to solve the problem before him; the mining engineer, on the other hand, who reasons scientifically—that is to say, with a knowledge of his own knowledge—is found not to know, and to fail in discovering the mineral.

"It is an experience we are continually encountering in other walks of life," continues Dr. Carpenter, "that particular persons are guided—some apparently by an original and others by *an acquired intuition*— to conclusions for which they can give no adequate reason, but which subsequent events prove to have been correct." And this, I take it, implies what I have been above insisting on, namely, that on becoming intense, knowledge seems also to become unaware of the grounds on which it rests, or that it has or requires grounds at all, or indeed even exists. The only issue between myself and Dr. Carpenter would appear to be that Dr. Carpenter, himself an acknowledged leader in the scientific world, restricts the term "scientific" to the people who know that they know, but are beaten by those who are not so conscious of their own knowledge; while I say that the term "scientific" should be applied (only that they would not like it) to the nice sensible people who know what's what rather than to the professorial classes.

And this is easily understood when we remember that the pioneer cannot hope to acquire any of the new sciences in a single lifetime so perfectly as to become unaware of his own knowledge. As a general rule, we observe him to be still in a state of active consciousness concerning whatever particular science he is extending, and as long as he is in this state he cannot know utterly. It is, as I have already so often insisted, those who do not know that they know so much who have the firmest grip of their knowledge: the best class, for example, of our English youth, who live much in the open air, and, as Lord Beaconsfield finely said, never read. These are the people who know best those things which are best worth knowing— that is to say, they are the most truly scientific.

Unfortunately, the apparatus necessary for this kind of science is so costly as to be within the reach of few, involving, as it does, an experience in the use of it for some preceding generations. Even those who are born with the means within their reach must take no less pains, and exercise no less self-control, before they can attain the perfect unconscious use of them, than would go to the making of a James Watt or a Stephenson; it is vain, therefore, to hope that this best kind of science can ever be put within the reach of the many; nevertheless it may be safely said that all the other and more generally recognised kinds of science are valueless except in so far as they minister to this the highest kind. They have no *raison d'être* unless they tend to do away with the necessity for work, and to diffuse good health, and that good sense which is above self-consciousness. They are to be encouraged because they have rendered the most fortunate kind of modern European possible, and because they tend to make possible a still more fortunate kind than any now existing. But the man who devotes himself to science cannot—with the rarest, if any, exceptions—belong to this most fortunate class himself. He occupies a lower place, both scientifically and morally, for it is not possible but that his drudgery should somewhat soil him both in mind and health of body, or, if this be denied, surely it must let him and hinder him in running the race for unconsciousness. We do not feel that it increases the glory of a king or great nobleman that he should excel in what is commonly called science. Certainly he should not go further than Prince Rupert's drops. Nor should he excel in music, art, literature, or theology—all which things are more or less parts of science. He should be above them all, save in so far as he can without effort reap renown from the labours of others. It is a *lâche* in him that he should write music or books, or paint pictures at all; but if he must do so, his work should be at best contemptible. Much as we must condemn Marcus Aurelius, we condemn James I. even more severely.

It is a pity there should exist so general a confusion of thought upon this subject, for it may be asserted without fear of contradiction that there is hardly any form of immorality now rife which produces more disastrous effects upon those who give themselves up to it, and upon society in general, than the so-called science of those who know that they know too well to be able to know truly. With very clever people—the people who know that they know—it is much as with the members of the early Corinthian Church, to whom St. Paul wrote, that if they looked their numbers over, they would not find many wise, nor powerful, nor well-born people among them. Dog-fanciers tell us that performing dogs never carry their tails; such dogs have eaten of the tree of knowledge, and are convinced of sin accordingly—they know that they know things, in respect of which, therefore, they are no longer under grace, but under the law, and they have yet so much grace left as to be ashamed. So with the human clever dog; he may speak with the tongues of men and angels, but so long as he knows that he knows, his tail will droop.

More especially does this hold in the case of those who are born to wealth and of old family. We must all feel that a rich young nobleman with a taste for science and principles is rarely a pleasant object. We do not understand the rich young man in the Bible who wanted to inherit eternal life, unless, indeed, he merely wanted to know whether there was not some way by which he could avoid dying, and even so he is hardly worth considering. Principles are like logic, which never yet made a good reasoner of a bad one, but might still be occasionally useful if they did not invariably contradict each other whenever there is any temptation to appeal to them. They are like fire, good servants but bad masters. As many people or more have been wrecked on principle as from want of principle. They are, as their name implies, of an elementary character, suitable for beginners only, and he who has so little mastered them as to have occasion to refer to them consciously, is out of place in the society of well-educated people. The truly scientific invariably hate him, and, for the most part, the more profoundly in proportion to the unconsciousness with which they do so.

If the reader hesitates, let him go down into the streets and look in the shop-windows at the photographs of eminent men, whether literary, artistic, or scientific, and note the work which the consciousness of knowledge has wrought on nine out of every ten of them; then let him go to the masterpieces of Greek and Italian art, the truest preachers of the truest gospel of grace; let him look at the Venus of Milo, the Discobolus, the St. George of Donatello. If it had pleased these people to wish to study, there was no lack of brains to do it with; but imagine "what a deal of scorn" would "look beautiful in the contempt and anger" of the Venus of Milo's lip if it were suggested to her that she should learn to read. Which, think you, knows most, the Theseus, or any modern professor taken at random? True, learning must have a great share in the advancement of beauty, inasmuch as beauty is but knowledge perfected and incarnate—but with the pioneers it is *sic vos non vobis;* the grace is not for them, but for those who come after. Science is like offences. It must needs come, but woe unto that man through whom it comes; for there cannot be much beauty where there is consciousness of knowledge, and while knowledge is still new it must in the nature of things involve much consciousness.

It is not knowledge, then, that is incompatible with beauty; there cannot be too much knowledge, but it must have passed through many people who it is to be feared must be both ugly and disagreeable, before beauty or grace will have anything to say to it; it must be so diffused throughout a man's whole being that he shall not be aware of it, or he will bear himself under it constrainedly as one under the law, and not as one under grace.

And grace is best, for where grace is, love is not distant. Grace! the old Pagan ideal whose charm even unlovely Paul could not withstand, but, as the legend tells us, his soul-fainted within him, his heart misgave him, and, standing alone on the seashore at dusk, he "troubled deaf heaven with his bootless cries," his thin voice pleading for grace after the flesh.

The waves came in one after another, the sea-gulls cried together after their kind, the wind rustled among the dried canes upon the sandbanks, and there came a voice from heaven saying, "Let My grace be sufficient for thee." Whereon, failing of the thing itself, he stole the word and strove to crush its meaning to the measure of his own limitations. But the true grace, with her groves and high places, and troops of young men and maidens crowned with flowers, and singing of love and youth and wine—the true grace he drove out into the wilderness—high up, it may be, into Piora, and into such-like places. Happy they who harboured her in her ill report.

It is common to hear men wonder what new faith will be adopted by mankind if disbelief in the Christian religion should become general. They seem to expect that some new theological or quasi-theological system will arise, which, *mutatis mutandis*, shall be Christianity over again. It is a frequent reproach against those who maintain that the supernatural element of Christianity is without foundation, that they bring forward no such system of their own. They pull down but cannot build. We sometimes hear even those who have come to the same conclusions as the destroyers say, that having nothing new to set up, they will not attack the old. But how can people set up a new superstition, knowing it to be a superstition? Without faith in

their own platform, a faith as intense as that manifested by the early Christians, how can they preach?
A new superstition will come, but it is in the very
essence of things that its apostles should have no suspicion of its real nature; that they should no more
recognise the common element between the new and the
old than the early Christians recognised it between
their faith and Paganism.   If they did, they would be
paralysed.   Others say that the new fabric may be seen
rising on every side, and that the coming religion is
science.   Certainly its apostles preach it without misgiving, but it is not on that account less possible that
it may prove only to be the coming superstition—like
Christianity, true to its true votaries, and, like Christianity, false to those who follow it introspectively.

It may well be we shall find we have escaped from
one set of taskmasters to fall into the hands of others
far more ruthless.   The tyranny of the Church is light
in comparison with that which future generations may
have to undergo at the hands of the doctrinaires.   The
Church did uphold a grace of some sort as the *sum-
mum bonum*, in comparison with which all so-called
earthly knowledge—knowledge, that is to say, which
had not passed through so many people as to have
become living and incarnate—was unimportant.   Do
what we may, we are still drawn to the unspoken
teaching of her less introspective ages with a force
which no falsehood could command.   Her buildings,
her music, her architecture, touch us as none other on
the whole can do; when she speaks there are many of
us who think that she denies the deeper truths of her
own profounder mind, and unfortunately her tendency
is now towards more rather than less introspection.
The more she gives way to this—the more she becomes

conscious of knowing—the less she will know. But still her ideal is in grace.

The so-called man of science, on the other hand, seems now generally inclined to make light of all knowledge, save of the pioneer character. His ideal is in self-conscious knowledge. Let us have no more Lo, here, with the professor; he very rarely knows what he says he knows; no sooner has he misled the world for a sufficient time with a great flourish of trumpets than he is toppled over by one more plausible than himself. He is but medicine-man, augur, priest, in its latest development; useful it may be, but requiring to be well watched by those who value freedom. Wait till he has become more powerful, and note the vagaries which his conceit of knowledge will indulge in. The Church did not persecute while she was still weak. Of course every system has had, and will have, its heroes, but, as we all very well know, the heroism of the hero is but remotely due to system; it is due not to arguments, nor reasoning, nor to any consciously recognised perceptions, but to those deeper sciences which lie far beyond the reach of self-analysis, and for the study of which there is but one schooling—to have had good forefathers for many generations.

Above all things let no unwary reader do me the injustice of believing in *me*. In that I write at all I am among the damned. If he must believe in anything, let him believe in the music of Handel, the painting of Giovanni Bellini, and in the thirteenth chapter of St. Paul's First Epistle to the Corinthians.

But to return. Whenever we find people knowing that they know this or that, we have the same story over and over again. They do not yet know it perfectly.

We come, therefore, to the conclusion that our knowledge and reasonings thereupon, only become perfect, assured, unhesitating, when they have become automatic, and are thus exercised without further conscious effort of the mind, much in the same way as we cannot walk nor read nor write perfectly till we can do so automatically.

APPLICATION OF FOREGOING CHAPTERS TO
CERTAIN HABITS ACQUIRED AFTER BIRTH
WHICH ARE COMMONLY CONSIDERED IN-
STINCTIVE.

(CHAPTER III. OF LIFE AND HABIT.)

WHAT is true of knowing is also true of willing.
The more intensely we will, the less is our will
deliberate and capable of being recognised as will at all.
So that it is common to hear men declare under certain
circumstances that they had no will, but were forced
into their own action under stress of passion or temptation. But in the more ordinary actions of life, we
observe, as in walking or breathing, that we do not
will anything utterly and without remnant of hesitation, till we have lost sight of the fact that we are
exercising our will.

The question, therefore, is forced upon us, how far
this principle extends, and whether there may not be
unheeded examples of its operation which, if we consider them, will land us in rather unexpected conclusions. If it be granted that consciousness of knowledge
and of volition vanishes when the knowledge and the
volition have become intense and perfect, may it not
be possible that many actions which we do without
knowing how we do them, and without any conscious
exercise of the will—actions which we certainly could

not do if we tried to do them, nor refrain from doing if for any reason we wished to do so—are done so easily and so unconsciously owing to excess of knowledge or experience rather than deficiency, we having done them too often, knowing how to do them too well, and having too little hesitation as to the method of procedure, to be capable of following our own action, without the derangement of such action altogether; or, in other cases, because we have so long settled the question that we have stowed away the whole apparatus with which we work in corners of our system which we cannot now conveniently reach?

It may be interesting to see whether we can find any class or classes of actions which link actions which for some time after birth we could not do at all, and in which our proficiency has reached the stage of unconscious performance obviously through repeated effort and failure, and through this only, with actions which we could do as soon as we were born, and concerning which it would at first sight appear absurd to say that they can have been acquired by any process in the least analogous to what we commonly call experience, inasmuch as the creature itself which does them has only just begun to exist, and cannot, therefore, in the very nature of things, have had experience.

Can we see that actions, for the acquisition of which experience is such an obvious necessity, that whenever we see the acquisition we assume the experience, gradate away imperceptibly into actions which seem, according to all reasonable analogy, to necessitate experience—of which, however, the time and place are so obscure, that they are not now commonly supposed to have any connection with *bonâ fide* experience at all.

Eating and drinking appear to be such actions. The

new-born child cannot eat, and cannot drink, but he can swallow as soon as he is born; and swallowing appears (as we may remark in passing) to have been an earlier faculty of animal life than that of eating with teeth. The ease and unconsciousness with which we eat and drink is clearly attributable to practice; but a very little practice seems to go a long way—a suspiciously small amount of practice—as though somewhere or at some other time there must have been more practice than we can account for. We can very readily stop eating or drinking, and can follow our own action without difficulty in either process; but as regards swallowing, which is the earlier habit, we have less power of self-analysis and control: when we have once committed ourselves beyond a certain point to swallowing, we must finish doing so,—that is to say, our control over the operation ceases. Also, a still smaller experience seems necessary for the acquisition of the power to swallow than appeared necessary in the case of eating; and if we get into a difficulty we choke, and are more at a loss how to become introspective than we are about eating and drinking.

Why should a baby be able to swallow—which one would have said was the more complicated process of the two—with so much less practice than it takes him to learn to eat? How comes it that he exhibits in the case of the more difficult operation all the phenomena which ordinarily accompany a more complete mastery and longer practice? Analogy points in the direction of thinking that the necessary experience cannot have been wanting, and that, too, not in such a quibbling sort as when people talk about inherited habit or the experience of the race, which, without explanation, is to plain-speaking persons very much the same, in regard to the individual, as no experience at all, but *bonâ fide* in the child's own person.

Breathing, again, is an action acquired after birth, generally with some little hesitation and difficulty, but still acquired in a time seldom longer, as I am informed, than ten minutes or a quarter of an hour. For an art which has to be acquired at all, there seems here, as in the case of eating, to be a disproportion between, on the one hand, the intricacy of the process performed, and on the other, the shortness of the time taken to acquire the practice, and the ease and unconsciousness with which its exercise is continued from the moment of acquisition.

We observe that in later life much less difficult and intricate operations than breathing require much longer practice before they can be mastered to the extent of unconscious performance. We observe also that the phenomena attendant on the learning by an infant to breathe are extremely like those attendant upon the repetition of some performance by one who has done it very often before, but who requires just a little prompting to set him off, on getting which, the whole familiar routine presents itself before him, and he repeats his task by rote. Surely then we are justified in suspecting that there must have been more *bonâ fide* personal recollection and experience, with more effort and failure on the part of the infant itself, than meet the eye.

It should be noticed, also that our control over breathing is very limited. We can hold our breath a little, or breathe a little faster for a short time, but we cannot do this for long, and after having gone without air for a certain time we must breathe.

Seeing and hearing require some practice before their free use is mastered, but not very much. They are so far within our control that we can see more by looking harder, and hear more by listening attentively—but they are beyond our control in so far as that we must see and hear the greater part of what presents itself to us as near, and at the same time unfamiliar, unless we turn away or shut our eyes, or stop our ears by a mechanical process; and when we do this it is a sign that we have already involuntarily seen or heard more than we wished. The familiar, whether sight or sound, very commonly escapes us.

Take again the processes of digestion, the action of the heart, and the oxygenisation of the blood—processes of extreme intricacy, done almost entirely unconsciously, and quite beyond the control of our volition.

Is it possible that our unconsciousness concerning our own performance of all these processes arises from over-experience?

Is there anything in digestion or the oxygenisation of the blood different in kind to the rapid unconscious action of a man playing a difficult piece of music on the piano? There may be in degree, but as a man who sits down to play what he well knows, plays on when once started, almost, as we say, mechanically, so, having eaten his dinner, he digests it as a matter of course, unless it has been in some way unfamiliar to him or he to it, owing to some derangement or occurrence with which he is unfamiliar, and under which therefore he is at a loss how to comport himself, as a player would be at a loss how to play with gloves on, or with gout in his fingers, or if set to play music upside down.

Can we show that all the acquired actions of childhood and after-life, which we now do unconsciously, or without conscious exercise of the will, are familiar acts—acts which we have already done a very great number of times ?

Can we also show that there are no acquired actions which we can perform in this automatic manner which were not at one time difficult, requiring attention, and liable to repeated failure, our volition failing to command obedience from the members which should carry its purposes into execution?

If so, analogy will point in the direction of thinking that other acts which we do even more unconsciously may only escape our power of self-examination and control because they are even more familiar—because we have done them oftener; and we may imagine that if there were a microscope which could show us the minutest atoms of consciousness and volition, we should find that even the apparently most automatic actions were yet done in due course, upon a balance of considerations, and under the deliberate exercise of the will.

We should also incline to think that even such an action as the oxygenisation of its blood by an infant of ten minutes' old, can only be done so well and so unconsciously, after repeated failures on the part of the infant itself.

True, as has been already implied, we do not immediately see when the baby could have made the necessary mistakes and acquired that infinite practice without which it could never go through such complex processes satisfactorily; we have therefore invented the word "heredity," and consider it as accounting for the phenomena; but a little reflection will show that though this word may be a very good way of stating the difficulty, it does nothing whatever towards removing it.*

* See page 228 of this book, "Remarks on Mr. Romanes' 'Mental Evolution in Animals.'"

Why should heredity enable a creature to dispense with the experience which we see to be necessary in all other cases before difficult operations can be performed successfully?

What is this talk that is made about the experience *of the race*, as though the experience of one man could profit another who knows nothing about him? If a man eats his dinner, it nourishes *him* and not his neighbour; if he learns a difficult art, it is *he* that can do it and not his neighbour. Yet, practically, we see that the vicarious experience, which seems so contrary to our common observation, does nevertheless appear to hold good in the case of creatures and their descendants. Is there, then, any way of bringing these apparently conflicting phenomena under the operation of one law? Is there any way of showing that this experience of the race, of which so much is said without the least attempt to show in what way it may or does become the experience of the individual, is in sober seriousness the experience of one single being only, repeating in a great many different ways certain performances with which it has become exceedingly familiar?

It comes to this—that we must either suppose the conditions of experience to differ during the earlier stages of life from those which we observe them to become during the heyday of any existence—and this would appear very gratuitous, tolerable only as a suggestion because the beginnings of life are so obscure, that in such twilight we may do pretty much whatever we please without fear of being found out—or that we must suppose continuity of life and sameness between living beings, whether plants or animals, and their descendants, to be far closer than we have hitherto believed; so that the experience of one person is

G

not enjoyed by his successor, so much as that the successor is *bonâ fide* an elongation of the life of his progenitors, imbued with their memories, profiting by their experiences—which are, in fact, his own until he leaves their bodies—and only unconscious of the extent of these memories and experiences owing to their vastness and already infinite repetition.

Certainly it presents itself to us as a singular coincidence—

I. That we are *most conscious of, and have most control over*, such habits as speech, the upright position, the arts and sciences—which are acquisitions peculiar to the human race, always acquired after birth, and not common to ourselves and any ancestor who had not become entirely human.

II. That we are *less conscious of, and have less control over*, the use of teeth, swallowing, breathing, seeing and hearing—which were acquisitions of our prehuman ancestry, and for which we had provided ourselves with all the necessary apparatus before we saw light, but which are still, geologically speaking, recent, or comparatively recent.

III. That we are *most unconscious of, and have least control over*, our digestion, which we have in common even with our invertebrate ancestry, and which is a habit of extreme antiquity.

There is something too like method in this for it to be taken as the result of mere chance—chance again being but another illustration of Nature's love of a contradiction in terms; for everything is chance, and nothing is chance. And you may take it that all is chance or nothing chance, according as you please, but you must not have half chance and half not chance— which, however, in practice is just what you *must* have.

Does it not seem as though the older and more confirmed the habit, the more unquestioning the act of volition, till, in the case of the oldest habits, the practice of succeeding existences has so formulated the procedure, that, on being once committed to such and such a line beyond a certain point, the subsequent course is so clear as to be open to no further doubt, and admit of no alternative, till the very power of questioning is gone, and even the consciousness of volition? And this too upon matters which, in earlier stages of a man's existence, admitted of passionate argument and anxious deliberation whether to resolve them thus or thus, with heroic hazard and experiment, which on the losing side proved to be vice, and on the winning virtue. For there was passionate argument once what shape a man's teeth should be, nor can the colour of his hair be considered as even yet settled, or likely to be settled for a very long time.

It is one against legion when a creature tries to differ from his own past selves. He must yield or die if he wants to differ widely, so as to lack natural instincts, such as hunger or thirst, or not to gratify them. It is more righteous in a man that he should "eat strange food," and that his cheek should "so much as lank not," than that he should starve if the strange food be at his command. His past selves are living in unruly hordes within him at this moment and overmastering him. "Do this, this, this, which we too have done, and found our profit in it," cry the souls of his forefathers within him. Faint are the far ones, coming and going as the sound of bells wafted on to a high mountain; loud and clear are the near ones, urgent as an alarm of fire. "Withhold," cry some. "Go on boldly," cry others. "Me, me, me, revert hitherward, my descendant," shouts one as it were from some high vantage-ground over the heads of the clamorous multitude. " Nay, but me, me, me," echoes another; and our former selves fight within us and wrangle for our possession. Have we not here what is commonly called an *internal tumult*, when dead pleasures and pains tug within us hither and thither? Then may the battle be decided by what people are pleased to call our own experience. Our own indeed! What is our own save by mere courtesy of speech? A matter of fashion. Sanction sanctifieth and fashion fashioneth. And so with death—the most inexorable of all conventions.

However this may be, we may assume it as an axiom with regard to actions acquired after birth, that we never do them automatically save as the result of long practice, and after having thus acquired perfect mastery over the action in question.

But given the practice or experience, and the intricacy of the process to be performed appears to matter very little. There is hardly anything conceivable as being done by man, which a certain amount of familiarity will not enable him to do, unintrospectively, and without conscious effort. " The most complex and difficult movements," writes Mr. Darwin, " can in time be performed without the least effort or consciousness." All the main business of life is done thus unconsciously or semi-unconsciously. For what is the main business of life? We work that we may eat and digest, rather than eat and digest that we may work; this, at any rate, is the normal state of things; the more important business then is that which is carried on unconsciously. So again, the action of the brain, which goes on prior to our realising the idea in which it results, is not perceived by the individual. So also all the deeper springs of action and conviction. The residuum with which we fret and worry ourselves is a mere matter of detail, as the higgling and haggling of the market, which is not over the bulk of the price, but over the last half-penny.

Shall we say, then, that a baby of a day old sucks (which involves the whole principle of the pump, and hence a profound practical knowledge of the laws of pneumatics and hydrostatics), digests, oxygenises its blood (millions of years before Sir Humphry Davy discovered oxygen), sees and hears—all most difficult and complicated operations, involving an unconscious knowledge of the facts concerning optics and acoustics, compared with which the conscious discoveries of Newton sink into utter insignificance? Shall we say that a baby can do all these things at once, doing them so well and so regularly, without being even able to direct its attention to them, and without mistake, and at the same time not know how to do them, and never have done them before?

Such an assertion would be a contradiction to the whole experience of mankind. Surely the *onus probandi* must rest with him who makes it.

A man may make a lucky hit now and again by what is called a fluke, but even this must be only a little in advance of his other performances of the same kind. He may multiply seven by eight by a fluke after a little study of the multiplication table, but he will not be able to extract the cube root of 4913 by a fluke, without long training in arithmetic, any more than an agricultural labourer would be able to operate successfully for cataract. If, then, a grown man cannot perform so simple an operation as that, we will say, for cataract, unless he have been long trained in other similar operations, and until he has done what comes to the same thing many times over, with what show of reason can we maintain that one who is so far less capable than a grown man, can perform such vastly more difficult operations, without knowing how to do them, and without ever having done them before? There is no sign of "fluke" about the circulation of a baby's blood.   There may perhaps be some little hesitation about its earliest breathing, but this, as a general rule, soon passes over, both breathing and circulation, within an hour after birth, being as regular and easy as at any time during life.   Is it reasonable, then, to say that the baby does these things without knowing how to do them, and without ever having done them before, and continues to do them by a series of lifelong flukes?

It would be well if those who feel inclined to hazard such an assertion would find some other instances of intricate processes gone through by people who know nothing about them, and who never had any practice therein.   What *is* to know how to do a thing?   Surely to do it.   What is proof that we know how to do a thing?   Surely the fact that we can do it.   A man shows that he knows how to throw the boomerang by throwing the boomerang.   No amount of talking or writing can get over this; *ipso facto*, that a baby breathes and makes its blood circulate, it knows how to do so; and the fact that it does not know its own knowledge is only proof of the perfection of that knowledge, and of the vast number of past occasions on which it must have been exercised already.   As has been said already, it is less obvious when the baby could have gained its experience, so as to be able so readily to remember exactly what to do; *but it is more easy to suppose that the necessary occasions cannot have been wanting, than that the power which we observe should have been obtained without practice and memory.*

If we saw any self-consciousness on the baby's part about its breathing or circulation, we might suspect that it had had less experience, or had profited less by its experience, than its neighbours—exactly in the same manner as we suspect a deficiency of any quality which we see a man inclined to parade. We all become introspective when we find that we do not know our business, and whenever we are introspective we may generally suspect that we are on the verge of unproficiency. Unfortunately, in the case of sickly children we observe that they sometimes do become conscious of their breathing and circulation, just as in later life we become conscious that we have a liver or a digestion. In that case there is always something wrong. The baby that becomes aware of its breathing does not know how to breathe and will suffer for his ignorance and incapacity, exactly in the same way as he will suffer in later life for ignorance and incapacity in any other respect in which his peers are commonly knowing and capable. In the case of inability to breathe, the punishment is corporal, breathing being a matter of fashion, so old and long settled that nature can admit of no departure from the established custom, and the procedure in case of failure is as much formulated as the fashion itself. In the case of the circulation, the whole performance has become one so utterly of rote, that the mere discovery that we could do it at all was considered one of the highest flights of human genius.

It has been said a day will come when the Polar ice shall have accumulated, till it forms vast continents many thousands of feet above the level of the sea, all of solid ice. The weight of this mass will, it is believed, cause the world to topple over on its axis, so that the earth will be upset as an ant-heap overturned by a ploughshare. In that day the icebergs will come crunching against our proudest cities, razing them from off the face of the earth as though they were made of rotten blotting-paper. There is no respect now of Handel nor of Shakespeare; the works of Rembrandt and Bellini fossilise at the bottom of the sea. Grace, beauty, and wit, all that is precious in music, literature, and art—all gone. In the morning there was Europe. In the evening there are no more populous cities nor busy hum of men, but a sea of jagged ice, a lurid sunset, and the doom of many ages. Then shall a scared remnant escape in places, and settle upon the changed continent when the waters have subsided—a simple people, busy hunting shellfish on the drying ocean beds, and with little time for introspection; yet they can read and write and sum, for by that time these accomplishments will have become universal, and will be acquired as easily as we now learn to talk; but they do so as a matter of course, and without self-consciousness. Also they make the simpler kinds of machinery too easily to be able to follow their own operations—the manner of their own apprenticeship being to them as a buried city. May we not imagine that, after the lapse of another ten thousand years or so, some one of them may again become cursed with lust of introspection, and a second Harvey may astonish the world by discovering that it can read and write, and that steam-engines do not grow, but are made? It may be safely prophesied that he will die a martyr, and be honoured in the fourth generation.

PERSONAL IDENTITY.

(CHAPTER V. OF LIFE AND HABIT.)

"STRANGE difficulties have been raised by some," says Bishop Butler, "concerning personal identity, or the sameness of living agents as implied in the notion of our existing now and hereafter, or indeed in any two consecutive moments." But in truth it is not easy to see the strangeness of the difficulty, if the words either "personal" or "identity" are used in any strictness.

Personality is one of those ideas with which we are so familiar that we have lost sight of the foundations upon which it rests. We regard our personality as a simple definite whole; as a plain, palpable, individual thing, which can be seen going about the streets or sitting indoors at home; as something which lasts us our lifetime, and about the confines of which no doubt can exist in the minds of reasonable people. But in truth this "we," which looks so simple and definite, is a nebulous and indefinable aggregation of many component parts which war not a little among themselves, our perception of our existence at all being perhaps due to this very clash of warfare, as our sense of sound and light is due to the jarring of vibrations. Moreover, as the component parts of our identity change from moment to moment, our personality becomes a thing

dependent upon time present, which has no logical
existence, but lives only upon the sufferance of times
past and future, slipping out of our hands into the domain
of one or other of these two claimants the moment we
try to apprehend it. And not only is our personality
as fleeting as the present moment, but the parts which
compose it blend some of them so imperceptibly into,
and are so inextricably linked on to, outside things
which clearly form no part of our personality, that
when we try to bring ourselves to book and determine
wherein we consist, or to draw a line as to where we
begin or end, we find ourselves baffled. There is
nothing but fusion and confusion.

Putting theology on one side, and dealing only with
the common sense of mankind, our body is certainly
part of our personality. With the destruction of our
bodies, our personality, as far as we can follow it, comes
to a full stop ; and with every modification of them it
is correspondingly modified. But what are the limits
of our bodies ? They are composed of parts, some of
them so unessential as to be hardly included in personality at all, and to be separable from ourselves without perceptible effect, as hair, nails, and daily waste of
tissue. Again, other parts are very important, as our
hands, feet, arms, legs, &c., but still are no essential
parts of our "self" or "soul," which continues to exist,
though in a modified condition, in spite of their amputation. Other parts, as the brain, heart, and blood, are
so essential that they cannot be dispensed with, yet it
is impossible to say that personality consists in any
one of them.

Each one of these component members of our personality is continually dying and being born again,
supported in this process by the food we eat, the water

we drink, and the air we breathe; which three things link us on, and fetter us down, to the organic and inorganic world about us. For our meat and drink, though no part of our personality before we eat and drink, cannot, after we have done so, be separated entirely from us without the destruction of our personality altogether, so far as we can follow it; and who shall say at what precise moment our food has or has not become part of ourselves? A famished man eats food; after a short time his whole personality is so palpably affected that we know the food to have entered into him and taken, as it were, possession of him; but who can say at what precise moment it did so? Thus we find that we melt away into outside things and are rooted into them as plants into the soil in which they grow, nor can any man say he consists absolutely in this or that, nor define himself so certainly as to include neither more nor less than himself; many undoubted parts of his personality being more separable from it, and changing it less when so separated, both to his own senses and those of other people, than other parts which are strictly speaking no parts at all.

A man's clothes, for example, as they lie on a chair at night are no part of him, but when he wears them they would appear to be so, as being a kind of food which warms him and hatches him, and the loss of which may kill him of cold. If this be denied, and a man's clothes be considered as no part of his self, nevertheless they, with his money, and it may perhaps be added his religious opinions, stamp a man's individuality as strongly as any natural feature can stamp it. Change in style of dress, gain or loss of money, make a man feel and appear more changed than having his chin shaved or his nails cut. In fact, as soon as we leave common parlance on one side, and try for a scientific definition of personality, we find that there is none possible, any more than there can be a demonstration of the fact that we exist at all—a demonstration for which, as for that of a personal God, many have hunted but which none have found. The only solid foundation is, as in the case of the earth's crust, pretty near the surface of things; the deeper we try to go, the damper, darker, and altogether more uncongenial we find it. There is no quagmire of superstition into which we may not be easily lured if we once cut ourselves adrift from those superficial aspects of things, in which alone our nature permits us to be comforted.

Common parlance, however, settles the difficulty readily enough (as indeed it settles most others if they show signs of awkwardness) by the simple process of ignoring it: we decline, and very properly, to go into the question of where personality begins and ends, but assume it to be known by every one, and throw the onus of not knowing it upon the over-curious, who had better think as their neighbours do, right or wrong, or there is no knowing into what villany they may not presently fall.

Assuming, then, that every one knows what is meant by the word " person " (and such superstitious bases as this are the foundations upon which all action, whether of man, beast, or plant, is constructed and rendered possible; for even the corn in the fields grows upon a superstitious basis as to its own existence, and only turns the earth and moisture into wheat through the conceit of its own ability to do so, without which faith it were powerless; and the lichen only grows upon the granite rock by first saying to itself, " I think I can do it ; " so that it would not be able

to grow unless it thought it could grow, and would not
think it could grow unless it found itself able to grow,
and thus spends its life arguing most virtuously in a
most vicious circle—basing action upon hypothesis,
which hypothesis is in turn based upon action)—assuming that we know what is meant by the word "person,"
we say that we are one and the same person from birth
till death, so that whatever is done by or happens to
any one between birth and death, is said to happen to
or be done by one individual.　This in practice is found
sufficient for the law courts and the purposes of daily
life, which, being full of hurry and the pressure of
business, can only tolerate compromise, or conventional
rendering of intricate phenomena.　When facts of
extreme complexity have to be daily and hourly dealt
with by people whose time is money, they must be
simplified, and treated much as a painter treats them,
drawing them in squarely, seizing the more important
features, and neglecting all that does not assert itself
as too essential to be passed over—hence the slang and
cant words of every profession, and indeed all language;
for language at best is but a kind of "patter," the only
way, it is true, in many cases, of expressing our ideas
to one another, but still a very bad way, and not for
one moment comparable to the unspoken speech which
we may sometimes have recourse to.　The metaphors
and *façons de parler* to which even in the plainest
speech we are perpetually recurring (as, for example,
in this last two lines, "plain," "perpetually," and "recurring," are all words based on metaphor, and hence
more or less liable to mislead) often deceive us, as
though there were nothing more than what we see and
say, and as though words, instead of being, as they are,
the creatures of our convenience, had some claim to be

the actual ideas themselves concerning which we are conversing.

This is so well expressed in a letter I have recently received from a friend, now in New Zealand, and certainly not intended by him for publication, that I shall venture to quote the passage, but should say that I do so without his knowledge or permission which I should not be able to receive before this book must be completed.

"Words, words, words," he writes, "are the stumbling-blocks in the way of truth. Until you think of things as they are, and not of the words that misrepresent them, you cannot think rightly. Words produce the appearance of hard and fast lines where there are none. Words divide; thus we call this a man, that an ape, that a monkey, while they are all only differentiations of the same thing. To think of a thing they must be got rid of: they are the clothes that thoughts wear—only the clothes. I say this over and over again, for there is nothing of more importance. Other men's words will stop you at the beginning of an investigation. A man may play with words all his life, arranging them and rearranging them like dominoes. If I could *think* to you without words you would understand me better."

If such remarks as the above hold good at all, they do so with the words "personal identity." The least reflection will show that personal identity in any sort of strictness is an impossibility. The expression is one of the many ways in which we are obliged to scamp our thoughts through pressure of other business which pays us better. For surely all reasonable people will feel that an infant an hour before birth, when in the eye of the law he has no existence, and could not be called a peer for another sixty minutes, though his father were a peer, and already dead,—surely such an embryo is more personally identical with the baby into which he develops within an hour's time than the born baby is so with itself (if the expression may be pardoned), one, twenty, or it may be eighty years after birth. There is more sameness of matter; there are fewer differences of any kind perceptible by a third person; there is more sense of continuity on the part of the person himself, and far more of all that goes to make up our sense of sameness of personality between an embryo an hour before birth and the child on being born, than there is between the child just born and the man of twenty. Yet there is no hesitation about admitting sameness of personality between these two last.

On the other hand, if that hazy contradiction in terms, "personal identity," be once allowed to retreat behind the threshold of the womb, it has eluded us once for all. What is true of one hour before birth is true of two, and so on till we get back to the impregnate ovum, which may fairly claim to have been personally identical with the man of eighty into which it ultimately developed, in spite of the fact that there is no particle of same matter nor sense of continuity between them, nor recognised community of instinct, nor indeed of anything which on a *primâ facie* view of the matter goes to the making up of that which we call identity.

There is far more of all these things common to the impregnate ovum and the ovum immediately before impregnation, or again between the impregnate ovum, and both the ovum before impregnation and the spermatozoon which impregnated it. Nor, if we admit personal identity between the ovum and the octogenarian, is there any sufficient reason why we should not admit it between the impregnate ovum and the two factors of which it is composed, which two factors are but offshoots from two distinct personalities, of which they are as much part as the apple is of the apple-tree; so that an impregnate ovum cannot without a violation of first principles be debarred from claiming personal identity with both its parents, and hence, by an easy chain of reasoning, *with each of the impregnate ova from which its parents were developed.*

So that each ovum when impregnate should be considered not as descended from its ancestors, but as being a continuation of the personality of every ovum in the chain of its ancestry, every which ovum *it actually is* as truly as the octogenarian *is* the same identity with the ovum from which he has been developed. The two cases stand or fall together.

This process cannot stop short of the primordial cell, which again will probably turn out to be but a brief resting-place. We therefore prove each one of us to *be actually* the primordial cell which never died nor dies, but has differentiated itself into the life of the world, all living beings whatever, being one with it, and members one of another.

To look at the matter for a moment in another light, it will be admitted that if the primordial cell had been killed before leaving issue, all its possible descendants would have been killed at one and the same time. It is hard to see how this single fact does not establish at the point, as it were, of a logical bayonet, an identity between any creature and all others that are descended from it.

The fencing (for it does not deserve the name of serious disputation) with which Bishop Butler meets his opponents is rendered possible by the laxness with which the words "identical" and "identity" are ordinarily used. Bishop Butler would not seriously deny that personality undergoes great changes between infancy and old age, and hence that it must undergo some change from moment to moment. So universally is this recognised, that it is common to hear it said of such and such a man that he is not at all the person he was, or of such and such another that he is twice the man he used to be—expressions than which none nearer the truth can well be found. On the other hand, those whom Bishop Butler is intending to confute would be the first to admit that, though there are many changes between infancy and old age, yet they come about in any one individual under such circumstances as we are all agreed in considering as the factors of personal identity rather than as hindrances thereto— that is to say that there has been no entire and permanent death on the part of the individual between any two phases of his existence, and that any one phase has had a lasting though perhaps imperceptible effect upon all succeeding ones. So that no one ever seriously argued in the manner supposed by Bishop Butler, unless with modifications and saving clauses, to which it does not suit his purpose to call attention.

.　.　.　.　.　.　.

No doubt it would be more strictly accurate to say "you are the now phase of the person I met last night," or "you are the being which has been evolved from the being I met last night," than "you are the person I met last night." But life is too short for the periphrases which would crowd upon us from every quarter, if we did not set our face against all that is under the surface of things, unless, that is to say, the going beneath the surface is, for some special chance of profit, excusable or capable of extenuation.

.   .   .   .

Take again the case of some weeping trees, whose boughs spring up into fresh trees when they have reached the ground, who shall say at what time they cease to be members of the parent tree ? In the case of cuttings from plants it is easy to elude the difficulty by making a parade of the sharp and sudden act of separation from the parent stock, but this is only a piece of mental sleight of hand ; the cutting remains as much part of its parent plant as though it had never been severed from it ; it goes on profiting by the experience which it had before it was cut off, as much as though it had never been cut off at all.   This will be more readily seen in the case of worms which have been cut in half.   Let a worm be cut in half, and the two halves will become fresh worms; which of them is the original worm ?. Surely both. Perhaps no simpler case than this could readily be found of the manner in which personality eludes us, the moment we try to investigate its real nature.   There are few ideas which on first consideration appear so simple, and none which becomes more utterly incapable of limitation or definition as soon as it is examined closely.

It has gone the way of species.   It is now generally held that species blend or have blended into one another ; so that any possibility of arrangement and apparent subdivision into definite groups, is due to the suppression by death both of individuals and whole genera, which, had they been now existing, would have linked all living beings by a series of gradations so subtle that little classification could have been attempted. What we have failed to see is that the individual is as much linked onto other individuals as the species is linked on to other species. How it is that the one great personality of life as a whole, should have split itself up into so many centres of thought and action, each one of which is wholly, or at any rate nearly unconscious of its connection with the other members, instead of having grown up into a huge polyp, or as it were coral reef or compound animal over the whole world, which should be conscious but of its own one single existence; how it is that the daily waste of this creature should be carried on by the conscious death of its individual members, instead of by the unconscious waste of tissue which goes on in the bodies of each individual (if indeed the tissue which we waste daily in our own bodies is so unconscious of its birth and death as we suppose); how, again, that the daily repair of this huge creature life should have become decentralised, and be carried on by conscious reproduction on the part of its component items, instead of by the unconscious nutrition of the whole from a single centre, as the nutrition of our own bodies would appear (though perhaps falsely) to be carried on; these are matters upon which I dare not speculate here, but on which some reflections may follow in subsequent chapters.

INSTINCT AS INHERITED MEMORY.

(CHAPTER XI. OF LIFE AND HABIT.)

OBVIOUSLY the memory of a habit or experience will not commonly be transmitted to offspring in that perfection which is called "instinct," till the habit or experience has been repeated in several generations with more or less uniformity; for otherwise the impression made will not be strong enough to endure through the busy and difficult task of reproduction. This of course involves that the habit shall have attained, as it were, equilibrium with the creature's sense of its own needs, so that it shall have long seemed the best course possible, leaving upon the whole and under ordinary circumstances little further to be desired, and hence that it should have been little varied during many generations, We should expect that it would be transmitted in a more or less partial, varying, imperfect, and intelligent condition before equilibrium had been attained; it would, however, continually tend towards equilibrium.

When this stage has been reached, as regards any habit, the creature will cease trying to improve; on which the repetition of the habit will become stable, and hence capable of more unerring transmission—but at the same time improvement will cease; the habit will become fixed, and be perhaps transmitted at an earlier and earlier age, till it has reached that date of manifestation which shall be found most agreeable to the other habits of the creature. It will also be manifested, as a matter of course, without further consciousness or reflection, for people cannot be always opening up settled questions; if they thought a matter all over yesterday they cannot think it all over again to-day, what they thought then they will think now, and will act upon their opinion; and this, too, even in spite sometimes of misgiving, that if they were to think still further they could find a still better course. It is not, therefore, to be expected that "instinct" should show signs of that hesitating and tentative action which results from knowledge that is still so imperfect as to be actively self-conscious; nor yet that it should grow or vary perceptibly unless under such changed conditions as shall baffle memory, and present the alternative of either invention—that is to say, variation—or death.

But every instinct must have passed through the laboriously intelligent stages through which human civilisations *and mechanical inventions* are now passing; and he who would study the origin of an instinct with its development, partial transmission, further growth, further transmission, approach to more unreflecting stability, and finally, its perfection as an unerring and unerringly transmitted instinct, must look to laws, customs, *and machinery* as his best instructors. Customs and machines are instincts *and organs* now in process of development; they will assuredly one day reach the unconscious state of equilibrium which we observe in the structures and instincts of bees and ants, and an approach to which may be found among some savage nations. We may reflect, however, not without pleasure, that this condition—the true millennium—is still distant. Nevertheless the ants and bees seem happy; perhaps more happy than when so many social questions were in as hot discussion among them as other and not dissimilar ones will one day be amongst ourselves.

And this, as will be apparent, opens up the whole question of the stability of species, which we cannot follow further here, than to say, that according to the balance of testimony, many plants and animals do appear to have reached a phase of being from which they are hard to move—that is to say, they will die sooner than be at the pains of altering their habits— true martyrs to their convictions. Such races refuse to see changes in their surroundings as long as they can, but when compelled to recognise them, they throw up the game because they cannot and will not, or will not and cannot, invent.

This is perfectly intelligible, for a race is nothing but a long-lived individual, and like any individual, or tribe of men whom we have yet observed, will have its special capacities and its special limitations, though, as in the case of the individual, so also with the race, it is exceedingly hard to say what those limitations are, and why, having been able to go so far, it should go no further. Every man and every race is capable of education up to a certain point, but not to the extent of being made from a sow's ear into a silk purse. The proximate cause of the limitation seems to lie in the absence of the wish to go further; the presence or absence of the wish will depend upon the nature and surroundings of the individual, which is simply a way of saying that one can get no further, but that as the song (with a slight alteration) says :—

" Some breeds do, and some breeds don't,
  Some breeds will, but this breed won't :
  I tried very often to see if it would,
  But it said it really couldn't, and I don't think it could."

M. Ribot in his work on Heredity[*] writes (p. 14):—
" The duckling hatched by the hen makes straight for
water." In what conceivable way can we account for
this, except on the supposition that the duckling knows
perfectly well what it can and what it cannot do with
water, owing to its recollection of what it did when it
was still one individuality with its parents, and hence,
when it was a duckling before ?

" The squirrel, before it knows anything of winter,
lays up a store of nuts. A bird when hatched in a cage
will, when given its freedom, build for itself a nest like
that of its parents, out of the same materials, and of
the same shape."

If this is not due to memory, " even an imperfect "
explanation of what else it can be due to, " would," to
quote from Mr. Darwin, " be satisfactory."

" Intelligence gropes about, tries this way and that,
misses its object, commits mistakes, and corrects them."

Yes. Because intelligence is of consciousness, and
consciousness is of attention, and attention is of uncertainty, and uncertainty is of ignorance or want of consciousness. Intelligence is not yet thoroughly up to
its business.

" Instinct advances with a mechanical certainty,
hence comes its unconscious character. It knows nothing either of ends, or of the means of attaining them :
it implies no comparison, judgment, or choice."

This is assumption. What is certain is that instinct
does not betray signs of self-consciousness as to its own

[*] Kegan Paul, 1875.

knowledge. It has dismissed reference to first principles, and is no longer under the law, but under the
grace of a settled conviction.

"All seems directed by thought."

Yes; because all *has been* in earlier existences
directed by thought.

"Without ever arriving at thought."

Because it has *got past thought*, and though "directed
by thought" originally, is now travelling in exactly the
opposite direction. It is not likely to reach thought
again, till people get to know worse and worse how to
do things, the oftener they practise them.

"And if this phenomenon appear strange, it must
be observed that analogous states occur in ourselves.
*All that we do from habit—walking, writing, or practis-
ing a mechanical act, for instance—all these and many
other very complex acts are performed without consciousness.*

"Instinct appears stationary. It does not, like
intelligence, seem to grow and decay, to gain and to
lose. It does not improve."

Naturally. For improvement can only as a general
rule be looked for along the line of latest development,
that is to say, in matters concerning which the creature
is being still consciously exercised. Older questions
are settled, and the solution must be accepted as final,
for the question of living at all would be reduced to an
absurdity, if everything decided upon one day was to
be undecided again the next; as with painting or
music, so with life and politics, let every man be fully
persuaded in his own mind, for decision with wrong
will be commonly a better policy than indecision—I
had almost added with right; and a firm purpose with
risk will be better than an infirm one with temporary

exemption from disaster. Every race has made its great blunders, to which it has nevertheless adhered, inasmuch as the corresponding modification of other structures and instincts was found preferable to the revolution which would be caused by a radical change of structure, with consequent havoc among a legion of vested interests. Rudimentary organs are, as has been often said, the survivals of these interests—the signs of their peaceful and gradual extinction as living faiths; they are also instances of the difficulty of breaking through any cant or trick which we have long practised, and which is not sufficiently troublesome to make it a serious object with us to cure ourselves of the habit.

"If it does not remain perfectly invariable, at least it only varies within very narrow limits; and though this question has been warmly debated in our day and is yet unsettled, we may yet say that in instinct immutability is the law, variation the exception."

This is quite as it should be. Genius will occasionally rise a little above convention, but with an old convention immutability will be the rule.

"Such," continues M. Ribot, "are the admitted characters of instinct."

Yes; but are they not also the admitted characters of habitual actions that are due to memory?

.   .   .   .

M. Ribot says a little further on: "Originally man had considerable trouble in taming the animals which are now domesticated; and his work would have been in vain had not heredity" (memory) "come to his aid. It may be said that after man has modified a wild animal to his will, there goes on in its progeny a silent conflict between two heredities" (memories), "the one tending to fix the acquired modifications and the other to preserve the primitive instincts. The latter often get the mastery, and only after several generations is training sure of victory. But we may see that in either case heredity" (memory) "always asserts its rights."

How marvellously is the above passage elucidated and made to fit in with the results of our recognised experience, by the simple substitution of the word "memory" for heredity.

.   .   .   .

I cannot refrain from bringing forward a few more instances of what I think must be considered by every reader as hereditary memory. Sydney Smith writes :—

"Sir James Hall hatched some chickens in an oven. Within a few minutes after the shell was broken, a spider was turned loose before this very youthful brood ; the destroyer of flies had hardly proceeded more than a few inches, before he was descried by one of these oven-born chickens, and, at one peck of his bill, immediately devoured. This certainly was not imitation. A female goat very near delivery died ; Galen cut out the young kid, and placed before it a bundle of hay, a bunch of fruit, and a pan of milk ; the young kid smelt to them all very attentively, and then began to lap the milk. This was not imitation. And what is commonly and rightly called instinct, cannot be explained away under the notion of its being imitation." (Lecture xvii. on Moral Philosophy.)

It cannot, indeed, be explained away under the notion of its being imitation, but I think it may well be so under that of its being memory.

Again, a little further on in the same lecture as that above quoted from, we find :—

"Ants and beavers lay up magazines. Where do they get their knowledge that it will not be so easy to collect food in rainy weather as it is in summer? Men and women know these things, because their grandpapas and grandmammas have told them so. Ants hatched from the egg artificially, or birds hatched in this manner, have all this knowledge by intuition, without the smallest communication with any of their relations. Now observe what the solitary wasp does; she digs several holes in the sand, in each of which she deposits an egg, though she certainly knows not (?) that an animal is deposited in that egg, and still less that this animal must be nourished with other animals. She collects a few green flies, rolls them up neatly in several parcels (like Bologna sausages), and stuffs one parcel into each hole where an egg is deposited. When the wasp worm is hatched, it finds a store of provision ready made; and what is most curious, the quantity allotted to each is exactly sufficient to support it, till it attains the period of wasphood, and can provide for itself. This instinct of the parent wasp is the more remarkable as it does not feed upon flesh itself. Here the little creature has never seen its parent; for by the time it is born, the parent is always eaten by sparrows; and yet, without the slightest education, or previous experience, it does everything that the parent did before it. Now the objectors to the doctrine of instinct may say what they please, but young tailors have no intuitive method of making pantaloons; a new-born mercer cannot measure diaper; nature teaches a cook's daughter nothing about sippets. All these things require with us seven years' apprenticeship; but insects are like Molière's persons of quality—they know everything (as Molière says) without having learnt anything. 'Les gens de qualité savent tout, sans avoir rien appris.'"

How completely all difficulty vanishes from the facts so pleasantly told in this passage when we bear in mind the true nature of personal identity, the ordinary working of memory, and the vanishing tendency of consciousness concerning what we know exceedingly well.

My last instance I take from M. Ribot, who writes:— "Gratiolet, in his *Anatomie Comparée du Système Nerveux*, states that an old piece of wolf's skin, with the hair all worn away, when set before a little dog, threw the animal into convulsions of fear by the slight scent attaching to it. The dog had never seen a wolf, and we can only explain this alarm by the hereditary transmission of certain sentiments, coupled with a certain perception of the sense of smell." ("Heredity," p. 43.)

I should prefer to say "we can only explain the alarm by supposing that the smell of the wolf's skin" —the sense of smell being, as we all know, more powerful to recall the ideas that have been associated with it than any other sense—"brought up the ideas with which it had been associated in the dog's mind during many previous existences"—he on smelling the wolf's skin remembering all about wolves perfectly well.

CONCLUDING REMARKS.

(FROM CHAPTER XV. OF LIFE AND HABIT.)

HERE, then, I leave my case, though well aware that I have crossed the threshold only of my subject. My work is of a tentative character, put before the public as a sketch or design for a, possibly, further endeavour, in which I hope to derive assistance from the criticisms which this present volume may elicit.* Such as it is, however, for the present I must leave it.

We have seen that we cannot do anything thoroughly till we can do it unconsciously, and that we cannot do anything unconsciously till we can do it thoroughly; this at first seems illogical; but logic and consistency are luxuries for the gods, and the lower animals, only. Thus a boy cannot really know how to swim till he can swim, but he cannot swim till he knows how to swim. Conscious effort is but the process of rubbing off the rough corners from these two contradictory statements, till they eventually fit into one another so closely that it is impossible to disjoin them.

Whenever we see any creature able to go through any complicated and difficult process with little or no effort—whether it be a bird building her nest, or a

* It is now (January 1884) more than six years since Life and Habit was published, but I have come across nothing which makes me wish to alter it to any material extent.

hen's egg making itself into a chicken, or an ovum turning itself into a baby—we may conclude that the creature has done the same thing on a very great number of past occasions.

We found the phenomena exhibited by heredity to be so like those of memory, and to be so inexplicable on any other supposition than that they were modes of memory, that it was easier to suppose them due to memory in spite of the fact that we cannot remember having recollected, than to believe that because we cannot so remember, therefore the phenomena cannot be due to memory.

We were thus led to consider "personal identity," in order to see whether there was sufficient reason for denying that the experience, which we must have clearly gained somewhere, was gained by us when we were in the persons of our forefathers ; we found, not without surprise, that unless we admitted that it might be so gained, in so far as that we once *actually were* our remotest ancestor, we must change our ideas concerning personality altogether.

We therefore assumed that the phenomena of heredity, whether as regards instinct or structure, were due to memory of past experiences, accumulated and fused till they had become automatic, or quasi automatic, much in the same way as after a long life—

> .   .   .   " Old experience doth attain
> To something like prophetic strain."

After dealing with certain phenomena of memory, but more especially with its abeyance and revival, we inquired what the principal corresponding phenomena of life and species should be, on the hypothesis that they were mainly due to memory.

I think I may say that we found the hypothesis fit

in with actual facts in a sufficiently satisfactory manner. We found not a few matters, as, for example, the sterility of hybrids, the principle underlying longevity, the phenomena of old age, and puberty as generally near the end of development, explain themselves with more completeness than I have yet heard of their being explained on any other hypothesis. Most indeed of these phenomena have been left hitherto without even an attempt at an explanation.

We considered the most important difficulty in the way of instinct as hereditary habit, namely, the structure and instincts of neuter insects; these are very unlike those of their parents, and cannot, apparently, be transmitted to offspring by individuals of the previous generation, in whom such structure and instincts appeared, inasmuch as these creatures are sterile. I do not say that the difficulty is wholly removed, inasmuch as some obscurity must be admitted to remain as to the manner in which the structure of the larva is aborted; this obscurity is likely to remain till we know more of the early history of civilisation among bees than I can find that we know at present; but I believe the difficulty was reduced to such proportions as to make it little likely to be felt in comparison with that of attributing instinct to any other cause than inherited habit, or memory on the part of offspring, of habits contracted in the persons of its ancestors.[*]

[*] It must be remembered that the late Mr. C. Darwin expressly denied that instinct and inherited habit are generally to be connected.—See Mr. Darwin's "Origin of Species," end of chapter viii., where he expresses his surprise that no one has hitherto adduced the instincts of neuter insects "against the well-known doctrine of inherited habit as advanced by Lamarck."

Mr. Romanes, in his "Mental Evolution in Animals" (November, 1883), refers to this passage of Mr. Darwin's, and endorses it with approbation (p. 297).

We then inquired what was the great principle underlying variation, and answered, with Lamarck, that it must be "sense of need;" and though not without being haunted by suspicion of a vicious circle, and also well aware that we were not much nearer the origin of life than when we started, we still concluded that here was the truest origin of species, and hence of genera; and that the accumulation of variations, which in time amounted to specific and generic differences, was due to intelligence and memory on the part of the creature varying, rather than to the operation of what Mr. Darwin has called "natural selection." At the same time we admitted that the course of nature is very much as Mr. Darwin has represented it, in this respect, in so far as that there is a struggle for existence, and that the weaker must go to the wall. But we denied that this part of the course of nature would lead to much, if any, accumulation of variation, unless the variation was directed mainly by intelligent sense of need, with continued personality and memory.

We conclude, therefore, that the small, apparently structureless, impregnate ovum from which we have each one of us sprung, has a potential recollection of all that has happened to each one of its ancestors prior to the period at which any such ancestor has issued from the bodies of its progenitors — provided, that is to say, a sufficiently deep, or sufficiently often-repeated, impression has been made to admit of its being remembered at all.

Each step of normal development will lead the impregnate ovum up to, and remind it of, its next ordinary course of action, in the same way as we, when we recite a well-known passage, are led up to each successive sentence by the sentence which has immediately preceded it.

And for this reason, namely, that as it takes two people "to tell" a thing—a speaker and a comprehending listener, without which last, though much may have been said, there has been nothing told—so also it takes two people, as it were, to "remember" a thing—the creature remembering, and the surroundings of the creature at the time it last remembered. Hence, though the ovum immediately after impregnation is instinct with all the memories of both parents, not one of these memories can normally become active till both the ovum itself, and its surroundings, are sufficiently like what they respectively were, when the occurrence now to be remembered last took place. The memory will then immediately return, and the creature will do as it did on the last occasion that it was in like case as now. This ensures that similarity of order shall be preserved in all the stages of development in successive generations.

Life then is the being possessed of memory. We are all the same stuff to start with; plants and animals only differ from one another because they remember different things; they grow up in the shapes they bear because these shapes are the embodiments of their ideas concerning their own past history; they are forms of faith or faiths of form whichever the reader chooses.

Hence the term "Natural History," as applied to the different plants and animals around us. For surely the study of natural history means only the study of plants and animals themselves, which, at the moment of using the words "Natural History," we assume to be the most important part of nature.

A living creature well supported by a mass of healthy ancestral memory is a young and growing creature, free from ache or pain, and thoroughly acquainted with its business so far, but with much yet to be reminded of. A creature which finds itself and its surroundings not so unlike those of its parents about the time of their begetting it, as to be compelled to recognise that it never yet was in any such position, is a creature in the heyday of life. A creature which begins to be aware of itself is one which is beginning to recognise that the situation is a new one.

It is the young and fair, then, who are the truly old and truly experienced; it is they who alone have a trustworthy memory to guide them; they alone know things as they are, and it is from them that, as we grow older, we must study if we would still cling to truth. The whole charm of youth lies in its advantage over age in respect of experience, and where this has for some reason failed, or been misapplied, the charm is broken. When we say that we are getting old, we should say rather that we are getting new or young, and are suffering from inexperience, which drives us into doing things which we do not understand, and lands us, eventually, in the utter impotence of death. The kingdom of heaven is the kingdom of little children.

SELECTIONS
FROM EVOLUTION, OLD AND NEW.*

—o—

*IMPOTENCE OF PALEY'S CONCLUSION. THE
TELEOLOGY OF THE EVOLUTIONIST.*

(FROM CHAPTER III. OF EVOLUTION, OLD AND NEW.)

IF we conceive of ourselves as looking simultaneously
upon a real foot, and upon an admirably constructed
artificial one, placed by the side of it, the idea of design,
and design by an intelligent living being with a body
and soul (without which, the use of the word design
is delusive), will present itself strongly to our minds
in connection both with the true foot and with the
model; but we find another idea asserting itself with
even greater strength, namely, that the design of the
true foot is infinitely more intricate, and yet is carried
into execution in far more masterly manner than that
of the model.   We not only feel that there is a wider
difference between the ability, time, and care which
have been lavished on the real foot and upon the
model, than there is between the skill and the time
taken to produce Westminster Abbey, and that be-
stowed upon a gingerbread cake stuck with sugar plums
so as to represent it, but also that these two objects
must have been manufactured on different principles.
We do not for a moment doubt that the real foot was
designed, but we are so astonished at the dexterity of

* Evolution, Old and New, was published in May, 1879.

the designer that we are at a loss for some time to
think who could have designed it, where he can live,
in what manner he studied, for how long, and by what
processes he carried out his design, when matured, into
actual practice. Until recently it was thought that
there was no answer to many of these questions, more
especially to those which bear upon the mode of manufacture. For the last hundred years, however, the
importance of a study has been recognised which does
actually reveal to us in no small degree the processes
by which the human foot is manufactured, so that in
our endeavour to lay our hands upon the points of
difference between the kind of design with which the
foot itself is designed, and the design of the model,
we turn naturally to the guidance of those who have
made this study their specialty; and a very wide difference does this study, embryology, at once reveal to us.

Writing of the successive changes through which
each embryo is forced to pass, the late Mr. G. H. Lewes
says that "none of these phases have any adaptation
to the future state of the animal, but are in positive
contradiction to it or are simply purposeless; whereas
all show stamped on them the unmistakable characters
of *ancestral* adaptation, and the progressions of organic
evolution. What does the fact imply? There is not
a single known example of a complex organism which
is not developed out of simpler forms. Before it can
attain the complex structure which distinguishes it,
there must be an evolution of forms similar to those
which distinguish the structure of organisms lower in
the series. On the hypothesis of a plan which pre-
arranged the organic world, nothing could be more
unworthy of a supreme intelligence than this inability
to construct an organism at once, without making several

previous tentative efforts, undoing to-day what was so carefully done yesterday, and *repeating for centuries the same tentatives in the same succession.* Do not let us blink this consideration. There is a traditional phrase much in vogue among the anthropomorphists, which arose naturally enough from a tendency to take human methods as an explanation of the Divine—a phrase which becomes a sort of argument—'The Great Architect.' But if we are to admit the human point of view, a glance at the facts of embryology must produce very uncomfortable reflections. For what should we say to an architect who was unable, or being able was obstinately unwilling, to erect a palace except by first using his materials in the shape of a hut, then pulling them down and rebuilding them as a cottage, then adding story to story and room to room, *not* with any reference to the ultimate purposes of the palace, but wholly with reference to the way in which houses were constructed in ancient times? What should we say to the architect who could not form a museum out of bricks and mortar, but was forced to begin as if going to construct a mansion, and after proceeding some way in this direction, altered his plan into a palace, and that again into a museum? Yet this is the sort of succession on which organisms are constructed. The fact has long been familiar; how has it been reconciled with infinite wisdom? Let the following passage answer for a thousand :—'The embryo is nothing like the miniature of the adult. For a long while the body in its entirety and in its details, presents the strangest of spectacles. Day by day and hour by hour, the aspect of the scene changes, and this instability is exhibited by the most essential parts no less than by the accessory parts. One would say that nature feels her

way, and only reaches the goal after many times missing the path ' (on dirait que la nature tâtonne et ne
conduit son œuvre à bon fin, qu'après s'être souvent
trompée)." *

The above passage does not, I think, affect the evidence for design which we adduced in the preceding
chapter.† However strange the process of manufacture
may appear, when the work comes to be turned out
the design is too manifest to be doubted.

If the reader were to come upon some lawyer's deed
which dealt with matters of such unspeakable intricacy
that it baffled his imagination to conceive how it could
ever have been drafted, and if in spite of this he were
to find the intricacy of the provisions to be made, ex-
ceeded only by the ease and simplicity with which the
deed providing for them was found to work in practice;
and after this, if he were to discover that the deed, by
whomsoever drawn, had nevertheless been drafted upon
principles which at first seemed very foreign to any
according to which he was in the habit of drafting
deeds himself, as for example, that the draftsman had
begun to draft a will as a marriage settlement, and so
forth—yet an observer would not, I take it, do either
of two things. He would not in the face of the result
deny the design, making himself judge rather of the
method of procedure than of the achievement. Nor
yet after insisting in the manner of Paley, on the
wonderful proofs of intention and on the exquisite provisions which were to be found in every syllable—thus
leading us up to the highest pitch of expectation—

---

* Quatrefages, "Metamorphoses de l'Homme et des Animaux," 1862,
p. 42 ; G. H. Lewes, "Physical Basis of Mind," 1877, p. 83.

† I have been unable, through want of space, to give this chapter
here.

would he present us with such an impotent conclusion as that the designer, though a living person and a true designer, was yet immaterial and intangible, a something, in fact, which proves to be a nothing; an omniscient and omnipotent vacuum.

Our observer would feel he need not have been at such pains to establish his design if this was to be the upshot of his reasoning. He would therefore admit the design, and by consequence the designer, but would probably ask a little time for reflection before he ventured to say who, or what, or where the designer was. Then gaining some insight into the manner in which the deed had been drawn, he would conclude that the draftsman was a specialist who had had long practice in this particular kind of work, but who now worked almost as it might be said automatically and without consciousness, and found it difficult to depart from a habitual method of procedure.

We turn, then, on Paley, and say to him: "We have admitted your design and your designer. Where is he? Show him to us. If you cannot show him to us as flesh and blood, show him as flesh and sap; show him as a living cell; show him as protoplasm. Lower than this we should not fairly go; it is not in the bond or *nexus* of our ideas that something utterly inanimate and inorganic should scheme, design, contrive, and elaborate structures which can make mistakes: it may elaborate low unerring things, like crystals, but it cannot elaborate those which have the power to err. Nevertheless, we will commit such abuse with our understandings as to waive this point, and we will ask you to show him to us as air which, if it cannot be seen yet can be felt, weighed, handled, transferred from place to place, be judged by its effects, and so forth; or if this may not be, give us half a grain of hydrogen, diffused through all space and invested with some of the minor attributes of matter; or if you cannot do this, give us an imponderable like electricity, or even the higher mathematics, but give us something or throw off the mask and tell us fairly out that it is your paid profession to hoodwink us on this matter if you can, and that you are but doing your best to earn an honest living."

We may fancy Paley as turning the tables upon us and as saying; " But you too have admitted a designer —you too then must mean a designer with a body and soul, who must be somewhere to be found in space, and who must live in time. Where is this your designer? Can you show him more than I can? Can you lay your finger on him and demonstrate him so that a child shall see him and know him, and find what was heretofore an isolated idea concerning him, combine itself instantaneously with the idea of the designer, we will say, of the human foot, so that no power on earth shall henceforth tear those two ideas asunder? Surely if you cannot do this, you too are trifling with words, and abusing your own mind and that of your reader. Where, then, is your designer of man? Who made him? And where, again, is your designer of beasts and birds, of fishes and of plants?"

Our answer is simple enough; it is that we can and do point to a living tangible person with flesh, blood, eyes, nose, ears, organs, senses, dimensions, who did of his own cunning after infinite proof of every kind of hazard and experiment scheme out and fashion each organ of the human body. This is the person whom we claim as the designer and artificer of that body, and he is the one of all others the best fitted for the task by his antecedents, and his practical knowledge of the requirements of the case—for he is man himself.

Not man, the individual of any given generation, but man in the entirety of his existence from the dawn of life onwards to the present moment. In like manner we say that the designer of all organisms is so incorporate with the organisms themselves—so lives, moves, and has its being in those organisms, and is so one with them—they in it, and it in them—that it is more consistent with reason and the common use of words to see the designer of each living form in the living form itself, than to look for its designer in some other place or person.

Thus we have a third alternative presented to us.

Mr. Charles Darwin· and his followers deny design, as having any appreciable share in the formation of organism at all.

Paley and the theologians insist on design, but upon a designer outside the universe and the organism.

The third opinion is that suggested in the first instance and carried out to a very high degree of development by Buffon. It was improved, and indeed, made almost perfect by Dr. Erasmus Darwin, but too much neglected by him after he had put it forward. It was borrowed, as I think we may say with some confidence, from Dr. Darwin by Lamarck, and was followed up by him ardently thenceforth, during the remainder of his life, though somewhat less perfectly comprehended by him than it had been by Dr. Darwin. It is that the design which has designed organisms, has resided within, and been embodied in, the organisms themselves.

FAILURE OF THE FIRST EVOLUTIONISTS TO SEE THEIR POSITION AS TELEOLOGICAL.

(CHAPTER IV. OF EVOLUTION, OLD AND NEW.)

IT follows from the doctrine of Dr. Erasmus Darwin. and Lamarck, if not from that of Buffon himself, that the majority of organs are as purposive to the evolutionist as to the theologian, and far more intelligibly so. Circumstances, however, prevented these writers from acknowledging this fact to the world, and perhaps even to themselves. Their *crux* was, as it still is to so many evolutionists, the presence of rudimentary organs, and the processes of embryological development. They would not admit that rudimentary and therefore useless organs were designed by a Creator to take their place once and for ever as part of a scheme whose main idea was, that every animal structure was to serve some useful end in connection with its possessor.

This was the doctrine of final causes as then commonly held; in the face of rudimentary organs it was absurd. Buffon was above all things else a plain matter of fact thinker, who refused to go far beyond the obvious. Like all other profound writers, he was, if I may say so, profoundly superficial. He felt that the aim of research does not consist in the knowing this or that, but in the easing of the desire to know or understand more completely—in the peace of mind which passeth all understanding. His was the perfection of a healthy

mental organism by which over effort is felt to be as
vicious and contemptible as indolence.   He knew this
too well to know the grounds of his knowledge, but we
smaller people who know it less completely, can see
that such felicitous instinctive tempering together of
the two great contradictory principles, love of effort
and love of ease, has underlain every healthy step of
all healthy growth, whether of vegetable or animal, from
the earliest conceivable time to the present moment.
Nothing is worth looking at which is seen either too
obviously or with too much difficulty.   Nothing is
worth doing or well done which is not done fairly
easily, and some little deficiency of effort is more pardonable than any very perceptible excess, for virtue
has ever erred on the side of self-indulgence rather
than of asceticism.

According to Buffon, then—as also according to
Dr. Darwin, who was just such another practical and
genial thinker, and who was distinctly a pupil of
Buffon, though a most intelligent and original one—
if an organ after a reasonable amount of inspection
appeared to be useless, it was to be called useless
without more ado, and theories were to be ordered out
of court if they were troublesome.   In like manner, if
animals breed freely *inter se* before our eyes, as for
example the horse and ass, the fact was to be noted,
but no animals were to be classed as capable of inter-
breeding until they had asserted their right to such
classification by breeding with tolerable certainty.   If,
again, an animal looked as if it felt, that is to say, if it
moved about pretty quickly or made a noise, it must be
held to feel; if it did neither of these things it did not
look as if it felt, and therefore it must be said not to
feel. *De non apparentibus et non existentibus eadem est*

lex was one of the chief axioms of their philosophy; no writers have had a greater horror of mystery or of ideas that have not become so mastered as to be, or to have been, superficial. Lamarck was one of those men of whom I believe it has been said that they have brain upon the brain. He had his theory that an animal could not feel unless it had a nervous system, and at least a spinal marrow—and that it could not think at all without a brain—all his facts, therefore, have to be made to square with this. With Buffon and Dr. Darwin we feel safe that however wrong they may sometimes be, their conclusions have always been arrived at on that fairly superficial view of things in which, as I have elsewhere said, our nature alone permits us to be comforted.

To these writers, then, the doctrine of final causes for rudimentary organs was a piece of mystification and an absurdity; no less fatal to any such doctrine were the processes of embryological development. It was plain that the commonly received teleology must be given up; but the idea of design or purpose was so associated in their minds with theological design that they avoided it altogether. They seem to have forgotten that an internal purpose is as much purpose as an external one; hence, unfortunately, though their whole theory of development is intensely purposive, it is the fact rather than the name of teleology which has hitherto been insisted upon, even by the greatest writers on evolution—the name having been most persistently denied even by those who were most insisting on the thing itself.

It is easy to understand the difficulty felt by the fathers of evolution when we remember how much had to be seen before the facts could lie well before them.

It was necessary to attain, firstly, to a perception of the unity of person between parents and offspring in successive generations; secondly, it must be seen that an organism's memory (within the limitations to which all memory is subject) goes back for generations beyond its birth, to the first beginnings in fact, of which we know anything whatever; thirdly, the latency of that memory, as of memory generally, till the associated ideas are reproduced, must be brought to bear upon the facts of heredity; and lastly, the unconsciousness with which habitual actions come to be performed, must be assigned as the explanation of the unconsciousness with which we grow and discharge most of our natural functions.

Buffon was too busy with the fact that animals descended with modification at all, to go beyond the development and illustration of this great truth. I doubt whether he ever saw more than the first, and that dimly, of the four considerations above stated.

Dr. Darwin was the first to point out the first two considerations; he did so with some clearness, but can hardly be said to have understood their full importance: the two latter ideas do not appear to have occurred to him.

Lamarck had little if any perception of any one of the four. When, however, they are firmly seized and brought into their due bearings one upon another, the facts of heredity become as simple as those of a man making a tobacco pipe, and rudimentary organs are seen to be essentially of the same character as the little rudimentary protuberance at the bottom of the pipe to which I referred in 'Erewhon.' *

These organs are now no longer useful, but they

* Page 210, first edition.

once were so, and were therefore once purposive, though
not so now.   They are the expressions of a bygone use-
fulness ; sayings, as it were, about which there was at
one time infinite wrangling, as to what both the meaning and the expression should best be, so that they then
had living significance in the mouths of those who
used them, though they have become such mere shib-
boleths and cant formulæ to ourselves that we think
no more of their meaning than we do of Julius Cæsar
in the month of July.   They continue to be reproduced
through the force of habit, and through indisposition to
get out of any familiar groove of action until it becomes
too unpleasant for us to remain in it any longer.   It
has long been felt that embryology and rudimentary
structures indicated community of descent.   Dr. Darwin
and Lamarck insisted on this, as have all subsequent
writers on evolution ; but the explanation why and
how the structures come to be repeated—namely, that
they are simply examples of the force of habit—can
only be perceived intelligently by those who admit such
unity between parents and offspring as that the self-
development of the latter can be properly called
habitual (as being a repetition of an act by one and
the same individual), and can only be fully sympathised with by those who recognise that if habit be
admitted as the key to the fact at all, the unconscious
manner in which the habit comes to be repeated is only
of a piece with all our other observations concerning
habit.   For the fuller development of the foregoing, I
must refer the reader to my work " Life and Habit."

The purposiveness, which even Dr. Darwin (and
Lamarck still less) seems never to have quite recognised in spite of their having insisted so much on what
amounts to the same thing, now comes into full view.

It is seen that the organs external to the body, and those internal to it, are the second as much as the first, things which we have made for our own convenience, and with a prevision that we shall have need of them; the main difference between the manufacture of these two classes of organs being, that we have made the one kind so often that we can no longer follow the processes whereby we make them, while the others are new things which we must make introspectively or not at all, and which are not yet so incorporate with our vitality as that we should think they grow instead of being manufactured. The manufacture of the tool, and the manufacture of the living organ prove therefore to be but two species of the same genus, which, though widely differentiated, have descended as it were from one common filament of desire and inventive faculty. The greater or less complexity of the organs goes for very little. It is only a question of the amount of intelligence and voluntary self-adaptation which we must admit, and this must be settled rather by an appeal to what we find in organism, and observe concerning it, than by what we may have imagined *à priori*.

Given a small speck of jelly with some power of slightly varying its actions in accordance with slightly varying circumstances and desires—given such a jelly-speck with a power of assimilating other matter, and thus of reproducing itself, given also that it should be possessed of a memory and a reproductive system, and we can show how the whole animal world can have descended it may be from an *amœba* without interference from without, and how every organ in every creature is designed at first roughly and tentatively but finally fashioned with the most consummate

perfection, by the creature which has had need of that
organ, which best knew what it wanted, and was never
satisfied till it had got that which was the best suited
to its varying circumstances in their entirety.   We can
even show how, if it becomes worth the Ethiopian's
while to try and change his skin, or the leopard's to
change his spots, they can assuredly change them
within a not unreasonable time and adapt their covering to their own will and convenience, and to that of
none other; thus what is commonly conceived of as
direct creation by God is moved back to a time and
space inconceivable in their remoteness, while the aim
and design so obvious in nature are shown to be still
at work around us, growing ever busier and busier, and
advancing from day to day both in knowledge and
power.

It was reserved for Mr. Charles Darwin and for
those who have too rashly followed him to deny purpose as having had any share in the development of
animal and vegetable organs; to see no evidence of
design in those wonderful provisions which have been
the marvel and delight of observers in all ages.   The
one who has drawn our attention more than perhaps
any other living writer to those very marvels of co-
adaptation, is the foremost to maintain that they are
the result not of desire and design, either within the
creature or without it, but of blind chance, working
no whither, and due but to the accumulation of innumerable lucky accidents.

"There are men," writes Professor Tyndal in the
Nineteenth Century for last November,* "and by no
means the minority, who, however wealthy in regard
to facts, can never rise into the region of principles;

* 1878.

and they are sometimes intolerant of those that can. They are formed to plod meritoriously on in the lower levels of thought; unpossessed of the pinions necessary to reach the heights, they cannot realise the mental act—the act of inspiration it might well be called— by which a man of genius, after long pondering and proving, reaches a theoretic conception which unravels and illuminates the tangle of centuries of observation and experiment. There are minds, it may be said in passing, who, at the present moment, stand in this relation to Mr. Darwin."

The more rhapsodical parts of the above must go for what they are worth, but I should be sorry to think that what remains conveyed a censure which might fall justly on myself. As I read the earlier part of the passage I confess that I imagined the conclusion was going to be very different from what it proved to be. Fresh from the study of the older men and also of Mr. Darwin himself, I failed to see that Mr. Darwin had "unravelled and illuminated" a tangled skein, but believed him, on the contrary, to have tangled and obscured what his predecessors had made in great part, if not wholly, plain. With the older writers, I had felt as though in the hands of men who wished to understand themselves and to make their reader understand them with the smallest possible exertion. The older men, if not in full daylight, at any rate saw in what quarter of the sky the dawn was breaking, and were looking steadily towards it. It is not they who have put their hands over their own eyes and ours, and who are crying out that there is no light, but chance and blindness everywhere.

K

THE TELEOLOGICAL EVOLUTION OF ORGANISM.

I HAVE stated the foregoing in what I take to be an extreme logical development, in order that the reader may more easily perceive the consequences of those premises which I am endeavouring to re-establish. But it must not be supposed that an animal or plant has ever conceived the idea of some organ widely different from any it was yet possessed of, and has set itself to design it in detail and grow towards it.

The small jelly-speck, which we call the amœba, has no organs save what it can extemporise as occasion arises. If it wants to get at anything, it thrusts out part of its jelly, which thus serves it as an arm or hand: when the arm has served its purpose, it is absorbed into the rest of the jelly, and has now to do the duty of a stomach by helping to wrap up what it has just purveyed. The small round jelly-speck spreads itself out and envelops its food, so that the whole creature is now a stomach, and nothing but a stomach. Having digested its food, it again becomes a jelly-speck, and is again ready to turn part of itself into hand or foot as its next convenience may dictate. It is not to be believed that such a creature as this, which is probably just sensitive to light and nothing more, should be able to form any conception of an eye and set itself to work to grow one, any more than it is believable that he who first observed the magnifying power of a dew-drop, or even he who first constructed a rude lens, should have had any idea in his mind of Lord Rosse's telescope with all its parts and appliances. Nothing could be well conceived more foreign to experience and common sense. Animals and plants have travelled to their present forms as a man has travelled to any one of his own most complicated inventions. Slowly, step by step, through many blunders and mischances which have worked together for good to those that have persevered in elasticity. They have travelled as man has travelled, with but little perception of a want till there was also some perception of a power, and with but little perception of a power till there was a dim sense of want ; want stimulating power, and power stimulating want ; and both so based upon each other that no one can say which is the true foundation, but rather that they must be both baseless and, as it were, meteoric in mid air. They have seen very little ahead of a present power or need, and have been then most moral, when most inclined to pierce a little into futurity, but also when most obstinately declining to pierce too far, and busy mainly with the present. They have been so far blindfolded that they could see but for a few steps in front of them, yet so far free to see that those steps were taken with aim and definitely, and not in the dark.

"Plus il a su," says Buffon, speaking of man, " plus il a pu, mais aussi moins il a fait, moins il a su.' This holds good wherever life holds good. Wherever there is life there is a moral government of rewards and punishments understood by the amœba neither better nor worse than by man. The history of organic development is the history of a moral struggle.

As for the origin of a creature able to feel want and power and as to what want and power spring from, we know nothing as yet, nor does it seem worth while to go into this question until an understanding has been come to as to whether the interaction of want and power in some low form or forms of life which could assimilate matter, reproduce themselves, vary their actions, and be capable of remembering, will or will not suffice to explain the development of the varied organs and desires which we see in the higher vertebrates and man. When this question has been settled, then it will be time to push our inquiries farther back.

But given such a low form of life as here postulated, and there is no force in Paley's pretended objection to the Darwinism of his time.

" Give our philosopher," he says, " appetencies ; give him a portion of living irritable matter (a nerve or the clipping of a nerve) to work upon ; give also to his in-cipient or progressive forms the power of propagating their like in every stage of their alteration ; and if he is to be believed, he could replenish the world with all the vegetable and animal productions which we now see in it."*

After meeting this theory with answers which need not detain us, he continues :—

" The senses of animals appear to me quite incapable of receiving the explanation of their origin which this theory affords. Including under the word ' sense ' the organ and the perception, we have no account of either. How will our philosopher get at vision or make an eye? Or, suppose the eye formed, would the perception

* " Nat. Theol." ch. xxiii.

follow ? The same of the other senses. And this objection holds its force, ascribe what you will to the hand of time, to the power of habit, to changes too slow to be observed by man, or brought within any comparison which he is able to make of past things with the present. Concede what you please to these arbitrary and unattested superstitions, how will they help you ? Here is no inception. No laws, no course, no powers of nature which prevail at present, nor any analogous to these would give commencement to a new sense; and it is in vain to inquire how that might proceed which would never *begin.*"

In answer to this, let us suppose that some inhabitants of another world were to see a modern philosopher so using a microscope that they should believe it to be a part of the philosopher's own person, which he could cut off from and join again to himself at pleasure, and suppose there were a controversy as to how this microscope had originated, and that one party maintained the man had made it little by little because he wanted it, while the other declared this to be absurd and impossible; I ask, would this latter party be justified in arguing that microscopes could never have been perfected by degrees through the preservation of and accumulation of small successive improvements inasmuch as men could not have begun to want to use microscopes until they had had a microscope which should show them that such an instrument would be useful to them, and that hence there is nothing to account for the *beginning* of microscopes, which might indeed make some progress when once originated, but which could never originate?

It might be pointed out to such a reasoner, firstly, that as regards any acquired power the various stages

in the acquisition of which he might be supposed able
to remember, he would find that logic notwithstanding,
the wish did originate the power, and yet was originated
by it, both coming up gradually out of something which
was not recognisable as either power or wish, and
advancing through vain beating of the air, to a vague
effort, and from this to definite effort with failure, and
from this to definite effort with success, and from this
to success with little consciousness of effort, and from
this to success with such complete absence of effort that
he now acts unconsciously and without power of introspection, and that, do what he will, he can rarely or
never draw a sharp dividing line whereat anything
shall be said to begin, though none less certain that
there has been a continuity in discontinuity, and a discontinuity in continuity between it and certain other
past things; moreover, that his opponents postulated
so much beginning of the microscope as that there
should be a dew-drop, even as our evolutionists start
with a sense of touch, of which sense all the others are
modifications, so that not one of them, but is resolvable
into touch by more or less easy stages; and secondly,
that the question is one of fact and of the more evident
deductions therefrom, and should not be carried back
to those remote beginnings where the nature of the
facts is so purely a matter of conjecture and inference.

No plant or animal, then, according to our view,
would be able to conceive more than a very slight improvement on its organisation at a given time, so clearly
as to make the efforts towards it that would result in
growth of the required modification; nor would these
efforts be made with any far-sighted perception of what
next and next and after, but only of what next; while
many of the happiest thoughts would come like all other

happy thoughts—thoughtlessly; by a chain of reasoning too swift and subtle for conscious analysis by the individual. Some of these modifications would be noticeable, but the majority would involve no more noticeable difference that can be detected between the length of the shortest day, and that of the shortest but one.

Thus a bird whose toes were not webbed, but who had under force of circumstances little by little in the course of many generations learned to swim, either from having lived near a lake, and having learnt the art owing to its fishing habits, or from wading about in shallow pools by the sea-side at low water and finding itself sometimes a little out of its depth and just managing to scramble over the intermediate yard or so between it and safety—such a bird did not probably conceive the idea of swimming on the water and set itself to learn to do so, and then conceive the idea of webbed feet and set itself to get webbed feet. The bird found itself in some small difficulty, out of which it either saw, or at any rate found that it could extricate itself by striking out vigorously with its feet and extending its toes as far as ever it could; it thus began to learn the art of swimming and conceived the idea of swimming synchronously, or nearly so; or perhaps wishing to get over a yard or two of deep water, and trying to do so without being at the trouble of rising to fly, it would splash and struggle its way over the water, and thus practically swim, though without much perception of what it had been doing. Finding that no harm had come to it, the bird would do the same again and again; it would thus presently lose fear, and would be able to act more calmly; then it would begin to find out that it could swim a little, and if its food lay much in the water so that it would be of great advantage to it to be able to alight and rest without being forced to return to land, it would begin to make a practice of swimming. It would now discover that it could swim the more easily according as its feet presented a more extended surface to the water; it would therefore keep its toes extended wherever it swam, and as far as in it lay, would make the most of whatever skin was already at the base of its toes. After many generations it would become web-footed, if doing as above described should have been found continuously convenient, so that the bird should have continuously used the skin about its toes as much as possible in this direction.

For there is a margin in every organic structure (and perhaps more than we imagine in things inorganic also), which will admit of references, as it were, side notes, and glosses upon the original text. It is on this margin that we may err or wander—the greatness of a mistake depending rather upon the extent of the departure from the original text, than on the direction that the departure takes. A little error on the bad side is more pardonable, and less likely to hurt the organism than a too great departure upon the right one. This is a fundamental proposition in any true system of ethics, the question what is too much or too sudden being decided by much the same higgling as settles the price of butter in a country market, and being as invisible as the link which connects the last moment of desire with the first of power and performance, and with the material result achieved.

It is on this margin that the fulcrum is to be found, whereby we obtain the little purchase over our structure, that enables us to achieve great results if we use it steadily, with judgment, and with neither too little effort nor too much. It is by employing this that those who have a fancy to move their ears or toes without moving other organs learn to do so. There is a man at the Agricultural Hall now [*] playing the violin with his toes, and playing it, as I am told, sufficiently well. The eye of the sailor, the wrist of the conjuror, the toe of the professional medium, are all found capable of development to an astonishing degree, even in a single lifetime; but in every case success has been attained by the simple process of making the best of whatever power a man has had at any given time, and by being on the look-out to take advantage of accident, and even of misfortune. If a man would learn to paint, he must not theorise concerning art, nor think much what he would do beforehand, but he must do *something*—whatever under the circumstances will come handiest and easiest to him; and he must do that something as well as he can. This will presently open the door for something else, and a way will show itself which no conceivable amount of searching would have discovered, but which yet could never have been discovered by sitting still and taking no pains at all. "Dans l'animal," says Buffon, "il y a moins de jugement que de sentiment." [†]

It may appear as though this were blowing hot and cold with the same breath, inasmuch as I am insisting that important modifications of structure have been always purposive; and at the same time am denying that the creature modified has had any far-seeing purpose in the greater part of all those actions which have at length modified both structure and instinct. Thus I say that a bird learns to swim without having

* 1878.   † "Oiseaux," vol. i. p. 5.

any purpose of learning to swim before it set itself to make those movements which have resulted in its being able to do so. At the same time I maintain that it has only learned to swim by trying to swim, and this involves the very purpose which I have just denied. The reconciliation of these two apparently irreconcilable contentions must be found in the consideration that the bird was not the less trying to swim, merely because it did not know the name we have chosen to give to the art which it was trying to master, nor yet how great were the resources of that art. A person, who knew all about swimming, if from some bank he could watch our supposed bird's first attempt to scramble over a short space of deep water, would at once declare that the bird was trying to swim—if not actually swimming. Provided then that there is a very little perception of, and prescience concerning, the means whereby the next desired end may be attained, it matters not how little in advance that end may be of present desire or faculties; it is still reached through purpose, and must be called purposive. Again, no matter how many of these small steps be taken, nor how absolute was the want of purpose or prescience concerning any but the one being actually taken at any given moment, this does not bar the result from having been arrived at through design and purpose. If each one of the small steps is purposive the result is purposive, though there was never purpose extended over more than one, two, or perhaps at most three steps at a time.

Returning to the art of painting for an example, are we to say that the proficiency which such a student as was supposed above will certainly attain, is not due to design, merely because it was not until he had already

become three parts excellent that he knew the full pur-
port of all that he had been doing?   When he began
he had but vague notions of what he would do.   He
had a wish to learn to represent nature, but the line
into which he has settled down has probably proved
very different from that which he proposed to himself
originally.   Because he has taken advantage of his
accidents, is it, therefore, one whit the less true that
his success is the result of his desires and his design?
The *Times* pointed out some time ago that the theory
which now associates meteors and comets in the most
unmistakable manner, was suggested by one accident,
and confirmed by another.   But the writer added well
that "such accidents happen only to the zealous student
of nature's secrets."   In the same way the bird that is
taking to the habit of swimming, and of making the
most of whatever skin it already has between its toes,
will have doubtless to thank accidents for no small
part of its progress; but they will be such accidents as
could never have happened to or been taken advantage
of by any creature which was not zealously trying to
make the most of itself—and between such accidents
as this, and design, the line is hard to draw; for if we
go deep enough we shall find that most of our design
resolves itself into as it were a shaking of the bag to
see what will come out that will suit our purpose, and
yet at the same time that most of our shaking of the
bag resolves itself into a design that the bag shall contain only such and such things, or thereabouts.

Again, the fact that animals are no longer conscious
of design and purpose in much that they do, but act
unreflectingly, and as we sometimes say concerning
ourselves "automatically" or "mechanically"—that
they have no idea whatever of the steps, whereby they

have travelled to their present state, and show no sign of doubt about what must have been at one time the subject of all manner of doubts, difficulties, and discussions—that whatever sign of reflection they now exhibit is to be found only in case of some novel feature or difficulty presenting itself; these facts do not bar that the results achieved should be attributed to an inception in reason, design and purpose, no matter how rapidly and as we call it instinctively, the creatures may now act.

For if we look closely at such an invention as the steam engine in its latest and most complicated developments, about which there can be no dispute but that they are achievements of reason, purpose and design, we shall find them present us with examples of all those features the presence of which in the handiwork of animals is too often held to bar reason and purpose from having had any share therein.

Assuredly such men as the Marquis of Worcester and Captain Savery had very imperfect ideas as to the upshot of their own action. The simplest steam engine now in use in England is probably a marvel of ingenuity as compared with the highest development which appeared possible to these two great men, while our newest and most highly complicated engines would seem to them more like living beings than machines. Many, again, of the steps leading to the present development have been due to action which had but little heed of the steam engine, being the inventions of attendants whose desire was to save themselves the trouble of turning this or that cock, and who were indifferent to any other end than their own immediate convenience. No step in fact along the whole route was ever taken with much perception of what would be the next step after the one being taken at any given moment.

Nor do we find that an engine made after any old and well-known pattern is now made with much more consciousnesss of design than we can suppose a bird's nest to be built with. The greater number of the parts of any such engine, are made by the gross as it were like screw and nuts, which are turned out by machinery and in respect of which the labour of design is now no more felt than is the design of him who first invented the wheel. It is only when circumstances require any modification in the article to be manufactured that thought and design will come into play again; but I take it few will deny that if circumstances compel a bird either to give up a nest three-parts built altogether, or to make some trifling deviation from its ordinary practice, it will in nine cases out of ten make such deviation as shall show that it had thought the matter over, and had on the whole concluded to take such and such a course, that is to say, that it had reasoned and had acted with such purpose as its reason had dictated.

And I imagine that this is the utmost that any one can claim even for man's own boasted powers. Set the man who has been accustomed to make engines of one type, to make engines of another type without any intermediate course of training or instruction, and he will make no better figure with his engines than a thrush would do if commanded by her mate to make a nest like a blackbird. It is vain then to contend that the ease and certainty with which an action is performed, even though it may have now become matter of such fixed habit that it cannot be suddenly and seriously modified without rendering the whole performance abortive, is any argument against that

action having been an achivement of design and reason
in respect of each one of the steps that have led to it;
and if in respect of each one of the steps then as regards the entire action; for we see our own most
reasoned actions become no less easy, unerring, automatic, and unconscious, than the actions which we call
instinctive when they have been repeated a sufficient
number of times.

.   .   .   .

If the foregoing be granted, and it be admitted that
the unconsciousness and seeming automatism with which
any action may be performed is no bar to its having a
foundation in memory, reason, and at one time consciously recognised effort—and this I believe to be the
chief addition which I have ventured to make to the
theory of Buffon and Dr. Erasmus Darwin—then the
wideness of the difference between the Darwinism of
eighty years ago and the Darwinism of to-day becomes
immediately apparent, and it also becomes apparent,
how important and interesting is the issue which is
raised between them.

According to the older Darwinism the lungs are just
as purposive as the corkscrew.   They, no less than the
corkscrew, are a piece of mechanism designed and
gradually improved upon and perfected by an intelligent creature for the gratification of its own needs.
True there are many important differences between
mechanism which is part of the body, and mechanism
which is no such part, but the differences are such as
do not affect the fact that in each case the result,
whether, for example, lungs or corkscrew, is due to
desire, invention, and design.

And now I will ask one more question, which may
seem, perhaps, to have but little importance, but which

I find personally interesting. I have been told by a reviewer, of whom upon the whole I have little reason to complain, that the theory I put forward in "Life and Habit," and which I am now again insisting on, is pessimism—pure and simple. I have a very vague idea what pessimism means, but I should be sorry to believe that I am a pessimist. Which, I would ask, is the pessimist? He who sees love of beauty, design, steadfastness of purpose, intelligence, courage, and every quality to which success has assigned the name of "worth" as having drawn the pattern of every leaf and organ now and in all past time, or he who sees nothing in the world of nature but a chapter of accidents and of forces interacting blindly?

BUFFON—MEMOIR.

(CHAPTER VIII. OF EVOLUTION, OLD AND NEW.)

BUFFON, says M. Flourens, was born at Montbar, on the 7th of September 1707; he died in Paris, at the Jardin du Roi, on the 16th of April 1788, aged 81 years. More than fifty of these years, as he used himself to say, he had passed at his writing-desk. His father was a councillor of the parliament of Burgundy. His mother was celebrated for her wit, and Buffon cherished her memory.

He studied at Dijon with much *éclat*, and shortly after leaving became accidentally acquainted with the Duke of Kingston, a young Englishman of his own age, who was travelling abroad with a tutor. The three travelled together in France and Italy, and Buffon then passed some months in England.

Returning to France, he translated Hales's Vegetable Statics and Newton's Treatise on Fluxions. He refers to several English writers on natural history in the course of his work, but I see he repeated spells the English name Willoughby, "Willulghby." He was appointed superintendent of the Jardin du Roi in 1739, and from thenceforth devoted himself to science.

In 1752 Buffon married Mdlle de Saint Bélin, whose beauty and charm of manner were extolled by all her contemporaries. One son was born to him, who entered the army, became a colonel, and I grieve to say, was guillotined at the age of twenty-nine, a few days only before the extinction of the Reign of Terror.

Of this youth, who inherited the personal comeliness and ability of his father, little is recorded except the following story. Having fallen into the water and been nearly drowned when he was about twelve years old, he was afterwards accused of having been afraid: "I was so little afraid," he answered, "that though I had been offered the hundred years which my grandfather lived, I would have died then and there, if I could have added one year to the life of my father;" then thinking for a minute, a flush suffused his face and he added, "but I should petition for one quarter of an hour in which to exult over the thought of what I was about to do."

On the scaffold he showed much composure, smiling half proudly, half reproachfully, yet wholly kindly upon the crowd in front of him. "Citoyens," he said, "Je me nomme Buffon," and laid his head upon the block.

The noblest outcome of the old and decaying order, overwhelmed in the most hateful birth frenzy of the new. So in those cataclysms and revolutions which take place in our own bodies during their development, when we seem studying in order to become fishes and suddenly make, as it were, different arrangements and resolve on becoming men—so, doubtless, many good cells must go, and their united death cry comes up, it may be, in the pain which an infant feels on teething.

But to return. The man who could be father of such a son, and who could retain that son's affection, as it is well known that Buffon retained it, may not perhaps always be strictly accurate, but it will be as well to pay attention to whatever he may think fit to

L

tell us. These are the only people whom it is worth while to look to and study from.

"Glory," said Buffon, after speaking of the hours during which he had laboured, "glory comes always after labour if she can—*and she generally can.*" But in his case she could not well help herself. "He was conspicuous," says M. Flourens, "for elevation and force of character, for a love of greatness and true magnificence in all he did. His great wealth, his handsome person, and graceful manners seemed in correspondence with the splendour of his genius, so that of all the gifts which Fortune has in it her power to bestow she had denied him nothing."

Many of his epigrammatic sayings have passed into proverbs: for example, that "genius is but a supreme capacity for taking pains." Another and still more celebrated passage shall be given in its entirety and with its original setting.

"Style," says Buffon, "is the only passport to posterity. It is not range of information, nor mastery of some little known branch of science, nor yet novelty of matter that will ensure immortality. Works that can claim all this will yet die if they are conversant about trivial objects only, or written without taste, genius, and true nobility of mind; for range of information, knowledge of details, novelty of discovery are of a volatile essence and fly off readily into other hands that know better how to treat them. The matter is foreign to the man, and is not of him; the manner is the man himself."*

"Le style, c'est l'homme même." Elsewhere he tells us what true style is, but I quote from memory and cannot be sure of the passage. "Le style," he says

* "Discours de Réception à l'Académie Française."

"est comme le bonheur; il vient de la douceur de l'âme."

Is it possible not to think of the following?—

"But whether there be prophecies they shall fail; whether there be tongues they shall cease; whether there be knowledge it shall vanish away . . . . and now abideth faith, hope and charity, these three; but the greatest of these is charity." *

* 1 Cor. xiii. 8, 13.

BUFFON'S METHOD—THE IRONICAL CHARACTER OF HIS WORK.

(CHAPTER IX. OF EVOLUTION, OLD AND NEW.)

BUFFON'S idea of a method amounts almost to the denial of the possibility of method at all. "The true method," he writes, "is the complete description and exact history of each particular object," * and later on he asks, "is it not more simple, more natural and more true to call an ass an ass, and a cat a cat, than to say, without knowing why, that an ass is a horse, and a cat a lynx?" †

He admits such divisions as between animals and vegetables, or between vegetables and minerals, but that done, he rejects all others that can be founded on the nature of things themselves. He concludes that one who could see living forms as a whole and without preconceived opinions, would classify animals according to the relations in which he found himself standing towards them :—

"Those which he finds most necessary and useful to him will occupy the first rank; thus he will give the precedence among the lower animals to the dog and the horse; he will next concern himself with those which without being domesticated, nevertheless occupy the same country and climate as himself, as for example

---

* Tom. i. p. 24, 1749.   † Tom. i. p. 40, 1749.

stags, hares, and all wild animals ; nor will it be till after
he has familiarised himself with all these that curiosity
will lead him to inquire what inhabitants there may be
in foreign climates, such as elephants, dromedaries, &c.
The same will hold good for fishes, birds, insects, shells,
and for all nature's other productions ; he will study
them in proportion to the profit which he can draw
from them ; he will consider them in that order in
which they enter into his daily life ; he will arrange
them in his head according to this order, which is in
fact that in which he has become acquainted with them,
and in which it concerns him to think about them,
This order—the most natural of all—is the one which
I have thought it well to follow in this volume.   My
classification has no more mystery in it than the reader
has just seen . . . it is preferable to the most profound and ingenious that can be conceived, for there is
none of all the classifications which ever have been
made or ever can be, which has not more of an arbitrary
character than this has.   Take it for all in all," he
concludes, " it is more easy, more agreeable, and more
useful, to consider things in their relation to ourselves
than from any other standpoint." *

  " Has it not a better effect not only in a treatise on
natural history, but in a picture or any work of art to
arrange objects in the order and place in which they are
commonly found, than to force them into association in
virtue of some theory of our own ?   Is it not better to
let the dog which has toes, come after the horse which
has a single hoof, in the same way as we see him follow
the horse in daily life, than to follow up the horse by
the zebra, an animal which is little known to us, and

* Vol. i. p. 34, 1749.

which has no other connection with the horse than the fact that it has a single hoof ? " *

Can we suppose that Buffon really saw no more connection than this ?   The writer whom we shall presently find † declining to admit any essential difference between the skeletons of man and of the horse, can here see no resemblance between the zebra and the horse, except that they each have a single hoof.   Is he to be taken at his word ?

It is perhaps necessary to tell the reader that Buffon carried the foregoing scheme into practice as nearly as he could in the first fifteen volumes of his Natural History.   He begins with man—and then goes on to the horse, the ass, the cow, sheep, goat, pig, dog, &c. One would be glad to know whether he found it always more easy to know in what order of familiarity this or that animal would stand to the majority of his readers than other classifiers have found it to know whether an individual more resembles one species or another ; probably he never gave the matter a thought after he had gone through the first dozen most familiar animals, but settled generally down into a classification which becomes more and more specific—as when he treats of the apes and monkeys—till he reaches the birds, when he openly abandons his original idea, in deference, as he says, to the opinion of " le peuple des naturalistes."

Perhaps the key to this piece of apparent extravagance is to be found in the word " mystérieuse." ‡ Buffon wished to raise a standing protest against mystery mongering.   Or perhaps more probably, he wished at once to turn to animals under domestication, so as to insist early on the main object of his work—the plasticity of animal forms.

* Tom. i. p. 36.   † See p. 173.   ‡ Tom. i. p. 33.

I am inclined to think that a vein of irony pervades the whole or much the greater part of Buffon's work, and that he intended to convey one meaning to one set of readers, and another to another; indeed, it is often impossible to believe that he is not writing between his lines for the discerning, what the undiscerning were not intended to see. It must be remembered that his Natural History has two sides,—a scientific and a popular one. May we not imagine that Buffon would be unwilling to debar himself from speaking to those who could understand him, and yet would wish like Handel and Shakespeare to address the many, as well as the few? But the only manner in which these seemingly irreconcilable ends could be attained, would be by the use of language which should be self-adjusting to the capacity of the reader. So keen an observer can hardly have been blind to the signs of the times which were already close at hand. Free-thinker though he was, he was also a powerful member of the aristocracy, and little likely to demean himself—for so he would doubtless hold it—by playing the part of Voltaire or Rousseau. He would help those who could see to see still further, but he would not dazzle eyes that were yet imperfect with a light brighter than they could stand. He would therefore impose upon people, as much as he thought was for their good; but, on the other hand, he would not allow inferior men to mystify them.

"In the private character of Buffon," says Sir William Jardine in a characteristic passage, "we regret there is not much to praise; his disposition was kind and benevolent, and he was generally beloved by his inferiors, followers, and dependants, which were numerous over his extensive property; he was strictly honourable,

and was an affectionate parent.   In early youth he had
entered into the pleasures and dissipations of life, and
licentious habits seem to have been retained to the end.
But the great blemish in such a mind was his declared
infidelity; it presents one of those exceptions among
the persons who have been devoted to the study of
nature ; and it is not easy to imagine a mind apparently
with such powers, scarcely acknowledging a Creator,
and when noticed, only by an arraignment for what
appeared wanting or defective in His great works.   So
openly, indeed, was the freedom of his religious opinions
expressed, that the indignation of the Sorbonne was
provoked.   He had to enter into an explanation which
he in some way rendered satisfactory ; and while he afterwards attended to the outward ordinances of religion,
he considered them as a system of faith for the multitude,
and regarded those most impolitic who most opposed
them." *

This is partly correct and partly not.   Buffon was a
free-thinker, and as I have sufficiently explained, a
decided opponent of the doctrine that rudimentary and
therefore useless organs were designed by a Creator in
order to serve some useful end throughout all time to
the creature in which they are found.

He was not, surely, to hide the magnificent conceptions which he had been the first to grasp, from
those who were worthy to receive them ; on the other
hand he would not tell the uninstructed what they
would interpret as a licence to do whatever they pleased,
inasmuch as there was no God.   What he did was to
point so irresistibly in the right direction, that a reader
of any intelligence should be in no doubt as to the
road he ought to take, and then to contradict himself

* The Naturalist's Library, vol. ii. p. 23. Edinburgh, 1843.

so flatly as to reassure those who would be shocked by a truth for which they were not yet ready. If I am right in the view which I have taken of Buffon's work, it is not easy to see how he could have formed a finer scheme, nor have carried it out more finely.

I should, however, warn the reader to be on his guard against accepting my view too hastily. So far as I know I stand alone in taking it. Neither Dr. Darwin, nor Flourens, nor Isidore Geoffroy, nor Mr. Charles Darwin see any subrisive humour in Buffon's pages; but it must be remembered that Flourens was a strong opponent of mutability, and probably paid but little heed to what Buffon said on this question; Isidore Geoffroy is not a safe guide, few men indeed less so. Mr. Charles Darwin seems to have adopted the one half of Isidore Geoffroy's conclusions without verifying either; and Dr. Erasmus Darwin, who has no small share of a very pleasant conscious humour, yet sometimes rises to such heights of unconscious humour, that Buffon's puny labour may well have been invisible to him. Dr. Darwin wrote a great deal of poetry, some of which was about the common pump. Miss Seward tells us, that he "illustrated this familiar object with a picture of Maternal Beauty administering sustenance to her infant." Buffon could not have done anything like this.

Buffon never, then, "arraigned the Creator for what was wanting or defective in His works;" on the contrary, whenever he was led up by an irresistible chain of reasoning to conclusions which should make men recast their ideas concerning the Deity, he invariably retreats under cover of an appeal to revelation. Naturally enough, the Sorbonne objected to an artifice which even Buffon could not conceal completely. They did not like being undermined ; like Buffon himself, they preferred imposing upon the people, to seeing others do so.   Buffon made his peace with the Sorbonne immediately, and, perhaps, from that time forward, contradicted himself a little more impudently than heretofore.

It is probably for the reasons above suggested that Buffon did not propound a connected scheme of evolution or descent with modification, but scattered his theory in fragments up and down his work in the prefatory remarks with which he introduces the more striking animals or classes of animals.   He never wastes evolutionary matter in the preface to an uninteresting animal ; and the more interesting the animal, the more evolution will there be commonly found. When he comes to describe the animal more familiarly—and he generally begins a fresh chapter or half chapter when he does so—he writes no more about evolution, but gives an admirable description, which no one can fail to enjoy, and which I cannot think is nearly so inaccurate as is commonly supposed.   These descriptions are the parts which Buffon intended for the general reader, expecting, doubtless, and desiring that such a reader should skip the dry parts he had been addressing to the more studious.   It is true the descriptions are written *ad captandum,* as are all great works, but they succeed in captivating, having been composed with all the pains a man of genius and of great perseverance could bestow upon them.   If I am not mistaken, he looked to these parts of his work to keep the whole alive till the time should come when the philosophical side of his writings should be understood and appreciated.

Thus the goat breeds with the sheep, and may therefore serve as the text for a dissertation on hybridism, which is accordingly given in the preface to this animal. The presence of rudimentary organs under a pig's hoof suggests an attack upon the doctrine of final causes in so far as it is pretended that every part of every animal or plant was specially designed with a view to the wants of the animal or plant itself, once and forever throughout all time. The dog with his great variety of breeds gives an opportunity for an article on the formation of breeds and sub-breeds by man's artificial selection. The cat is not honoured with any philosophical reflection, and comes in for nothing but abuse. The hare suggests the rabbit, and the rabbit is a rapid breeder, although the hare is an unusually slow one; but this is near enough, so the hare shall serve us for the theme of a discourse on the geometrical ratio of increase and the balance of power which may be observed in nature. When we come to the carnivora, additional reflections follow upon the necessity for death, and even for violent death; this leads to the question whether the creatures that are killed suffer pain; here, then, will be the proper place for considering the sensations of animals generally.

Perhaps the most pregnant passage concerning evolution is to be found in the preface to the ass, which is so near the beginning of the work as to be only the second animal of which Buffon treats after having described man himself. It points strongly in the direction of his having believed all animal forms to have been descended from one single common ancestral type. Buffon did not probably choose to take his very first opportunity in order to insist upon matter that should point in this direction; but the considerations were too important to be deferred long, and are accordingly put forward under cover of the ass, his second animal.

When we consider the force with which Buffon's conclusion is led up to; the obviousness of the conclusion itself when the premises are once admitted; the impossibility that such a conclusion should be again lost sight of if the reasonableness of its being drawn had been once admitted; the position in his scheme which is assigned to it by its propounder; the persistency with which he demonstrates during forty years thereafter that the premises, which he has declared should establish the conclusion in question, are indisputable;—when we consider, too, that we are dealing with a man of unquestionable genius, and that the times and circumstances of his life were such as would go far to explain reserve and irony—is it, I would ask, reasonable to suppose that Buffon did not, in his own mind, and from the first, draw the inference to which he leads his reader, merely because from time to time he tells the reader, with a shrug of the shoulders, that *he* draws no inferences opposed to the Book of Genesis? Is it not more likely that Buffon intended his reader to draw his inferences for himself, and perhaps to value them all the more highly on that account?

The passage to which I am alluding is as follows :—

" If from the boundless variety which animated nature presents to us, we choose the body of some animal or even that of man himself to serve as a model with which to compare the bodies of other organised beings, we shall find that though all these beings have an individuality of their own, and are distinguished from one another by differences of which the gradations are infinitely subtle, there exists at the same time a

primitive and general design which we can follow for
a long way, and the departures from which (*dégénéra-
tions*) are far more gentle than those from mere outward resemblance. For not to mention organs of
digestion, circulation, and generation, which are common to all animals, and without which the animal
would cease to be an animal, and could neither continue to exist nor reproduce itself—there is none the
less even in those very parts which constitute the main
difference in outward appearance, a striking resemblance
which carries with it irresistibly the idea of a single
pattern after which all would appear to have been
conceived. The horse, for example—what can at first
sight seem more unlike mankind? Yet when we compare man and horse point by point and detail by detail,
is not our wonder excited rather by the points of
resemblance than of difference that are to be found
between them? Take the skeleton of a man; bend
forward the bones in the region of the pelvis, shorten
the thigh bones, and those of the leg and arm, lengthen
those of the feet and hands, run the joints together,
lengthen the jaws, and shorten the frontal bone, finally,
lengthen the spine, and the skeleton will now be that
of a man no longer, but will have become that of a
horse—for it is easy to imagine that in lengthening
the spine and the jaws we shall at the same time have
increased the number of the vertebræ, ribs, and teeth.
It is but in the number of these bones, which may be
considered accessory, and by the lengthening, shortening,
or mode of attachment of others, that the skeleton of
the horse differs from that of the human body. . . .
We find ribs in man, in all the quadrupeds, in birds,
in fishes, and we may find traces of them as far down
as the turtle, in which they seem still to be sketched

out by means of furrows that are to be found beneath
the shell.   Let it be remembered that the foot of the
horse, which seems so different from a man's hand, is,
nevertheless, as.M. Daubenton has pointed out, composed of the same bones, and that we have at the end
of each of our fingers a nail corresponding to the hoof
of a horse's foot.   Judge, then, whether this hidden
resemblance is not more marvellous than any outward differences—whether this constancy to a single
plan of structure which we may follow from man to
the quadrupeds, from the quadrupeds to the cetacea,
from the cetacea to birds, from birds to reptiles, from
reptiles to fishes—in which all such essential parts as
heart, intestines, spine are invariably found—whether,
I say, this does not seem to indicate that the Creator
when He made them would use but a single main idea,
though at the same time varying it in every conceivable
way, so that man might admire equally the magnificence
of the execution and the simplicity of the design.[*]

" If we regard the matter thus, not only the ass and
the horse, *but even man himself, the apes, the quadrupeds, and all animals might be regarded but as forming
members of one and the same family.*   But are we to
conclude that within this vast family which the Creator
has called into existence out of nothing, there are
other and smaller families, projected as it were by
Nature, and brought forth by her in the natural course
of events and after a long time, of which some contain
but two members, as the ass and the horse, others many
members, as the weasel, martin, stoat, ferret, &c., and
that on the same principle there are families of vegetables, containing ten, twenty, or thirty plants, as the
case may be ?   If such families had any real existence

[*] Tom. iv. p. 381, 1753.

they could have been formed only by crossing, by the accumulation of successive variations (*variation successive*), and by degeneration from an original type; but if we once admit that there are families. of plants and animals, so that the ass may be of the family of the horse, and that the one may only differ from the other through degeneration from a common ancestor, we might be driven to admit that the ape is of the family of man, that he is but a degenerate man, and that he and man have had a common ancestor, even as the ass and horse have had. It would follow then that every family, whether animal or vegetable, had sprung from a single stock, which after a succession of generations had become higher in the case of some of its descendants and lower in that of others."

What inference could be more aptly drawn? But it was not one which Buffon was going to put before the general public. He had said enough for the discerning, and continues with what is intended to make the conclusions they should draw even plainer to them, while it conceals them still more carefully from the general reader.

" The naturalists who are so ready to establish families among animals and vegetables, do not seem to have sufficiently considered the consequences which should follow from their premises, for these would limit direct creation to as small a number of forms as any one might think fit (reduisoient le produit immédiat de la création, àun nombre d'individus aussi petit que l'on voudroit). *For if it were once shown that we had right grounds for establishing these families; if the point were once gained that among animals and vegetables there had been, I do not say several species, but even a single one, which had been produced in the course of direct descent from another species ; if for example it could be once shown that the ass was but a degeneration from the horse —then there is no further limit to be set to the power of nature, and we should not be wrong in supposing that with sufficient time she could have evolved all other organised forms from one primordial type (et l'on n'auroit pas tort de supposer, que d'un seul être elle a su tirer avec le temps tous les autres êtres organisés)."*

Buffon now felt that he had sailed as near the wind as was desirable. His next sentence is as follows :—

"But no ! It is certain *from revelation* that all animals have alike been favoured with the grace of an act of direct creation, and that the first pair of every species issued full formed from the hands of the Creator." *

This might be taken as *bond fide,* if it had been written by Bonnet, but it is impossible to accept it from Buffon. It is only those who judge him at second hand, or by isolated passages, who can hold that he failed to see the consequences of his own premises. No one could have seen more clearly, nor have said more lucidly, what should suffice to show a sympathetic reader the conclusion he ought to come to. Even when ironical, his irony is not the ill-natured irony of one who is merely amusing himself at other people's expense, but the serious and legitimate irony of one who must either limit the circle of those to whom he appeals, or must know how to make the same language appeal differently to the different capacities of his readers, and who trusts to the good sense of the discerning to understand the difficulty of his position and make due allowance for it.

The compromise which he thought fit to put before

---

* Tom. iv. p. 383, 1753 (this was the first volume on the lower animals).

the public was that "Each species has a type of which
the principal features are engraved in indelible and eternally permanent characters, while all accessory touches
vary." * It would be satisfactory to know where an
accessory touch is supposed to begin and end.

And again :—

"The essential characteristics of every animal have
been conserved without alteration in their most important parts. . . . The individuals of each genus still
represent the same forms as they did in the earliest
ages, especially in the case of the larger animals" (so
that the generic forms even of the larger animals prove
not to be the same, but only "especially" the same as
in the earliest ages). †

This transparently illogical position is maintained
ostensibly from first to last, much in the same spirit
as in the two foregoing passages, written at intervals
of thirteen years. But they are to be read by the
light of the earlier one—placed as a lantern to the
wary upon the threshold of his work in 1753—to the
effect that a single, well-substantiated case of degeneration would make it conceivable that all living beings
were descended from but one common ancestor. If
after having led up to this by a remorseless logic, a
man is found five-and-twenty years later still sub-
stantiating cases of degeneration, as he has been sub-
stantiating them unceasingly in thirty quartos during
the whole interval, there should be little question how
seriously we are to take him when he wishes us to
stop short of the conclusions he has told us we ought to
draw from the premises that he has made it the business of his life to establish—especially when we know
that he has a Sorbonne to keep a sharp eye upon him.

* Tom. xiii. p. 1765.   † Sup. tom. v. p. 27, 1778.

I believe that if the reader will bear in mind the twofold, serious and ironical, character of Buffon's work he will understand it, and feel an admiration for it which will grow continually greater and greater the more he studies it, otherwise he will miss the whole point.

Buffon on one of the early pages of his first volume protested against the introduction of either *"plaisanterie"* or *" équivoque "* (p. 25) into a serious work. But I have observed that there is an unconscious irony in most disclaimers of this nature. When a writer begins by saying that he has "an ineradicable tendency to make things clear," we may infer that we are going to be puzzled; so when he shows that he is haunted by a sense of the impropriety of allowing humour to intrude into his work, we may hope to be amused as well as interested. As showing how far the objection to humour which he expressed upon his twenty-fifth page succeeded in carrying him safely over his twenty-sixth and twenty-seventh, I will quote the following, which begins on page twenty-six :—

"Aldrovandus is the most learned and laborious of all naturalists; after sixty years of work he has left an immense number of volumes behind him, which have been printed at various times, the greater number of them after his death. It would be possible to reduce them to a tenth part if we could rid them of all useless and foreign matter, and of a prolixity which I find almost overwhelming; were this only done, his books should be regarded as among the best we have on the subject of natural history in its entirety. The plan of his work is good, his classification distinguished for its good sense, his dividing lines well marked, his descriptions sufficiently accurate—monotonous it is true, but painstaking ; the historical part of his work is less good ; it is often confused and fabulous, and the author shows too manifestly the credulous tendencies of his mind.

"While going over his work, I have been struck with that defect, or rather excess, which we find in almost all the books of a hundred or a couple of hundred years ago, and which prevails still among the Germans—I mean with that quantity of useless erudition with which they intentionally swell out their works, and the result of which is that their subject is overlaid with a mass of extraneous matter on which they enlarge with great complacency, but with no consideration whatever for their readers. They seem, in fact, to have forgotten what they have to say in their endeavour to tell us what has been said by other people.

"I picture to myself a man like Aldrovandus, after he has once conceived the design of writing a complete natural history. I see him in his library reading, one after the other, ancients, moderns, philosophers, theologians, jurisconsults, historians, travellers, poets, and reading with no other end than with that of catching at all words and phrases which can be forced from far or near into some kind of relation with his subject. I see him copying all these passages, or getting them copied for him, and arranging them in alphabetical order. He fills many portfolios with all manner of notes, often taken without either discrimination or research, and at last sets himself to write with a resolve that not one of all these notes shall remain unused. The result is that when he comes to his account of the cow or of the hen, he will tell us all that has ever yet been said about cows or hens ; all that the ancients ever thought about them; all that has ever been imagined concerning their virtues, characters, and courage; every purpose to which they have ever yet been put; every story of every old woman that he can lay hold of; all the miracles which certain religions have ascribed to them; all the superstitions they have given rise to; all the metaphors and allegories which poets have drawn from them; the attributes that have been assigned to them; the representations that have been made of them in hieroglyphics and armorial bearings, in a word all the histories and all fables in which there was ever yet any mention either of a cow or hen. How much natural history is likely to be found in such a lumber-room? and how is one to lay one's hand upon the little that there may actually be?" *

It is hoped that the reader will see Buffon, much as Buffon saw the learned Aldrovandus. He should see him going into his library, &c., and quietly chuckling to himself as he wrote such a passage as the one in which we lately found him saying that the larger animals had "especially" the same generic forms as they had always had. And the reader should probably see Daubenton chuckling also.

* Tom. i. p. 28, 1749.

EXTRACTS FROM UNCONSCIOUS MEMORY.

——o——

RECAPITULATION AND STATEMENT OF AN OBJECTION.

(CHAPTER X. OF UNCONSCIOUS MEMORY.[*])

THE true theory of unconscious action is that of Professor Hering, from whose lecture[†] it is no strained conclusion to gather that he holds the action of all living beings, from the moment of conception to that of fullest development, to be founded in volition and design, though these have been so long lost sight of that the work is now carried on, as it were, departmentally and in due course according to an official routine which can hardly be departed from.

This involves the older " Darwinism " and the theory of Lamarck, according to which the modification of living forms has been effected mainly through the needs of the living forms themselves, which vary with varying conditions—the survival of the fittest (which, as I see Mr. H. B. Baildon has just said, " sometimes comes to mean merely the survival of the survivors "[‡])

* Unconscious Memory was published December, 1880.
† See Unconscious Memory, chap. vi.
‡ The Spirit of Nature, p. 39. J. A. Churchill & Co. 1880.

being taken as a matter of course. According to this view of evolution, there is a remarkable analogy between the development of living organs, or tools, and that of those organs or tools external to the body which has been so rapid during the last few thousand years.

Animals and plants, according to Professor Hering, are guided throughout their development, and preserve the due order in each step they take, through memory of the course they took on past occasions when in the persons of their ancestors. I am afraid I have already too often said that if this memory remains for long periods together latent and without effect, it is because the vibrations of the molecular substance of the body which are its supposed explanation are during these periods too feeble to generate action, until they are augmented in force through an accession of similar vibrations issuing from exterior objects; or, in other words, until recollection is stimulated by a return of the associated ideas. On this the internal agitation becomes so much enhanced, that equilibrium is visibly disturbed, and the action ensues which is proper to the vibrations of the particular substance under the particular conditions. This, at least, is what I suppose Professor Hering to intend.

Leaving the explanation of memory on one side, and confining ourselves to the fact of memory only, a caterpillar on being just hatched is supposed, according to this theory, to lose its memory of the time it was in the egg, and to be stimulated by an intense but unconscious recollection of the action taken by its ancestors when they were first hatched. It is guided in the course it takes by the experience it can thus command. Each step it takes recalls a new recollection, and thus it goes through a development as a performer performs a piece of music, each bar leading his recollection to the bar that should next follow.

In Life and Habit will be found examples of the manner in which this view solves a number of difficulties for the explanation of which the leading men of science express themselves at a loss. The following from Professor Huxley's recent work upon the crayfish may serve for an example. Professor Huxley writes:—

"It is a widely received notion that the energies of living matter have a tendency to decline and finally disappear, and that the death of the body as a whole is a necessary correlate of its life. That all living beings sooner or later perish needs no demonstration, but it would be difficult to find satisfactory grounds for the belief that they needs must do so. The analogy of a machine, that sooner or later must be brought to a standstill by the wear and tear of its parts, does not hold, inasmuch as the animal mechanism is continually renewed and repaired; and though it is true that individual components of the body are constantly dying, yet their places are taken by vigorous successors. A city remains notwithstanding the constant death-rate of its inhabitants; and such an organism as a crayfish is only a corporate unity, made up of innumerable partially independent individualities."—*The Crayfish*, p. 127.

Surely the theory which I have indicated above makes the reason plain why no organism can permanently outlive its experience of past lives. The death of such a body corporate as the crayfish is due to the social condition becoming more complex than there is memory of past experience to deal with. Hence social disruption, insubordination, and decay. The crayfish dies as a state dies, and all states that we have heard of die sooner or later. There are some savages who have not yet arrived at the conception that death is the necessary end of all living beings, and who consider even the gentlest death from old age as violent and abnormal; so Professor Huxley seems to find a difficulty in seeing that though a city commonly outlives many generations of its citizens, yet cities and states are in the end no less mortal than individuals. " The city," he says, " remains." Yes, but not for ever. When Professor Huxley can find a city that will last for ever, he may wonder that a crayfish does not last for ever.

I have already here and elsewhere said all that I can yet bring forward in support of Professor Hering's theory; it now remains for me to meet the most troublesome objection to it that I have been able to think of—an objection which I had before me when I wrote Life and Habit, but which then as now I believe to be unsound. Seeing, however, that a plausible case can be made out for it, I will state it and refute it here. When I say refute it, I do not mean that I shall have done with it—for it is plain that it opens up a vaster question in the relations between the so-called organic and inorganic worlds—but that I will refute the supposition that it any way militates against Professor Hering's theory.

" Why," it may be asked, " should we go out of our way to invent unconscious memory—the existence of which must at the best remain an inference*—when the observed fact that like antecedents are invariably followed by like consequents should be sufficient for our purpose ? Why should the fact that a given kind

---

* I have put these words into the mouth of my supposed objector, and shall put others like them, because they are characteristic ; but nothing can become so well known as to escape being an inference.

of chrysalis in a given condition will always become a butterfly within a certain time be connected with memory when it is not pretended that memory has anything to do with the invariableness with which oxygen and hydrogen when mixed in certain proportions make water?"

We assume confidently that if a drop of water were decomposed into its component parts, and if these were brought together again, and again decomposed and again brought together any number of times over, the results would be invariably the same, whether decomposition or combination, yet no one will refer the invariableness of the action during each repetition, to recollection by the gaseous molecules of the course taken when the process was last repeated. On the contrary, we are assured that molecules in some distant part of the world which had never entered into such and such a known combination themselves, nor held concert with other molecules that had been so combined, and which, therefore, could have had no experience and no memory, would none the less act upon one another in that one way in which other like combinations of atoms have acted under like circumstances, as readily as though they had been combined and separated and recombined again a hundred or a hundred thousand times. It is this assumption, tacitly made by every man, beast, and plant in the universe, throughout all time and in every action of their lives, that has made any improvement in action possible—for it is this which lies at the root of the power to profit by experience. I do not exactly know *why* we make this assumption, and I cannot find out that any one else knows much better than myself, but I do not recommend any one to dispute it.

As we admit of no doubt concerning the main result, so we do not suppose an alternative to lie before any atom of any molecule at any moment during the process of combination. This process is, in all probability, an exceedingly complicated one, involving a multitude of actions and subordinate processes, which follow one upon the other, and each one of which has a beginning, a middle, and an end, though they all come to pass in what appears to be an instant of time. Yet at no point do we conceive of any atom as swerving ever such a little to right or left of a determined course, but invest each one of them with so much of the divine attributes as that with it there shall be no variableness neither shadow of turning.

We attribute this regularity of action to what we call the necessity of things, as determined by the nature of the atoms and the circumstances in which they are placed. We say that only one proximate result can ever arise from any given combination. If, then, so great uniformity of action as nothing can exceed is manifested by atoms to which no one will impute memory, why this desire for memory, as though it were the only way of accounting for regularity of action in living beings? Sameness of action may be seen abundantly where there is no room for anything that we can consistently call memory. In these cases we say that it is due to sameness of substance in same circumstances.

The most cursory reflection upon our actions will show us that it is no more possible for living action to have more than one set of proximate consequents at any given time than for oxygen and hydrogen when mixed in the proportions proper for the formation of water. Why then not recognise this fact, and ascribe repeated similarity of living action to the reproduction of the necessary antecedents, with no more sense of connection between the steps in the action, or memory of similar action taken before, than we suppose on the part of oxygen and hydrogen molecules between the several occasions on which they may have been disunited and reunited ?

A boy catches the measles not because he remembers having caught them in the persons of his father and mother, but because he is a fit soil for a certain kind of seed to grow upon. In like manner he should be said to grow his nose because he is a fit combination for a nose to spring from. Dr. X———'s father died of *angina pectoris* at the age of forty-nine; so did Dr. X———. Can it be pretended that Dr. X——— remembered having died of *angina pectoris* at the age of forty-nine when in the person of his father, and accordingly, when he came to be forty-nine years old himself, died also ? For this to hold, Dr. X———'s father must have begotten him after he was dead; for the son could not remember the father's death before it happened.

As for the diseases of old age, so very commonly inherited, they are developed for the most part not only long after the average age of reproduction, but at a time when no appreciable amount of memory of any previous existence can remain; for a man will not have many male ancestors who become parents at over sixty years old, nor female ancestors who did so at over forty. By our own showing, therefore, recollection can have nothing to do with the matter. Yet who can doubt that gout is due to inheritance as much as eyes and noses ? In what respects do the two things differ so that we should refer the inheritance of eyes and noses to memory, while denying any connection between memory and gout? We may have a ghost of a pretence for saying that a man grows a nose by rote, or even that he catches the measles or whooping-cough by rote; but do we mean to say that he develops the gout by rote in his old age if he comes of a gouty family? If, then, rote and red-tape have nothing to do with the one, why should they with the other?

Remember also the cases in which aged females develop male characteristics. Here are growths, often of not inconsiderable extent, which make their appearance during the decay of the body, and grow with greater and greater vigour in the extreme of old age, and even for days after death itself. It can hardly be doubted that an especial tendency to develop these characteristics runs as an inheritance in certain families; here then is perhaps the best case that can be found of a development strictly inherited, but having clearly nothing whatever to do with memory. Why should not all development stand upon the same footing?

A friend who had been arguing with me for some time as above, concluded with the following words :—

"If you cannot be content with the similar action of similar substances (living or non-living) under similar circumstances—if you cannot accept this as an ultimate fact, but consider it necessary to connect repetition of similar action with memory before you can rest in it and be thankful—be consistent, and introduce this memory which you find so necessary into the inorganic world also. Either say that a chrysalis becomes a butterfly because it is the thing that it is, and, being that kind of thing, must act in such and such a manner and in such a manner only, so that the act of one generation has no more to do with the act of the next than the fact of cream being churned into butter in a dairy one day has to do with other cream being churn-able into butter in the following week—either say this or else develop some mental condition—which I have no doubt you will be very well able to do if you feel the want of it—in which you can make out a case for saying that oxygen and hydrogen on being brought together, and cream on being churned, are in some way acquainted with, and mindful of, action taken by other cream, and other oxygen and hydrogen on past occasions."

I felt inclined to reply that my friend need not twit me with being able to develop a mental organism if I felt the need of it, for his own ingenious attack on my position, and indeed every action of his life, was but an example of this omnipresent principle.

When he was gone, however, I thought over what he had been saying. I endeavoured to see how far I could get on without volition and memory, and reasoned as follows:—A repetition of like antecedents will be certainly followed by a repetition of like consequents, whether the agents be men and women or chemical substances. "If there be two cowards perfectly similar in every respect, and if they be subjected in a perfectly similar way to two terrifying agents, which are themselves perfectly similar, there are few who will not expect a perfect similarity in the running away, even though ten thousand years intervene between the original combination and its repetition." * Here certainly there is no coming into play of memory, more than in the pan of cream on two successive churning days, yet the action is similar.

A clerk in an office has an hour in the middle of the day for dinner. About half-past twelve he begins to

* Erewhon, chap. xxiii.

feel hungry; at one he takes down his hat and leaves the office. He does not yet know the neighbourhood, and on getting down into the street asks a policeman at the corner which is the best eating-house within easy distance. The policeman tells him of three houses, one of which is a little farther off than the other two, but is cheaper. Money being a greater object to him than time, the clerk decides on going to the cheaper house. He goes, is satisfied, and returns.

Next day he wants his dinner at the same hour, and —it will be said—remembering his satisfaction of yesterday, will go to the same place as before. But what has his memory to do with it? Suppose him to have forgotten all the circumstances of the preceding day from the moment of his beginning to feel hungry onward, though in other respects sound in mind and body, and unchanged generally. At half-past twelve he would begin to be hungry; but his beginning to be hungry cannot be connected with his remembering having begun to be hungry yesterday. He would begin to be hungry just as much whether he remembered or no. At one o'clock he again takes down his hat and leaves the office, not because he remembers having done so yesterday, but because he wants his hat to go out with. Being again in the street, and again ignorant of the neighbourhood (for he remembers nothing of yesterday), he sees the same policeman at the corner of the street, and asks him the same question as before; the policeman gives him the same answer, and money being still an object to him, the cheapest eating-house is again selected; he goes there, finds the same *menu*, makes the same choice for the same reasons, eats, is satisfied, and returns.

What similarity of action can be greater than this,

and at the same time more incontrovertible? But it has nothing to do with memory; on the contrary, it is just because the clerk has no memory that his action of the second day so exactly resembles that of the first. As long as he has no power of recollecting, he will day after day repeat the same actions in exactly the same way, until some external circumstances, such as his being sent away, modify the situation. Till this or some other modification occurs, he will day after day go down into the street without knowing where to go; day after day he will see the same policeman at the corner of the same street, and (for we may as well suppose that the policeman has no memory too) he will ask and be answered, and ask and be answered, till he and the policeman die of old age. This similarity of action is plainly due to that—whatever it is—which ensures that like persons or things when placed in like circumstances shall behave in a like manner.

Allow the clerk ever such a little memory, and the similarity of action will disappear; for the fact of remembering what happened to him on the first day he went out in search of dinner will be a modification in him in regard to his then condition when he next goes out to get his dinner. He had no such memory on the first day, and he has upon the second. Some modification of action must ensue upon this modification of the actor, and this is immediately observable. He wants his dinner, indeed, goes down into the street, and sees the policeman as yesterday, but he does not ask the policeman; he remembers what the policeman told him and what he did, and therefore goes straight to the eating-house without wasting time: nor does he dine off the same dish two days running, for he remembers what he had yesterday and likes variety. If, then, similarity of action is rather hindered than promoted by memory, why introduce it into such cases as the repetition of the embryonic processes by successive generations? The embryos of a well-fixed breed, such as the goose, are almost as much alike as water is to water, and by consequence one goose comes to be almost as like another as water to water. Why should it not be supposed to become so upon the same grounds—namely, that it is made of the same stuffs, and put together in like proportions in the same manner?

ON CYCLES.

(CHAPTER XI. OF UNCONSCIOUS MEMORY.)

THE one faith on which all normal living beings consciously or unconsciously act, is that like antecedents will be followed by like consequents. This is the
one true and catholic faith, undemonstrable, but except a
living being believe which, without doubt it shall perish
everlastingly. In the assurance of this all action is taken.

But if this fundamental article is admitted, it follows
that if ever a complete cycle were formed, so that the
whole universe of one instant were to repeat itself
absolutely in a subsequent one, no matter after what
interval of time, then the course of the events between
these two moments would go on repeating itself for
ever and ever afterwards in due order, down to the
minutest detail, in an endless series of cycles like a
circulating decimal. For the universe comprises everything; there could therefore be no disturbance from
without. Once a cycle, always a cycle.

Let us suppose the earth of given weight, moving with
given momentum in a given path, and under given
conditions in every respect, to find itself at any one time
conditioned in all these respects as it was conditioned
at some past moment; then it must move exactly in
the same path as the one it took when at the beginning
of the cycle it has just completed, and must therefore
in the course of time fulfil a second cycle, and therefore

N

a third, and so on for ever and ever, with no more chance of escape than a circulating decimal has, if the circumstances have been reproduced with perfect accuracy as to draw it into such a whirlpool.

We see something very like this actually happen in the yearly revolutions of the planets round the sun. But the relations between, we will say, the earth and the sun are not reproduced absolutely. These relations deal only with a small part of the universe, and even in this small part the relation of the parts *inter se* has never yet been reproduced with the perfection of accuracy necessary for our argument. They are liable, moreover, to disturbance from events which may or may not actually occur (as, for example, our being struck by a comet, or the sun's coming within a certain distance of another sun), but of which, if they do occur, no one can foresee the effects. Nevertheless the conditions have been so nearly repeated that there is no appreciable difference in the relations between the earth and sun on one New Year's Day and on another, nor is there reason for expecting such change within any reasonable time.

If there is to be an eternal series of cycles involving the whole universe, it is plain that not one single atom must be excluded. Exclude a single molecule of hydrogen from the ring, or vary the relative positions of two molecules only, and the charm is broken; an element of disturbance has been introduced, of which the utmost that can be said is that it may not prevent the ensuing of a long series of very nearly perfect cycles before similarity in recurrence is destroyed, but which must inevitably prevent absolute identity of repetition. The movement of the series becomes no longer a cycle, but spiral, and convergent or divergent at a greater or less rate according to circumstances.

We cannot conceive of all the atoms in the universe standing twice over in absolutely the same relation each one of them to every other. There are too many of them, and they are too much mixed; but, as has been just said, in the planets and their satellites we do see large groups of atoms whose movements recur with some approach to precision. The same holds good also with certain comets and with the sun himself. The result is that our days and nights and seasons follow one another with nearly perfect regularity from year to year, and have done so for as long time as we know anything for certain. A vast preponderance of all the action that takes place around us is cyclical action.

Within the great cycle of the planetary revolution of our own earth, and as a consequence thereof, we have the minor cycle of the seasons; these generate atmospheric cycles. Water is evaporated from the ocean and conveyed to mountain-ranges, where it is cooled, and whence it returns again to the sea. This cycle of events is being repeated again and again with little appreciable variation. The tides, and winds in certain latitudes, go round and round the world with what amounts to continuous regularity. There are storms of wind and rain called cyclones. In the case of these, the cycle is not very complete, the movement, therefore, is spiral, and the tendency to recur is comparatively soon lost. It is a common saying that history repeats itself, so that anarchy will lead to despotism and despotism to anarchy; every nation can point to instances of men's minds having gone round and round so nearly in a perfect cycle that many revolutions have occurred before the cessation of a tendency to recur. Lastly, in the generation of plants and animals we have, perhaps, the most striking and common example of the inevitable tendency of all action to repeat itself when it has once proximately done so. Let only one living being have once succeeded in producing a being like itself, and thus have returned, so to speak, upon itself, and a series of generations must follow of necessity, unless some matter interfere which had no part in the original combination, and, as it may happen, kill the first reproductive creature or all its descendants within a few generations. If no such mishap occurs as this, and if the recurrence of the conditions is sufficiently perfect, a series of generations follows with as much certainty as a series of seasons follows upon the cycle of the relations between the earth and sun.

Let the first periodically recurring substance—we will say A—be able to recur or reproduce itself, not once only, but many times over, as A^1, A^2, &c.; let A also have consciousness and a sense of self-interest, which qualities must, *ex hypothesi*, be reproduced in each one of its offspring; let these get placed in circumstances which differ sufficiently to destroy the cycle in theory without doing so practically—that is to say, to reduce the rotation to a spiral, but to a spiral with so little deviation from perfect cycularity as for each revolution to appear practically a cycle, though after many revolutions the deviation becomes perceptible; then some such differentiations of animal and vegetable life as we actually see follow as matters of course. A^1 and A^2 have a sense of self-interest as A had, but they are not precisely in circumstances similar to A's, nor, it may be, to each other's; they will therefore act somewhat differently, and every living being is modified by a change of action. Having become modified, they follow the spirit of A's action more essentially in begetting a creature like themselves than in begetting one like A; for the essence of A's act was not the reproduction of A, but the reproduction of a creature like the one from which it sprung —that is to say, a creature bearing traces in its body of the main influences that have worked upon its parent.

Within the cycle of reproduction there are cycles upon cycles in the life of each individual, whether animal or plant. Observe the action of our lungs and heart, how regular it is, and how a cycle having been once established, it is repeated many millions of times in an individual of average health and longevity. Remember also that it is this periodicity—this inevitable tendency of all atoms in combination to repeat any combination which they have once repeated, unless forcibly prevented from doing so—which alone renders nine-tenths of our mechanical inventions of practical use to us. There is not internal periodicity about a hammer or a saw, but there is in the steam-engine or watermill when once set in motion. The actions of these machines recur in a regular series, at regular intervals, with the unerringness of circulating decimals.

When we bear in mind, then, the omnipresence of this tendency in the world around us, the absolute freedom from exception which attends its action, the manner in which it holds equally good upon the vastest and the smallest scale, and the completeness of its accord with our ideas of what must inevitably happen when a like combination is placed in circumstances like those in which it was placed before— when we bear in mind all this, is it possible not to connect the facts together, and to refer cycles of living generations to the same unalterableness in the action of like matter under like circumstances which makes

Jupiter and Saturn revolve round the sun, or the piston of a steam-engine move up and down as long as the steam acts upon it?

But who will attribute memory to the hands of a clock, to a piston-rod, to air or water in a storm or in course of evaporation, to the earth and planets in their circuits round the sun, or to the atoms of the universe, if they too be moving in a cycle vaster than we can take account of? *   And if not, why introduce it into the embryonic development of living beings, when there is not a particle of evidence in support of its actual presence, when regularity of action can be ensured just as well without it as with it, and when at the best it is considered as existing under circumstances which it baffles us to conceive, inasmuch as it is supposed to be exercised without any conscious recollection? Surely a memory which is exercised without any consciousness of recollecting is only a periphrasis for the absence of any memory at all.†

* It must be remembered that this passage is put as if in the mouth of an objector.

† Mr. Herbert Spencer denies that there can be memory without a "tolerably deliberate succession of psychical states." *   So that practically he denies that there can be any such thing as "unconscious memory."   Nevertheless a few pages later on he says that " conscious memory passes into unconscious or organic memory."†   It is plain, therefore, that he could after all find no expression better suited for his purpose.

Mr. Romanes is, I think, right in setting aside Mr. Spencer's limitation of memory to conscious memory.   He writes, "Because I have so often seen the sun shine that my memory of it as shining has become automatic, I see no reason why my memory of this fact, simply on account of its perfection, should be called no memory."

* Principles of Psychology, I., 447.
† Ibid. p. 452.
‡ Mental Evolution in Animals, p. 130.

REFUTATION — MEMORY AT ONCE A PROMOTER
AND A DISTURBER OF UNIFORMITY OF ACTION
AND STRUCTURE.

(CHAPTER XII. OF UNCONSCIOUS MEMORY.)

TO meet the objections in the two foregoing chapters, I need do little more than show that the fact of certain often inherited diseases and developments, whether of youth or old age, being obviously not due to a memory on the part of offspring of like diseases and developments in the parents, does not militate against supposing that embryonic and youthful development generally is due to memory.

This is the main part of the objection; the rest resolves itself into an assertion that there is no evidence in support of instinct and embryonic development being due to memory, and a contention that the necessity of each particular moment in each particular case is sufficient to account for the facts without the introduction of memory.

I will deal with these two last points briefly first. As regards the evidence in support of the theory that instinct and growth are due to a rapid unconscious memory of past experiences and developments in the persons of the ancestors of the living form in which they appear, I must refer my readers to Life and Habit, and to the translation of Professor Hering's lecture given in Chapter VI. of Unconscious Memory.

I will only repeat here that a chrysalis, we will say, is as much one and the same person with the chrysalis of its preceding generation, as this last is one and the same person with the egg or caterpillar from which it sprang. You cannot deny personal identity between two successive generations without sooner or later denying it during the successive stages in the single life of what we call one individual; nor can you admit personal identity through the stages of a long and varied life (embryonic and post-natal) without admitting it to endure through an endless series of generations.

The personal identity of successive generations being admitted, the possibility of the second of two generations remembering what happened to it in the first is obvious. The *à priori* objection, therefore, is removed, and the question becomes one of fact—does the offspring act as if it remembered?

The answer to this question is not only that it does so act, but that it is not possible to account for either its development or its early instinctive actions upon any other hypothesis than that of its remembering, and remembering exceedingly well.

The only alternative is to declare with Von Hartmann that a living being may display a vast and varied information concerning all manner of details, and be able to perform most intricate operations, independently of experience and practice. Once admit knowledge independent of experience, and farewell to sober sense and reason from that moment.

Firstly, then, we show that offspring has had every facility for remembering; secondly, that it shows every appearance of having remembered; thirdly, that no other hypothesis except memory can be brought forward, so as to account for the phenomena of instinct and heredity generally, which is not easily reducible to an absurdity. Beyond this we do not care to go, and must allow those to differ from us who require further evidence.

As regards the argument that the necessity of each moment will account for likeness of result, without there being any need for introducing memory, I admit that likeness of consequents is due to likeness of antecedents, and I grant this will hold as good with embryos as with oxygen and hydrogen gas; what will cover the one will cover the other, for the writs of the laws common to all matter run within the womb as freely as elsewhere; but admitting that there are combinations into which living beings enter with a faculty called memory which has its effects upon their conduct, and admitting that such combinations are from time to time repeated (as we observe in the case of a practised performer playing a piece of music which he has committed to memory), then I maintain that though, indeed, the likeness of one performance to its immediate predecessor is due to likeness of the combinations immediately preceding the two performances, yet memory plays so important a part in both these combinations as to make it a distinguishing feature in them, and therefore proper to be insisted upon. We do not, for example, say that Herr Joachim played such and such a sonata without the music, because he was such and such an arrangement of matter in such and such circumstances, resembling those under which he played without music on some past occasion. This goes without saying; we say only that he played the music by heart or by memory, as he had often played it before.

To the objector that a caterpillar becomes a chrysalis not because it remembers and takes the action taken by its fathers and mothers in due course before it, but because when matter is in such a physical and mental state as to be called caterpillar, it must perforce assume presently such another physical and mental state as to be called chrysalis, and that therefore there is no memory in the case—to this objector I rejoin that the offspring caterpillar would not have become so like the parent as to make the next or chrysalis stage a matter of necessity, unless both parent and offspring had been influenced by something that we usually call memory. For it is this very possession of a common memory which has guided the offspring into the path taken by, and hence to a virtually same condition with, the parent, and which guided the parent in its turn to a state virtually identical with a corresponding state in the existence of its own parent. To memory, therefore, the most prominent place in the transaction is assigned rightly.

To deny that will guided by memory has anything to do with the development of embryos seems like denying that a desire to obstruct has anything to do with the recent conduct of certain members in the House of Commons. What should we think of one who said that the action of these gentlemen had nothing to do with a desire to embarrass the Government, but was simply the necessary outcome of the chemical and mechanical forces at work, which being such and such, the action which we see is inevitable, and has therefore nothing to do with wilful obstruction? We should answer that there was doubtless a great deal of chemical and mechanical action in the matter; perhaps, for aught we knew or cared, it was all chemical and mechanical; but if so, then a desire to obstruct parliamentary business is involved in certain kinds of chemical and mechanical action, and that the kinds involving this had preceded the recent proceedings of the members in question. If asked to prove this, we can get no further than that such action as has been taken has never been seen except as following after and in consequence of a desire to obstruct; that this is our nomenclature, and that we can no more be expected to change it than to change our mother tongue at the bidding of a foreigner.

A little reflection will convince the reader that he will be unable to deny will and memory to the embryo without at the same time denying their existence everywhere, and maintaining that they have no place in the acquisition of a habit, nor indeed in any human action. He will feel that the actions, and the relation of one action to another which he observes in embryos is such as is never seen except in association with and as a consequence of will and memory. He will therefore say that it is due to will and memory. To say that these are the necessary outcome of certain antecedents is not to destroy them: granted that they are —a man does not cease to be a man when we reflect that he has had a father and mother, neither do will and memory cease to be will and memory on the ground that they cannot come causeless. They are manifest minute by minute to the perception of all people who can keep out of lunatic asylums, and this tribunal, though not infallible, is nevertheless our ultimate court of appeal—the final arbitrator in all disputed cases.

We must remember that there is no action, however original or peculiar, which is not in respect of far the greater number of its details founded upon memory. If a desperate man blows his brains out—an action which he can do once in a lifetime only, and which none of his ancestors can have done before leaving off-spring—still nine hundred and ninety-nine thousandths of the movements necessary to achieve his end consist of habitual movements—movements, that is to say, which were once difficult, but which have been practised and practised by the help of memory until they are now performed automatically. We can no more have an action than a creative effort of the imagination cut off from memory. Ideas and actions seem almost to resemble matter and force in respect of the impossibility of originating or destroying them; nearly all that are, are memories of other ideas and actions, transmitted but not created, disappearing but not perishing.

It appears, then, that when in Chapter X. we supposed the clerk who wanted his dinner to forget on a second day the action he had taken the day before, we still, without perhaps perceiving it, supposed him to be guided by memory in all the details of his action, such as his taking down his hat and going out into the street. We could not, indeed, deprive him of all memory without absolutely paralysing his action.

Nevertheless new ideas, new faiths, and new actions do in the course of time come about, the living expressions of which we may see in the new forms of life which from time to time have arisen and are still arising, and in the increase of our own knowledge and mechanical inventions. But it is only a very little new that is added at a time, and that little is generally due to the desire to attain an end which cannot be attained by any of the means for which there exists a perceived precedent in the memory. When this is the case, either the memory is further ransacked for any forgotten shreds of details a combination of which may serve the desired purpose; or action is taken in the dark, which sometimes succeeds and becomes a fertile source of further combinations; or we are brought to a dead stop. All action is random in respect of any of the minute actions which compose it that are not done in consequence of memory, real or supposed. So that random, or action taken in the dark, or illusion, lies at the very root of progress.

I will now consider the objection that the phenomena of instinct and embryonic development ought not to be ascribed to memory, inasmuch as certain other phenomena of heredity, such as gout, cannot be ascribed to it.

Those who object in this way forget that our actions fall into two main classes: those which we have often repeated before by means of a regular series of subordinate actions beginning and ending at a certain tolerably well-defined point—as when Herr Joachim plays a sonata in public, or when we dress or undress ourselves; and actions the details of which are indeed guided by memory, but which in their general scope and purpose are new—as when we are being married, or presented at court.

At each point in any action of the first of the two kinds above referred to there is a memory (conscious or unconscious according to the less or greater number of times the action has been repeated), not only of the steps in the present and previous performances which have led up to the particular point that may be selected, *but also of the particular point itself;* there is therefore, at each point in a habitual performance, a memory at once of like antecedents *and of a like present.*

If the memory, whether of the antecedent or the present, were absolutely perfect; that is to say, if the vibrations in the nervous system (or, if the reader likes it better, if the molecular change in the particular nerves affected—for molecular change is only a change in the character of the vibrations going on within the molecules—it is nothing else than this)—if the vibrations in the particular nerves affected by any occurrence continued on each fresh repetition of the occurrence in their full original strength and without having been interfered with by any other vibrations; and if, again, the new waves running into the faint old ones from exterior objects and restoring the lapsed molecular state of the nerves to a pristine condition were absolutely identical in character on each repetition of the occurrence with the waves that ran in upon the last occasion, then there would be no change in the action, and no modification or improvement could take place. For though indeed the latest performance would always have one memory more than the latest but one to guide it, yet the memories being identical, it would not matter how many or how few they were.

On any repetition, however, the circumstances, external or internal, or both, never are absolutely identical: there is some slight variation in each individual case, and some part of this variation is remembered, with approbation or disapprobation as the case may be.

The fact, therefore, that on each repetition of the action there is one memory more than on the last but one, and that this memory is slightly different from its predecessor, is seen to be an inherent and, *ex hypothcsi*, necessarily disturbing factor in all habitual action— and the life of an organism should, as has been sufficiently insisted on, be regarded as the habitual action of a single individual, namely, of the organism itself, and of its ancestors. This is the key to accumulation of improvement, whether in the arts which we assidu-

ously practise during our single life, or in the structures
and instincts of successive generations. The memory
does not complete a true circle, but is, as it were, a
spiral slightly divergent therefrom, It is no longer a
perfectly circulating decimal. Where, on the other
hand, there is no memory of a like present, where, in
fact, the memory is not, so to speak, spiral, there is no
accumulation of improvement. The effect of any variation is not transmitted, and is not thus pregnant of
still further change.

As regards the second of the two classes of actions
above referred to—those, namely which are not recur-
rent or habitual, *and at no point of which is there a memory of a past present like the one which is present now*
—there will have been no accumulation of strong and
well-knit memory as regards the action as a whole, but
action, if taken at all, will be taken upon disjointed
fragments of individual actions (our own and those of
other people) pieced together with a result more or less
satisfactory according to circumstances.

But it does not follow that the action of two people
who have had tolerably similar antecedents and are
placed in tolerably similar circumstances should be
more unlike each other in this second case than in the
first. On the contrary, nothing is more common than to
observe the same kind of people making the same kind
of mistake when placed for the first time in the same
kind of new circumstances. I did not say that there
would be no sameness of action without memory of a
like present. There may be sameness of action proceeding from a memory, conscious or unconscious, of
like antecedents, and *a presence only of like presents
without recollection of the same.*

The sameness of action of like persons placed under

like circumstances for the first time, resembles the sameness of action of inorganic matter under the same combinations. Let us for a moment suppose what we call non-living substances to be capable of remembering their antecedents, and that the changes they undergo are the expressions of their recollections. Then I admit, of course, that there is not memory in any cream, we will say, that is about to be churned of the cream of the preceding week, but the common absence of such memory from each week's cream is an element of sameness between the two. And though no cream can remember having been churned before, yet all cream in all time has had nearly identical antecedents, and has therefore nearly the same memories and nearly the same proclivities. Thus, in fact, the cream of one week is as truly the same as the cream of another week from the same cow, pasture, &c., as anything is ever the same with anything; for the having been subjected to like antecedents engenders the closest similarity that we can conceive of, if the substances were like to start with. Same is as same does.

The manifest absence of any connecting memory (or memory of like presents) from certain of the phenomena of heredity, such as, for example, the diseases of old age, is now seen to be no valid reason for saying that such other and far more numerous and important phenomena as those of embryonic development are not phenomena of memory. Growth and the diseases of old age do indeed, at first sight, appear to stand on the same footing. The question, however, whether certain results are due to memory or no must be settled not by showing that two combinations, neither of which can remember the other (as between each other), may yet generate like results, and therefore, considering the memory theory disposed of for all other cases, but by the evidence we may be able to adduce in any particular case that the second agent has actually remembered the conduct of the first. Such evidence must show firstly that the second agent cannot be supposed able to do what it is plain he can do, except under the guidance of memory or experience, and secondly, that the second agent has had every opportunity of remembering. When the first of these' tests fails, similarity of action on the part of two agents need not be connected with memory of a like present as well as of like antecedents; when both fail, similarity of action should be referred to memory of like antecedents only.

Returning to a parenthesis a' few pages back, in which I said that consciousness of memory would be less or greater according to the greater or fewer number of times that the act had been repeated, it may be observed as a corollary to this, that the less consciousness of memory the greater the uniformity of action, and *vice versâ*. For the less consciousness involves the memory's being more perfect, through a larger number (generally) of repetitions of the act that is remembered; there is therefore a less proportionate difference in respect of the number of recollections of this particular act between the most recent actor and the most recent but one. This is why very old civilisations, as those of many insects, and the greater number of now living organisms, appear to the eye not to change at all.

For example, if an action has been performed only ten times, we will say by A, B, C, &c., who are similar in all respects, except that A acts without recollection, B with recollection of A's action, C with recollection of both B's and A's, while J remembers the course taken by A, B, C, D, E, F, G, H, and I—the possession of a

o

memory by B will indeed so change his action, as compared with A's, that it may well be hardly recognisable. We saw this in our example of the clerk who asked the policeman the way to the eating-house on one day, but did not ask him the next, because he remembered; but C's action will not be so different from B's as B's from A's, for though C will act with a memory of two occasions on which the action has been performed, while B recollects only the original performance by A, yet B and C both act with the guidance of a memory and experience of some kind, while A acted without any. Thus the clerk referred to in Chapter X. will act on the third day much as he acted on the second —that is to say, he will see the policeman at the corner of the street, but will not question him.

When the action is repeated by J for the tenth time, the difference between J's repetition of it and I's will be due solely to the difference between a recollection of nine past performances by J against only eight by I, and this is so much proportionately less than the difference between a recollection of two performances and of only one, that a less modification of action should be expected. At the same time consciousness concerning an action repeated for the tenth time should be less acute than on the first repetition. Memory, therefore, though tending to disturb similarity of action less and less continually, must always cause some disturbance. At the same time the possession of a memory on the successive repetitions of an action after the first, and, perhaps, the first two or three, during which the recollection may be supposed still imperfect, will tend to ensure uniformity, for it will be one of the elements of sameness in the agents—they both acting by the light of experience and memory.

During the embryonic stages and in childhood we are almost entirely under the guidance of a practised and powerful memory of circumstances which have been often repeated, not only in detail and piecemeal, but as a whole, and under many slightly varying conditions ; thus the performance has become well averaged and matured in its arrangements, so as to meet all ordinary emergencies. We therefore act with great unconsciousness and vary our performances little. Babies are much more alike than persons of middle age.

. Up to the average age at which our ancestors have had children during many generations, we are still guided in great measure by memory; but the variations in external circumstances begin to make themselves perceptible in our characters. In middle life we live more and more continually upon the piecing together of details of memory drawn from our personal experience, that is to say, upon the memory of our own antecedents ; and this resembles the kind of memory we hypothetically attached to cream a little time ago. It is not surprising, then, that a son who has inherited his father's tastes and constitution, and who lives much as his father had done, should make the same mistakes as his father did when he reaches his father's age— we will say of seventy—though he cannot possibly remember his father's having made the mistakes. It were to be wished we could, for then we might know better how to avoid gout, cancer, or what not. And it is to be noticed that the developments of old age are generally things we should be glad enough to avoid if we knew how to do so.

. *CONCLUSION.*

IF we observed the resemblance between successive generations to be as close as that between distilled water and distilled water through all time, and if we observed that perfect unchangeableness in the action of living beings which we see in what we call chemical and mechanical combinations, we might indeed suspect that memory had as little place among the causes of their action as it can have in anything, and that each repetition, whether of a habit or the practice of art, or of an embryonic process in successive generations, was as original as the " Origin of Species " itself, for all that memory had to do with it. I submit, however, that in the case of the reproductive forms of life we see just so much variety, in spite of uniformity, as is consistent with a repetition involving not only a nearly perfect similarity in the agents and their circumstances, but also the little departure therefrom that is inevitably involved in the supposition that a memory of like presents as well as of like antecedents (as distinguished from a memory of like antecedents only) has played a part in their development—a cyclical memory, if the expression may be pardoned.

There is life infinitely lower and more minute than any which our most powerful microscopes reveal to us, but let us leave this upon one side and begin with the amœba. Let us suppose that this "structureless" morsel of protoplasm is, for all its "structurelessness," composed of an infinite number of living molecules, each one of them with hopes and fears of its own, and all dwelling together like Tekke Turcomans, of whom we read that they live for plunder only, and that each man of them is entirely independent, acknowledging no constituted authority, but that some among them exercise a tacit and undefined influence over the others. Let us suppose these molecules capable of memory, both in their capacity as individuals and as societies, and able to transmit their memories to their descendants from the traditions of the dimmest past to the experiences of their own lifetime. Some of these societies will remain simple, as having had no history, but to the greater number unfamiliar, and therefore striking, incidents will from time to time occur, which, when they do not disturb memory so greatly as to kill, will leave their impression upon it. The body or society will remember these incidents and be modified by them in its conduct, and therefore more or less in its internal arrangements, which will tend inevitably to specialisation. This memory of the most striking events of varied lifetimes I maintain, with Professor Hering, to be the differentiating cause, which, accumulated in countless generations, has led up from the amœba to man. If there had been no such memory, the amœba of one generation would have exactly resembled the amœba of the preceding, and a perfect cycle would have been established; the modifying effects of an additional memory in each generation have made the cycle into a spiral, and into a spiral whose eccentricities, in the outset hardly perceptible, is becoming greater and greater with increasing longevity and more complex social and mechanical inventions.

We say that the chicken grows the horny tip to its beak with which it ultimately pecks its way out of its shell, because it remembers having grown it before, and the use it made of it. We say that it made it on the same principles as a man makes a spade or a hammer, that is to say, as the joint result both of desire and experience. When I say experience, I mean, experience not only of what will be wanted, but also of the details of all the means that must be taken in order to effect this. Memory, therefore, is supposed to guide the chicken not only in respect of the main design, but in respect also of every atomic action, so to speak, which goes to make up the execution of this design. It is not only the suggestion of a plan which is due to memory, but, as Professor Hering has so well said, it is the binding power of memory which alone renders any consolidation or coherence of action possible, inasmuch as without this no action could have parts subordinate one to another, yet bearing upon a common end; no part of an action, great or small, could have reference to any other part, much less to a combination of all the parts; nothing, in fact, but ultimate atoms of actions could ever happen—these bearing the same relation to such an action, we will say, as a railway journey from London to Edinburgh as a single molecule of hydrogen to a gallon of water.

If asked how it is that the chicken shows no sign of consciousness concerning this design, nor yet of the steps it is taking to carry it out, we reply that such unconsciousness is usual in all cases where an action, and the design which prompts it, have been repeated exceedingly often. If, again, we are asked how we account for the regularity with which each step is taken in its due order, we answer that this too is characteristic of actions that are done habitually— they being very rarely misplaced in respect of any part.

When I wrote Life and Habit, I had arrived at the conclusion that memory was the most essential characteristic of life, and went so far as to say, " Life is that property of matter whereby it can remember —matter which can remember is living," I should perhaps have written, " Life is the being possessed of a memory—the life of a thing at any moment is the memories which at that moment it retains;" and I would modify the words that immediately follow, namely, " Matter which cannot remember is dead;" for they imply that there is such a thing as matter which cannot remember anything at all, and this on fuller consideration I do not believe to be the case; I can conceive of no matter which is not able to re-member a little, and which is not living in respect of what it can remember. I do not see how action of any kind (chemical as much as vital) is conceivable without the supposition that every atom retains a memory of certain antecedents. I cannot, however, at this point, enter upon the reasons which have com-pelled me to join the many who are now adopting this conclusion. Whether these would be deemed sufficient or no, at any rate we cannot believe that a system of self-reproducing associations should develop from the simplicity of the amœba to the complexity of the human body without the presence of that memory which can alone account at once for the resemblances and the differences between successive generations, for the arising and the accumulation of divergences

—for the tendency to differ and the tendency not to differ.

At parting, therefore, I would recommend the reader to see every atom in the universe as living and able to feel and to remember, but in a humble way. He must have life eternal, as well as matter eternal ; and the life and the matter must be joined together inseparably as body and soul to one another. Thus he will see God everywhere, not as those who repeat phrases conventionally, but as people who would have their words taken according to their most natural and legitimate meaning; and he will feel that the main difference between him and many of those who oppose him lies in the fact that whereas both he and they use the same language, his opponents only half mean what they say, while he means it entirely.

The attempt to get a higher form of a life from a lower one is in accordance with our observation and experience. It is therefore proper to be believed. The attempt to get it from that which has absolutely no life is like trying to get something out of nothing. The millionth part of a farthing put out to interest at ten per cent. will in five hundred years become over a million pounds, and so long as we have any millionth of a millionth of the farthing to start with, our getting as many million pounds as we have a fancy for is only a question of time, but without the initial millionth of a millionth of a millionth part, we shall get no increment whatever. A little leaven will leaven the whole lump, but there must be *some* leaven.

We should endeavour to see the so-called inorganic as living, in respect of the qualities it has in common with the organic, rather than the organic as non-living in respect of the qualities it has in common with the inorganic. True, it would be hard to place one's self on the same moral platform as a stone, but this is not necessary; it is enough that we should feel the stone to have a moral platform of its own, though that platform embraces little more than a profound respect for the laws of gravitation, chemical affinity, &c. As for the difficulty of conceiving a body as living that has not got a reproductive system—we should remember that neuter insects are living but are believed to have no reproductive system. Again, we should bear in mind that mere assimilation involves all the essentials of reproduction, and that both air and water possess this power in a very high degree. The essence of a reproductive system, then, is found low down in the scheme of nature.

At present our leading men of science are in this difficulty; on the one hand their experiments and their theories alike teach them that spontaneous generation ought not to be accepted; on the other, they must have an origin for the life of the living forms, which, by their own theory, have been evolved, and they can at present get this origin in no other way than by *Deus ex machinâ* method, which they reject as unproved, or spontaneous generation of living from non-living matter, which is no less foreign to their experience. As a general rule, they prefer the latter alternative. So Professor Tyndall, in his celebrated article (*Nineteenth Century*, November 1878), wrote:—

"The theory of evolution in its complete form involves the assumption that at some period or other of the earth's history there occurred what would be now called 'spontaneous generation.'"[1] And so Professor Huxley—

* Nineteenth Century, Nov. 1878, p. 826.

"It is argued that a belief in abiogenesis is a necessary corollary from the doctrine of Evolution. This may be" [which I submit is equivalent here to "is"] "true of the occurrence of abiogenesis at some time." *

Professor Huxley goes on to say that however this may be, abiogenesis (or spontaneous generation) is not respectable and will not do at all now. There may have been one case once; this may be winked at, but it must not occur again. "It is enough," he writes, "that a single particle of living protoplasm should once have appeared on the globe as the result of no matter what agency. In the eyes of a consistent [!] evolutionist any further [!] independent formation of protoplasm would be sheer waste"—and the sooner the Almighty gets to understand that He must not make that single act of special creation into a precedent the better for Him.

Professor Huxley, in fact, excuses the single case of spontaneous generation which he appears to admit, because however illegitimate, it was still "only a very little one," and came off a long time ago in a foreign country. For my own part I think it will prove in the end more convenient if we say that there is a low kind of livingness in every atom of matter, and adopt Life eternal as no less inevitable a conclusion than matter eternal.

It should not be doubted that wherever there is vibration or motion there is life and memory, and that there is vibration and motion at all times in all things.

The reader who takes the above position will find that he can explain the entry of what he calls death among what he calls the living, whereas he could by

* Encyclopedia Britannica, Art. Biology, 9th ed., Vol. 3, p. 689.

no means introduce life into his system if he started without it. Death is deducible; life is not deducible. Death is a change of memories; it is not the destruction of all memory. It is as the liquidation of one company each member of which will presently join a new one, and retain a trifle even of the old cancelled memory, by way of greater aptitude for working in concert with other molecules. This is why animals feed on grass and on each other, and cannot proselytise or convert the rude ground before it has been tutored in the first principles of the higher kinds of association.

Again, I would recommend the reader to beware of believing anything in this book unless he either likes it, or feels angry at being told it. If required belief in this or that makes a man angry, I suppose he should, as a general rule, swallow it whole then and there upon the spot, otherwise he may take it or leave it as he likes.

I have not gone far for my facts, nor yet far from them; all on which I rest are as open to the reader as to me. If I have sometimes used hard terms, the probability is that I have not understood them, but have done so by a slip, as one who has caught a bad habit from the company he has been lately keeping. They should be skipped.

Do not let the reader be too much cast down by the bad language with which professional scientists obscure the issue, nor by their seeming to make it their business to fog us under the pretext of removing our difficulties. It is not the ratcatcher's interest to catch all the rats; and, as Handel observed so sensibly, "Every professional gentleman must do his best for to live." The art of some of our philosophers, however, is sufficiently transparent, and consists too often in saying " organism which . . . must be classified among fishes," * instead of " fish " and then proclaiming that they have " an ineradicable tendency to try to make things clear." †

If another example is required, here is the following from an article than which I have seen few with which I more completely agree, or which have given me greater pleasure. If our men of science would take to writing in this way, we should be glad enough to follow them. The passage I refer to runs thus :—

"Professor Huxley speaks of a 'verbal fog by which the question at issue may be hidden ;' is there no verbal fog in the statement that *the œtiology of crayfishes resolves itself into a gradual evolution in the course of the mesozoic and subsequent epochs of the world's history of these animals from a primitive astacomorphous form ?* Would it be fog or light that would envelop the history of man if we say that the existence of man was explained by the hypothesis of his gradual evolution from a primitive anthropomorphous form ? I should call this fog, not light." ‡

Especially let him mistrust those who are holding forth about protoplasm, and maintaining that this is the only living substance. Protoplasm may be, and perhaps is, the *most* living part of an organism, as the most capable of retaining vibrations, of a certain character, but this is the utmost that can be claimed for it. I have noticed, however, that protoplasm has not been buoyant lately in the scientific market.

Having mentioned protoplasm, I may ask the reader to note the breakdown of that school of philosophy

* Professor Huxley, Encycl. Brit., 9th ed., Art. Evolution, p. 750.
† " Hume," by Professor Huxley, p. 45.
‡ "The Philosophy of Crayfishes," by the Right Rev. the Lord Bishop of Carlisle. Nineteenth Century for October 1880, p. 636.

which divided the *ego* from the *non ego*. The proto-plasmists, on the one hand, are whittling away at *ego*, till they have reduced it to a little jelly in certain parts of the body, and they will whittle away this too presently, if they go on as they are doing now.

Others, again, are so unifying the *ego* and the *non ego*, that with them there will soon be as little of the *non ego* left as there is of the *ego* with their opponents. Both, however, are so far agreed as that we know not where to draw the line between the two, and this renders nugatory any system which is founded upon a distinction between them.

The truth is, that all classification whatever, when we examine its *raison d'être* closely, is found to be arbitrary—to depend on our sense of our own convenience, and not on any inherent distinction in the nature of the things themselves. Strictly speaking, there is only one thing and one action. The universe, or God, and the action of the universe as a whole.

Lastly, I may predict with some certainty that before long we shall find the original Darwinism of Dr. Erasmus Darwin (with an infusion of Professor Hering into the bargain) generally accepted instead of the neo-Darwinism of to-day, and that the variations whose accumulation results in species will be recognised as due to the wants and endeavours of the living forms in which they appear, instead of being ascribed to chance, or, in other words, to unknown causes, as by Mr. Charles Darwin's system. We shall have some idyllic young naturalists bringing up Dr. Erasmus Darwin's note on *Trapa natans,** and Lamarck's kindred passage on the descent of *Ranunculus hederaceus* from

* Les Amours des Plantes, p. 360. Paris, 1800.

Ranunculus aquatilis [*] as fresh discoveries, and be told with much happy simplicity, that those animals and plants which have felt the need of such a structure have developed it, while those which have not wanted it have gone without it. Thus it will be declared, every leaf we see around us, every structure of the minutest insect, will bear witness to the truth of the "great guess" of the greatest of naturalists concerning the memory of living matter.[†]

I dare say the public will not object to this, and am very sure that none of the admirers of Mr. Charles Darwin or Mr. Wallace will protest against it; but it may be as well to point out that this was not the view of the matter taken by Mr. Wallace in 1858 when he and Mr. Darwin first came forward as preachers of natural selection. At that time Mr. Wallace saw clearly enough the difference between the theory of "natural selection" and that of Lamarck. He wrote :—

"The hypothesis of Lamarck—that progressive changes in species have been produced by the attempts of animals to increase the development of their own organs and thus modify their structure and habits—has been repeatedly and easily refuted by all writers on the subject of varieties and species, . . . but the view here developed renders such a hypothesis quite unnecessary . . . The powerful retractile talons of the falcon and the cat tribes have not been produced or increased by the volition of those animals, . . . neither did the giraffe acquire its long neck by desiring to reach the foliage of the more lofty shrubs, and constantly stretching its neck

---

[*] Philosophie Zoologique, tom. i. p. 231. Ed. M. Martin. Paris, 1873.

[†] Those who read the three following chapters will see that these words, written in 1880, have come out near the truth in 1884.

for this purpose, but because any varieties which occurred among its antitypes with a longer neck than usual *at once secured a fresh range of pasture over the same ground as their short-necked companions, and on the first scarcity of food were thereby enabled to outlive them* " (italics in original).*

This is absolutely the neo-Darwin doctrine, and a denial of the mainly fortuitous character of the variations in animal and vegetable forms cuts at its root. That Mr. Wallace, after years of reflection, still adhered to this view, is proved by his heading a reprint of the paragraph just quoted from † with the words " Lamarck's hypothesis very different from that now advanced ; " nor do any of his more recent works show that he has modified his opinion. It should be noted that Mr. Wallace does not call his work Contributions to the Theory of Evolution, but to that of Natural Selection.

Mr. Darwin, with characteristic caution, only commits himself to saying that Mr. Wallace has arrived at *almost* (italics mine) the same general conclusions as he, Mr. Darwin, has done ; ‡ but he still, as in 1859, declares that it would be " a serious error to suppose that the greater number of instincts have been acquired by habit in one generation and then transmitted by inheritance to succeeding generations," § and he still

* Journal of the Proceedings of the Linnean Society. Williams & Norgate, 1858, p. 61.
† Contributions to the Theory of Natural Selection, 2d ed., 1871, p. 41.
‡ Origin of Species, p. 1, ed. 1872.
§ Origin of Species, 6th ed., p. 206. I ought in fairness to Mr Darwin to say that he does not hold the error to be quite as serious as he once did. It is now " a serious error " only ; in 1859 it was " most serious error."— *Origin of Species,* 1st ed., p. 209.

comprehensively condemns the "well-known doctrine of inherited habit, as advanced by Lamarck." *

As for the statement in the passage quoted from Mr. Wallace, to the effect that Lamarck's hypothesis "has been repeatedly and easily refuted by all writers on the subject of varieties and species," it is a very surprising one. I have searched Evolution literature in vain for any refutation of the Erasmus Darwinian system (for this is what Lamarck's hypothesis really is), which need make the defenders of that system at all uneasy. The best attempt at an answer to Erasmus Darwin that has yet been made is Paley's Natural Theology, which was throughout obviously written to meet Buffon and the Zoonomia. It is the manner of theologians to say that such and such an objection "has been refuted over and over again," without at the same time telling us when and where; it is to be regretted that Mr. Wallace has here taken a leaf out of the theologians' book. His statement is one which will not pass muster with those whom public opinion is sure in the end to follow.

Did Mr. Herbert Spencer, for example, "repeatedly and easily refute" Lamarck's hypothesis in his brilliant article in the *Leader*, March 20, 1852? On the contrary, that article is expressly directed against those "who cavalierly reject the hypothesis of Lamarck and his followers." This article was written six years before the words last quoted from Mr. Wallace; how absolutely, however, does the word "cavalierly" apply to them!

Does Isidore Geoffrey, again, bear Mr. Wallace's assertion out better? In 1859—that is to say but a short time after Mr. Wallace had written—he wrote as follows :—

---

* Origin of Species, 1st ed., p. 242 ; 6th ed., p. 233.

"Such was the language which Lamarck heard during his protracted old age, saddened alike by the weight of years and blindness; this was what people did not hesitate to utter over his grave yet barely closed, and what indeed they are still saying—commonly too without any knowledge of what Lamarck maintained, but merely repeating at secondhand bad caricatures of his teaching.

"When will the time come when we may see Lamarck's theory discussed—and, I may as well at once say, refuted in some important points *—with at any rate the respect due to one of the most illustrious masters of our science? And when will this theory, the hardihood of which has been greatly exaggerated, become freed from the interpretations and commentaries by the false light of which so many naturalists have followed their opinion concerning it? If its author is to be condemned, let it be, at any rate, not before he has been heard." †

In 1873 M. Martin published his edition of Lamarck's *Philosophie Zoologique*. He was still able to say, with, I believe, perfect truth, that Lamarck's theory has "never yet had the honour of being discussed seriously." ‡

Professor Huxley in his article on Evolution is no less cavalier than Mr. Wallace. He writes: §—

"Lamarck introduced the conception of the action of an animal on itself as a factor in producing modification."

Lamarck did nothing of the kind. It was Buffon and Dr. Darwin who introduced this, but more especially Dr. Darwin. The accuracy of Professor

---

* I never could find what these particular points were.

† Isidore Geoffrey, Hist. Nat. Gen., tom. ii. p. 407, 1859.

‡ M. Martin's edition of the Philosophie Zoologique (Paris, 1873), Introduction, p. vi.

§ Encyclopædia Britannica, 9th ed., p. 750.

P

Huxley's statements about the history and literature of evolution is like the direct interference of the Deity—it vanishes whenever and wherever I have occasion to test it.

"But *a little consideration showed*" (italics mine) "that though Lamarck had seized what, as far as it goes, is a true cause of modification, it is a cause the actual effects of which are wholly inadequate to account for any considerable modification in animals, and which can have no influence whatever in the vegetable world," &c.

I should be very glad to come across some of the "little consideration" which will show this. I have searched for it far and wide, and have never been able to find it.

I think Professor Huxley has been exercising some of his ineradicable tendency to try to make things clear in the article on Evolution, already so often quoted from. We find him (p. 750) pooh-poohing Lamarck, yet on the next page he says, "How far 'natural selection' suffices for the production of species remains to be seen." And this when "natural selection" was already so nearly of age! Why, to those who know how to read between a philosopher's lines the sentence comes to very nearly the same as a declaration that the writer has no great opinion of "natural selection." Professor Huxley continues, "Few can doubt that, if not the whole cause, it is a very important factor in that operation." A philosopher's words should be weighed carefully, and when Professor Huxley says, "few can doubt," we must remember that he may be including himself among the few whom he considers to have the power of doubting on this matter. He does not say "few will," but "few can " doubt, as though it were only the enlightened who would have the power of doing so. Certainly " nature "—for that is what " natural selection " comes to—is rather an important factor in the operation, but we do not gain much by being told so. If however, Professor Huxley neither believes in the origin of species, through sense of need on the part of animals themselves, nor yet in " natural selection," we should be glad to know what he does believe in.

The battle is one of greater importance than appears at first sight. It is a battle between teleology and non-teleology, between the purposiveness and the non-purposiveness of the organs in animal and vegetable bodies. According to Erasmus Darwin, Lamarck, and Paley, organs are purposive; according to Mr. Darwin and his followers, they are not purposive. But the main arguments against the system of Dr. Erasmus Darwin are arguments which, so far as they have any weight, tell against evolution generally. Now that these have been disposed of, and the prejudice against evolution has been overcome, it will be seen that there is nothing to be said against the system of Erasmus Darwin and Lamarck which does not tell with far greater force against that of Mr. Charles Darwin and Mr. Wallace.

REMARKS ON MR. ROMANES' MENTAL EVOLUTION IN ANIMALS.*

I HAVE said on page 96 of this book that the word "heredity" may be a very good way of stating the difficulty which meets us when we observe the reappearance of like characteristics, whether of body or mind, in successive generations, but that it does nothing whatever towards removing it.

It is here that Mr. Herbert Spencer, the late Mr. G. H. Lewes, and Mr. Romanes fail. Mr. Herbert Spencer does indeed go so far in one place as to call instinct "organised memory,"† and Mr. G. H. Lewes attributes many instincts to what he calls the "lapsing of intelligence."‡ So does Mr. Herbert Spencer,§ whom Mr. Romanes should have known that Mr. Lewis was following. Mr. Romanes, in his recent work, Mental Evolution in Animals (November, 1883), endorses this, and frequently uses such expressions as "the lifetime of the species,"‖ "hereditary experience,"¶ and "hereditary memory and instinct," ** but none of these writers (and indeed no writer that I know of except Professor Hering of Prague, for a translation of whose address on this subject I must refer the reader

* Kegan Paul & Co., 1883.
† Principles of Psychology, Vol. I. p. 445.   ‡ Ibid. I. 456.
§ Problems of Life and Mind, first series, Vol. I., 3rd ed. 1874, p. 141, and Problem I. 21.
‖ P. 33.   ¶ P. 77.   ** P. 115.

to my book Unconscious Memory) has shown a comprehension of the fact that these expressions are unexplained so long as "heredity," whereby they explain
them, is unexplained ; and none of them sees the
importance of emphasizing Memory, and making it
as it were the keystone of the system.

Mr. Spencer may very well call instinct "organised
memory" if he means that offspring can remember—within the limitations to which all memory is subject—what
happened to it while it was yet in the person or persons of its parent or parents ; but if he does not mean
this, his use of the word "memory," his talk about
"the experience of the race," and other expressions of
kindred nature, are delusive.   If he does mean this, it
is a pity he has nowhere said so.

Professor Hering does mean this, and makes it clear
that he does so.   He does not catch the ball and let
it slip through his fingers again, but holds it firmly.
"It is to memory," he says, "that we owe almost all
that we have or are ; our ideas and conceptions are its
work ; our every thought and movement are derived
from this source.   Memory connects the countless
phenomena of our existence into a single whole, and
as our bodies would be scattered into the dust of their
component atoms if they were not held together by the
cohesion of matter, so our consciousness would be
broken up into as many moments as we had lived
seconds, but for the binding and unifying force of
Memory." *   And he proceeds to show that Memory
persists between generations exactly as it does between
the various stages in the life of the individual.   If I
could find any such passage as the one I have just

* Translation of Professor Hering's address on "Memory as an
Organised Function of Matter," Unconscious Memory, p. 116.

quoted, in Mr. Herbert Spencer's, Mr. Lewes's, or Mr. Romanes' works, I should be only too glad to quote it, but I know of nothing comparable to it for definiteness of idea, thoroughness and consistency.

No reader indeed can rise from a perusal of Mr. Herbert Spencer's, or Mr. G. H. Lewes', work with an adequate—if indeed with any—impression that the phenomena of heredity are in fact phenomena of memory ; that heredity, whether as regards body or mind, is only possible because each generation is linked on to and made one with its predecessor by the possession of a common and abiding memory, in as far as bodily existence was common—that is to say, until the substance of the one left the substance of the other ; and that this memory is exactly of the same general character as that which enables us to remember what we did half an hour ago—strong under the same circumstances as those under which this familiar kind of memory is strong, and weak under those under which it is weak. Mr. Spencer and Mr. Lewes have even less conception of the connection between heredity and memory than Dr. Erasmus Darwin had at the close of the last century.*

Mr. Lewes' position was briefly this. He denied that there could be any knowledge independent of experience, but he could not help seeing that young animals come into the world furnished with many organs which they use with great dexterity at a very early age. This looks as if they are acting on knowledge acquired independently of experience. "No," says Mr. Lewes, "not so. They are born with the organs—I cannot tell how or why, but heredity explains all that, and having once got the organs, the objects

---

* See Zoonomia, Vol. I. p. 484.

that come into contact with them in daily life naturally produce the same effect as on the parents, just as oxygen coming into contact with the right quantity of hydrogen will make water; hence even the first time the offspring come into contact with any given object they act as their parents did." The idea of the young having got their experience in a past generation does not seem to have even crossed his mind.

"What marvel is there," he asks, "that constant conditions acting upon structures which are similar should produce similar results? It is in this sense that the paradox of Leibnitz is true, and we can be said 'to acquire an innate idea;' only the idea is not acquired independently of experience, but through the process of experience similar to that which originally produced it."*

The impression left upon me is that he is all at sea for want of the clue with which Professor Hering would have furnished him, and that had that clue been presented to him a dozen years or so earlier than it was he would have adopted it.

As regards Mr. Romanes the case is different. His recent work, Mental Evolution in Animals,† shows that he is well aware of the direction which modern opinion is taking, and in several places he so writes as to warrant me in claiming his authority in support of the views which I have been insisting on for several years past.

Thus Mr. Romanes says that the analogies between the memory with which we are familiar in daily life and hereditary memory "are so numerous and pre-

* Problems of Life and Mind, I. pp. 239, 240: 1874.
† Kegan Paul. November, 1883.

cise" as to justify us in considering them to be of essentially the same kind.*

Again he says that although the memory of milk shown by newborn infants is "at all events in large part hereditary, it is none the less memory" of a certain kind.†

Two lines lower down he writes of "hereditary memory or instinct," thereby implying that instinct is "hereditary memory." "It makes no essential difference," he says, "whether the past sensation was actually experienced by the individual itself, or bequeathed it, so to speak, by its ancestors.‡ For it makes no essential difference whether the nervous changes . . . were occasioned during the lifetime of the individual or during that of the species, and afterwards impressed by heredity on the individual."

Lower down on the same page he writes :—

"As showing how close is the connection between hereditary memory and instinct," &c.

And on the following page :—

"And this shows how closely the phenomena of hereditary memory are related to those of individual memory : at this stage . . . it is practically impossible to disentangle the effects of hereditary memory from those of the individual."

Again :—

"Another point which we have here to consider is the part which heredity has played in forming the perceptive faculty of the individual prior to its own experience. We have already seen that heredity plays an important part in forming memory of ancestral experiences, and thus it is that many animals come

* Mental Evolution in Animals, p. 113.   † Ibid. p. 115.
‡ Ibid. p. 116. Kegan Paul. Nov. 1883.

into the world with their power of perception already largely developed. . . . The wealth of ready-formed information, and therefore of ready-made powers of perception, with which many newly-born or newly-hatched animals are provided, is so great and so precise that it scarcely requires to be supplemented by the subsequent experience of the individual."[*]

Again :—

"Instincts probably owe their origin and development to one or other of two principles.

"I. The first mode of origin consists in natural selection or survival of the fittest, continuously preserving actions, &c. &c. . . .

"II. The second mode of origin is as follows :—By the effects of habit in successive generations, actions which were originally intelligent become as it were stereotyped into permanent instincts. Just as in the lifetime of the individual adjustive actions which were originally intelligent may by frequent repetition become automatic, so in the lifetime of species actions originally intelligent may by frequent repetition and heredity so write their effects on the nervous system that the latter is prepared, even before individual experience, to perform adjustive actions mechanically which in previous generations were performed intelligently. This mode of origin of instincts has been appropriately called (by Lewes—see Problems of Life and Mind [†]) the 'lapsing of intelligence.'"[‡]

Later on :—

"That 'practice makes perfect' is a matter, as I have previously said, of daily observation. Whether

* Mental Evolution in Animals, p. 131. Kegan Paul. Nov. 1883.
† Vol. I., 3rd ed. 1874, p. 141, and Problem I. 21.
‡ Mental Evolution in Animals, pp. 177, 178. Nov. 1883.

we regard a juggler, a pianist, or a billiard-player, a child learning his lesson or an actor his part by frequently repeating it, or a thousand other illustrations of the same process, we see at once that there is truth in the cynical definition of a man as a 'bundle of habits.' And the same of course is true of animals." [*]

From this Mr. Romanes goes on to show "that automatic actions and conscious habits may be inherited," [†] and in the course of doing this contends that "instincts may be lost by disuse, and conversely that they may be acquired as instincts by the hereditary transmission of ancestral experience." [‡]

On another page Mr. Romanes says :—

"Let us now turn to the second of these two assumptions, viz., that some at least among migratory birds must possess, by inheritance alone, a very precise knowledge of the particular direction to be pursued. It is without question an astonishing fact that a young cuckoo should be prompted to leave its foster parents at a particular season of the year, and without any guide to show the course previously taken by its own parents, but this is a fact which must be met by any theory of instinct which aims at being complete. Now upon our own theory it can only be met by taking it to be due to inherited memory." [§]

Mr. Romanes says in a note that this theory was first advanced by Canon Kingsley in *Nature*, January 18, 1867, a piece of information which I learn for the first time; otherwise, as I need hardly say, I should have called attention to it in my own books on evolution. *Nature* did not begin to appear till the end of 1869, and I can find no communication from Canon

---

* Mental Evolution in Animals, p. 193.   † Ibid. p. 195.
‡ Ibid. p. 296. Nov. 1883.   § Ibid. p. 192. Nov. 1883.

Kingsley bearing upon hereditary memory in any number of *Nature* prior to the date of Canon Kingsley's death; but no doubt Mr. Romanes has only made a slip in his reference. Mr. Romanes also says that the theory connecting instinct with inherited memory "has since been independently 'suggested' by many writers."

A little lower Mr. Romanes says: "Of what kind, then, is the inherited memory on which the young cuckoo (if not also other migratory birds) depends? We can only answer, of the same kind, whatever this may be, as that upon which the old bird depends." *

I have given above most of the more marked passages which I have been able to find in Mr. Romanes' book which attribute instinct to memory, and which admit that there is no fundamental difference between the kind of memory with which we are all familiar and hereditary memory as transmitted from one generation to another. But throughout his work there are passages which suggest, though less obviously, the same inference.

The passages I have quoted show that Mr. Romanes is upholding the same opinions as Professor Hering's and my own, but their effect and tendency is more plain here than in Mr. Romanes' own book, where they are overlaid by nearly 400 long pages of matter which is not always easy of comprehension.

The late Mr. Darwin himself, indeed—whose mantle seems to have fallen more especially and particularly on Mr. Romanes—could not contradict himself more hopelessly than Mr. Romanes often does. Indeed in one of the very passages I have quoted in order to show that Mr. Romanes accepts the phenomena of heredity as

* Mental Evolution in Animals, p. 296. Nov. 1883.

phenomena of memory, he speaks of "heredity as playing an important part *in forming memory* of ancestral experiences;" so that whereas I want him to say that the phenomena of heredity are due to memory, he will have it that the memory is due to the heredity,[*] which seems to me absurd.

Over and over again Mr. Romanes insists that it is heredity which does this or that. Thus it is "*heredity with natural selection which adapt* the anatomical plan of the ganglia."[†] It is heredity which impresses nervous changes on the individual.[‡] "In the lifetime of species actions originally intelligent may by frequent repetition *and heredity*," &c.[§]; but he nowhere tells us what heredity is any more than Messrs. Herbert Spencer, Darwin, and Lewes have done. This, however, is exactly what Professor Hering, whom I have unwittingly followed, does. He resolves all phenomena of heredity, whether in respect of body or mind, into phenomena of memory. He says in effect, "A man grows his body as he does, and a bird makes her nest as she does, because both man and bird remember having grown body and made nest as they now do, or very nearly so, on innumerable past occasions." He thus reduces life from an equation of say 100 unknown quantities to one of 99 only by showing that heredity and memory, two of the original 100 unknown quantities, are in reality part of one and the same thing.

That he is right Mr. Romanes seems to me to admit, though in a very unsatisfactory way.

* See page 228.
† Mental Evolution in Animals, p. 33. Nov. 1883.
‡ Ibid. p. 116.   § Ibid. p. 178.

REMARKS ON MR. ROMANES' MENTAL EVOLUTION IN ANIMALS—(continued).

I WILL give examples of my meaning.

Mr. Romanes says on an early page, "The most fundamental principle of mental operation is that of memory, for this is the *conditio sine quâ non* of all mental life" (page 35).

I do not understand Mr. Romanes to hold that there is any living being which has no mind at all, and I do understand him to admit that development of body and mind are closely interdependent.

If then, "the most fundamental principle" of mind is memory, it follows that memory enters also as a fundamental principle into development of body. For mind and body are so closely connected that nothing can enter largely into the one without correspondingly affecting the other.

On a later page, indeed, Mr. Romanes speaks point-blank of the new-born child as "*embodying* the results of a great mass of *hereditary experience*" (p. 77), so that what he is driving at can be collected by those who take trouble, but is not seen until we call up from our own knowledge matter whose relevancy does not appear on the face of it, and until we connect passages many pages asunder, the first of which may easily be forgotten before we reach the second. There can be no doubt, however, that Mr. Romanes does in reality, like Professor Hering and myself, regard development, whether of mind or body, as due to memory, for it is nonsense indeed to talk about "hereditary experience" or "hereditary memory" if anything else is intended.

I have said above that on page 113 of his recent work Mr. Romanes declares the analogies between the memory with which we are familiar in daily life, and hereditary memory, to be "so numerous and precise" as to justify us in considering them as of one and the same kind.

This is certainly his meaning, but, with the exception of the words within inverted commas, it is not his language.   His own words are these :—

"Profound, however, as our ignorance unquestionably is concerning the physical substratum of memory, I think we are at least justified in regarding this substratum as the same both in ganglionic or organic, and in conscious or psychological memory, seeing that the analogies between them are so numerous and precise. Consciousness is but an adjunct which arises when the physical processes, owing to infrequency of repetition, complexity of operation, or other causes, involve what I have before called ganglionic friction."

I submit that I have correctly translated Mr. Romanes' meaning, and also that we have a right to complain of his not saying what he has to say in words which will involve less "ganglionic friction" on the part of the reader.

Another example may be found on p. 43 of Mr. Romanes' book.   "Lastly," he writes, "just as innumerable special mechanisms of muscular co-ordinations are found to be inherited, innumerable special associations of ideas are found to be the same, and in one

case as in the other the strength of the organically im-
posed connection is found to bear a direct proportion
to the frequency with which in the history of the
species it has occurred."

Mr. Romanes is here intending what the reader will
find insisted on on p. 98 of the present volume; but
how difficult he has made what could have been said
intelligibly enough, if there had been nothing but the
reader's comfort to be considered. Unfortunately that
seems to have been by no means the only thing of
which Mr. Romanes was thinking, or why, after implying and even saying over and over again that instinct is inherited habit due to inherited memory,
should he turn sharply round on p. 297 and praise
Mr. Darwin for trying to snuff out " the well-known
doctrine of inherited habit as advanced by Lamarck " ?
The answer is not far to seek. It is because Mr. Romanes did not merely want to tell us all about instinct,
but wanted also, if I may use a homely metaphor, to
hunt with the hounds and run with the hare at one
and the same time.

I remember saying that if the late Mr. Darwin " had
told us what the earlier evolutionists said, why they
said it, wherein he differed from them, and in what
way he proposed to set them straight, he would have
taken a course at once more agreeable with usual
practice, and more likely to remove misconception from
his own mind and from those of his readers."* This I
have no doubt was one of the passages which made
Mr. Romanes so angry with me. I can find no better
words to apply to Mr. Romanes himself. He knows
perfectly well what others have written about the connection between heredity and memory, and he knows

* Evolution, Old and New, pp. 357, 358.

no less well that so far as he is intelligible at all he is taking the same view that they have taken. If he had begun by saying what they had said and had then improved on it, I for one should have been only too glad to be improved upon.

Mr. Romanes has spoiled his book just because this plain old-fashioned method of procedure was not good enough for him. One-half the obscurity which makes his meaning so hard to apprehend is due to exactly the same cause as that which has ruined so much of the late Mr. Darwin's work—I mean to a desire to appear to be differing altogether from others with whom he knew himself after all to be in substantial agreement. He adopts, but (probably quite unconsciously) in his anxiety to avoid appearing to adopt, he obscures what he is adopting.

Here, for example, is Mr. Romanes' definition of instinct :—

" Instinct is reflex action into which there is imported the element of consciousness. The term is therefore a generic one, comprising all those faculties of mind which are concerned in conscious and adaptive action, antecedent to individual experience, without necessary knowledge of the relation between means employed and ends attained, but similarly performed under similar and frequently recurring circumstances by all the individuals of the same species." *

If Mr. Romanes would have been content to build frankly upon Professor Hering's foundation, the soundness of which he has elsewhere abundantly admitted, he might have said—

" Instinct is knowledge or habit acquired in past generations—the new generation remembering what

* Mental Evolution in Animals, p. 159. Kegan Paul & Co., 1883.

happened to it before it parted company with the old."
Then he might have added as a rider—

"If a habit is acquired as a new one, during any
given lifetime, it is not an instinct. If having been
acquired in one lifetime it is transmitted to offspring,
it is an instinct in the offspring though it was not an
instinct in the parent. If the habit is transmitted
partially, it must be considered as partly instinctive
and partly acquired."

This is easy; it tells people how they may test any
action so as to know what they ought to call it; it leaves
well alone by avoiding all such debatable matters as
reflex action, consciousness, intelligence, purpose, knowledge of purpose, &c.; it both introduces the feature
of inheritance which is the one mainly distinguishing
instinctive from so-called intelligent actions, and shows
the manner in which these last pass into the first, that
is to say, by way of memory and habitual repetition;
finally it points the fact that the new generation is
not to be looked upon as a new thing, but (as Dr.
Erasmus Darwin long since said *) as "a branch or
elongation" of the one immediately preceding it.

But then to have said this would have made it too
plain that Mr. Romanes was following some one else.
Mr. Romanes should remember that no one would
mind how much he took if he would only take it well.
But this is what those who take without due acknow-
ledgment never do.

In Mr. Darwin's case it is hardly possible to exaggerate the waste of time, money, and trouble that has
been caused by his not having been content to appear
as descending with modification like other people from
those who went before him. It will take years to get

* Zoonomia, Vol. I. p. 484.

Q

the evolution theory out of the mess in which Mr. Darwin has left it. He was heir to a discredited truth ; he left behind him an accredited fallacy. Mr. Romanes, if he is not stopped in time, will get the theory connecting heredity and memory into just such another muddle as Mr. Darwin has got Evolution, for surely the writer who can talk about "*heredity being able to work up* the faculty of homing into the instinct of migration,"* or of "the principle of (natural) selection combining with that of lapsing intelligence to the formation of a joint result,"† is little likely to depart from the usual methods of scientific procedure with advantage either to himself or any one else. Fortunately Mr. Romanes is not Mr. Darwin, and though he has certainly got Mr. Darwin's mantle, and got it very much too, it will not on Mr. Romanes' shoulders hide a good deal that people were not going to observe too closely while Mr. Darwin wore it.

* Mental Evolution in Animals, p. 297. Kegan Paul & Co., 1883.
† Ibid. p. 201.

REMARKS ON MR. ROMANES' MENTAL EVOLUTION IN ANIMALS—(concluded).

I GATHER that in the end the late Mr. Darwin himself admitted the soundness of the view which the reader will have found insisted upon in the extracts from my earlier books given in this volume. Mr. Romanes quotes a letter written by Mr. Darwin in the last year of his life, in which he speaks of an intelligent action gradually becoming "*instinctive, i.e., memory transmitted from one generation to another.*"*

Briefly, the stages of Mr. Darwin's opinion upon the subject of hereditary memory are as follows:—

1859. "It would be *the most serious error* to suppose that the greater number of instincts have been acquired by habit in one generation and transmitted by inheritance to succeeding generations."† And this more especially applies to the instincts of many ants.

1876. "It would be *a serious error* to suppose" &c., as before. ‡

1881. "We should remember *what a mass of inherited knowledge* is crowded into the minute brain of a worker ant." §

1881 or 1882. Speaking of a given habitual action

* Mental Evolution in Animals, p. 301. November, 1883.
† Origin of Species, Ed. I. p. 209.
‡ Ibid., Ed. VI. 1876, p. 206.
§ Formation of Vegetable Mould, &c., p. 98.

Mr. Darwin writes:—" It does not seem to me at all incredible that this action [and why this more than any other habitual action?] should then become instinctive:" *i.e., memory transmitted from one generation to another.**

And yet in 1839 or thereabouts, Mr. Darwin had pretty nearly grasped the conception from which until the last year or two of his life he so fatally strayed; for in his contribution to the volumes giving an account of the voyages of the *Adventure* and *Beagle*, he wrote: " Nature by making habit omnipotent and its effects hereditary, has fitted the Fuegian for the climate and productions of his country " (p. 237).

What is the secret of the long departure from the simple common-sense view of the matter which he took when he was a young man? I imagine simply what I have referred to in the preceding chapter,—over-anxiety to appear to be differing from his grandfather, Dr. Erasmus Darwin, and Lamarck.

I believe I may say that Mr. Darwin before he died not only admitted the connection between memory and heredity, but came also to see that he must readmit that design in organism which he had so many years opposed. For in the preface to Hermann Müller's Fertilisation of Flowers, † which bears a date only a very few weeks prior to Mr. Darwin's death, I find him saying:—" Design in nature has for a long time deeply interested many men, and though the subject must now be looked at from a somewhat different point of view from what was formerly the case, it is not on that account rendered less interesting." This is mused

---

* Quoted by Mr. Romanes as written in the last year of Mr. Darwin's life.

† Macmillan, 1883.

forth as a general gnome, and may mean anything or nothing: the writer of the letterpress under the hieroglyph in Old Moore's Almanac could not be more guarded; but I think I know what it does mean.

I cannot of course be sure; Mr. Darwin did not probably intend that I should; but I assume with confidence that whether there is design in organism or no, there is at any rate design in this passage of Mr. Darwin's. This, we may be sure, is not a fortuitous variation; and moreover it is introduced for some reason which made Mr. Darwin think it worth while to go out of his way to introduce it. It has no fitness in its connection with Hermann Müller's book, for what little Hermann Müller says about teleology at all is to condemn it; why then should Mr. Darwin muse here of all places in the world about the interest attaching to design in organism? Neither has the passage any connection with the rest of the preface. There is not another word about design, and even here Mr. Darwin. seems mainly anxious to face both ways, and pat design as it were on the head while not committing himself to any proposition which could be disputed.

The explanation is sufficiently obvious. Mr. Darwin wanted to hedge. He saw that the design which his works had been mainly instrumental in pitchforking out of organisms no less manifestly designed than a burglar's jemmy is designed, had nevertheless found its way back again, and that though, as I insisted in Evolution, Old and New, and Unconscious Memory, it must now be placed within the organism instead of outside it, as " was formerly the case," it was not on that account any the less——design, as well as interesting.

I should like to have seen Mr. Darwin say this more explicitly. Indeed I should have liked to have seen

Mr. Darwin say anything at all about the meaning of
which there could be no mistake, and without contra-
dicting himself elsewhere; but this was not Mr. Darwin's
manner.

In passing I will give another example of Mr.
Darwin's manner when he did not quite dare even to
hedge. It is to be found in the preface which he
wrote to Professor Weismann's Studies in the Theory
of Descent, published in 1882.

"Several distinguished naturalists," says Mr. Darwin,
"maintain with much confidence that organic beings
tend to vary and to rise in the scale, independently of
the conditions to which they and their progenitors have
been exposed; whilst others maintain that all variation
is due to such exposure, though the manner in which
the environment acts is as yet quite unknown. At the
present time there is hardly any question in biology of
more importance than this of the nature and causes of
variability, and the reader will find in the present work
an able discussion on the whole subject which will
probably lead him to pause before he admits the existence of an innate tendency to perfectibility "—or
towards *being able to be perfected.*

I could find no able discussion upon the whole subject
in Professor Weismann's book. There was a little something here and there, but not much.

Mr Herbert Spencer has not in his more recent
works said anything which enables me to appeal to
his authority.

I imagine that if he had got hold of the idea that
heredity was only a mode of memory before 1870,
when he published the second edition of his Principles
of Psychology, he would have gladly adopted it, for he
seems continually groping after it, and aware of it as

near him, though he is never able to grasp it. He probably failed to grasp it because Lamarck had failed. He could not adopt it in his edition of 1880, for this is evidently printed from stereos taken from the 1870 edition, and no considerable alteration was therefore possible.

The late Mr. G. H. Lewes did not get hold of the memory theory, probably because neither Mr. Spencer nor any of the well-known German philosophers had done so. Mr. Romanes, as I think I have shown, actually has adopted it, but he does not say where he got it from. I suppose from reading Canon Kingsley in *Nature* some years before *Nature* began to exist, or (for has not the mantle of Mr. Darwin fallen upon him?) he has thought it all out independently; but however Mr. Romanes may have reached his conclusion, he must have done so comparatively recently, for when he reviewed my book, Unconscious Memory, [*] he scoffed at the very theory which he is now adopting.

Of the view that " there is thus a race memory, as there is an individual memory, and that the expression of the former constitutes the phenomena of heredity "— for it is thus Mr. Romanes with fair accuracy describes the theory I was supporting—he wrote:

" Now this view, in which Mr. Butler was anticipated by Prof. Hering, is interesting if advanced merely as an illustration ; but to imagine that it maintains any truth of profound significance, or that it can possibly be fraught with any benefit to science, is simply absurd. The most cursory thought is enough to show," &c. &c.

" We can understand," he continued, " in some measure how an alteration in brain structure when once

[*] Nature, Jan. 27, 1881.

made should be permanent, . . . but we cannot understand how this alteration is transmitted to progeny
through structures so unlike the brain as are the pro-
ducts of the generative glands.   And we merely stultify
ourselves if we suppose that the problem is brought
any nearer to a solution by asserting that a future individual while still in the germ has already participated,
say in the cerebral alterations of its parents," &c.   Mr.
Romanes could find no measure of abuse strong enough
for me,—as any reader may see who feels curious
enough to turn to Mr. Romanes' article in *Nature*
already referred to.

As for Evolution, Old and New, he said I had
written it "in the hope of gaining some notoriety by
deserving and perhaps receiving a contemptuous refutation from " Mr. Darwin.*   In my reply to Mr. Romanes I said, " I will not characterise this accusation
in the terms which it merits."†   Mr. Romanes, in the
following number of *Nature*, withdrew his accusation
and immediately added, " I was induced to advance it
because it seemed the only rational motive that could
have led to the publication of such a book."   Again I
will not characterise such a withdrawal in the terms
it merits, but I may say in passing that if Mr. Romanes
thinks the motive he assigned to me " a rational one,"
his view of what is rational and mine differ.   It does
not commend itself as " rational" to me, that a man
should spend a good deal of money and two or three
years of work in the hope of deserving a contemptuous refutation from any one—not even from Mr.
Darwin.   But then Mr. Romanes has written such a
lot about reason and intelligence.

The reply to Evolution, Old and New, which I actu-

* Nature, Jan. 27, 1881.   † Ibid., Feb. 3, 1881.

ally did get from Mr. Darwin, was one which I do not see advertised among Mr. Darwin's other works now, and which I venture to say never will be advertised among them again—not at least until it has been altered. I have seen no reason to leave off advertising Evolution, Old and New, and Unconscious Memory.

I have never that I know of seen Mr. Romanes, but am told that he is still young. I can find no publication of his indexed in the British Museum Catalogue earlier than 1874, and then it was only about Christian Prayer. Mr. Romanes was good enough to advise me to turn painter or homœopathist;* as he has introduced the subject, and considering how many years I am his senior, I might be justified (if it could be any pleasure to me to do so) in suggesting to him too what I should imagine most likely to tend to his advancement in life; but there are examples so bad that even those who have no wish to be any better than their neighbours may yet decline to follow them, and I think Mr. Romanes' is one of these. I will not therefore find him a profession.

But leaving this matter on one side, the point I wish to insist on is that Mr. Romanes is saying almost in my own words what less than three years ago he was very angry with me for saying. I do not think that under these circumstances much explanation is necessary as to the reasons which have led Mr. Romanes to fight so shy of any reference to Life and Habit, Evolution, Old and New, and Unconscious Memory—works in which, if I may venture to say so, the theory connecting the phenomena of heredity with memory has been not only "suggested," but so far established that even Mr. Romanes has been led to think the matter over inde-

* Nature, Jan. 27, 1881.

pendently and to arrive at the same general conclusion as myself.

Curiously enough, Mr. Grant Allen too has come to much the same conclusions as myself, after having attacked me, though not so fiercely, as Mr. Romanes has done.   In 1879 he said in the *Examiner* (May 17) that the teleological view put forward in Evolution, Old and New, was "just the sort of mystical nonsense from which " he " had hoped Mr. Darwin had for ever saved us."   And so in the *Academy* on the same day he said that no "one-sided argument" (referring to Evolution, Old and New) could ever deprive Mr. Darwin of the "place which he had eternally won in the history of human thought by his magnificent achievement."

A few years, and Mr. Allen entertains a very different opinion of Mr. Darwin's magnificent achievement.

"There are only two conceivable ways," he writes, "in which any increment of brain power can ever have arisen in any individual.   The one is the Darwinian way, by 'spontaneous variation,' that is to say by variation due to minute physical circumstances affecting the individual in the germ.   The other is the Spencerian way, by functional increment, that is to say by the effect of increased use and constant exposure to varying circumstances during conscious life." *

Mr. Allen must know very well, or if he does not he has no excuse at any rate for not knowing, that the theory according to which increase of brain power or any other bodily or mental power is due to use, is no more Mr. Spencer's than the theory of gravitation is, except in so far as that Mr. Spencer has adopted it. It is the theory which every one except Mr. Allen

* Mind, October, 1883.

associates with Erasmus Darwin and Lamarck, but more especially (and on the whole I suppose justly) with Lamarck.

"I venture to think," continues Mr. Allen, "that the first way [Mr. Darwin's], if we look it clearly in the face, will be seen to be *practically unthinkable;* and that we have therefore no alternative but to accept the second."

These writers go round so quickly and so completely that there is no keeping pace with them. "As to Materialism," he writes presently, "surely it is more profoundly materialistic to suppose that mere physical causes operating on the germ can determine minute physical and material changes in the brain, which will in turn make the individuality what it is to be, than to suppose *that all brains are what they are in virtue of antecedent function.* The one creed makes the man depend mainly upon the accidents of molecular physics in a colliding germ cell and sperm cell; *the other makes him depend mainly upon the doings and gains of his ancestors as modified and altered by himself.*"

Here is a sentence taken almost at random from the body of the article :—

"We are always seeing something which adds to our total stock of memories ; we are always learning and doing something new. The vast majority of these experiences are similar in kind to those already passed through by our ancestors : they add nothing to the inheritance of the race. . . . Though they leave physical traces on the individual, they do not so far affect the underlying organisation of the brain as to make the development of after-brains somewhat different from previous ones. But there are certain functional activities which do tend so to alter the development of after-brains; certain novel or sustained activities which apparently ·result in the production of new correlated brain elements or brain connections hereditarily transmissible as increased potentialities of similar activity in the offspring."

Of Natural Selection Mr. Allen writes much, as Professor Mivart and others have been writing for many years past.

" It seems to me," he says, " easy to understand how survival of the fittest may result in progress starting from such functionally produced gains, but impossible to understand how it could result in progress if it had to start in mere accidental structural increments due to spontaneous variation alone." *

Mr. Allen may say this now, but until lately he has been among the first to scold any one else who said so.

And this is how the article concludes :—

"The first hypothesis (Mr Darwin's) is one that throws no light upon any of the facts.   The second hypothesis (which Mr. Allen is pleased to call Mr. Herbert Spencer's) is one that explains them all with transparent lucidity." †

So that Mr. Darwin, according to Mr. Allen, is clean out of it.   Truly when Mr. Allen makes stepping-stones of his dead selves, he jumps upon them to some tune.   But then Mr. Darwin is dead now.   I have not heard of his having given Mr. Allen any manuscripts as he gave Mr. Romanes.   I hope Mr. Herbert Spencer will not give him any.   If I was Mr. Spencer and found my admirers crowning me with Lamarck's laurels, I think I should have something to say to them.

---

* *Mind* for October 1883, p. 498.
† Ibid., p. 505, October 1883.

What are we to think of a writer who declares that the theory that specific and generic changes are due to use and disuse "explains *all the facts* with transparent lucidity"?

Lamarck's hypothesis is no doubt a great help and a great step toward Professor Hering's; it makes a known cause underlie variations, and thus is free from those fatal objections which Professor Mivart and others have brought against the theory of Messrs. Darwin and Wallace; but how does the theory that use develops an organism explain why offspring repeat the organism at all? How does the Lamarckian hypothesis explain the sterility of hybrids, for example? The sterility of hybrids has been always considered one of the great *cruces* in connection with any theory of Evolution. How again does it explain reversion to long-lost characters and the resumption of feral characteristics? the phenomena of old age? the principle that underlies longevity? the reason why the reproductive system is generally the last to arrive at maturity, and why few further developments take place in any organism after this has been fully developed? the sterility of many animals under captivity? the development in both males and females, under certain circumstances, of the characteristics of the opposite sex? the latency of memory? the unconsciousness with which we develop, and with which instinctive actions are performed? How does any theory advanced either by Lamarck, Mr. Herbert Spencer, or Mr. Darwin explain, or indeed throw light upon these facts until supplemented with the explanation given of them in Life and Habit—for which I must refer the reader to that work itself?

People may say what they like about "the experience of the race," * "the registration of experiences continued for numberless generations," † "infinity of experiences," ‡ "lapsed intelligence," &c., but until they make Memory, in the most uncompromising sense of the word, the key to all the phenomena of Heredity, they will get little help to the better understanding of the difficulties above adverted to. Add this to the theory of Buffon, Erasmus Darwin, and Lamarck, and the points which I have above alluded to receive a good deal of "lucidity."

But to return to Mr. Romanes: however much he and Mr. Allen may differ about the merits of Mr. Darwin, they were at any rate not long since cordially agreed in vilipending my unhappy self, and are now saying very much what I have been saying for some years past. I do not deny that they are capable witnesses. They will generally see a thing when a certain number of other people have come to do so. I submit that, no matter how grudgingly they give their evidence, the tendency of that evidence is sufficiently clear to show that the opinions put forward in Life and Habit, Evolution, Old and New, and Unconscious Memory, deserve the attention of the reader.

I may perhaps deal with Mr. Romanes' recent work more fully in the sequel to Life and Habit on which I am now engaged. For the present it is enough to say that if he does not mean what Professor Hering and, *longo intervallo,* myself do, he should not talk about habit or experience as between successive generations, and that if he does mean what we do—which I suppose he does—he should have said so much more clearly and consistently than he has.

* Principles of Psychology, I. 422.
† Ibid. I. 424.   ‡ Ibid. I. 424.

POSTSCRIPT.

THIS afternoon (March 7, 1884), the copies of this book being ready for issue, I see Mr. Romanes' letter to the *Athenæum* of this day, and get this postscript pasted into the book after binding.

Mr. Romanes corrects his reference to the passage in which he says that Canon Kingsley first advanced the theory that instinct is inherited memory (" M. E. in Animals," p. 296). Canon Kingsley's words are to be found in *Fraser*, June, 1867, and are as follows :—

" Yon wood-wren has had enough to make him sad, if only he recollects it; and if he can recollect his road from Morocco hither he maybe recollects likewise what happened on the road : the long weary journey up the Portuguese coast, and through the gap between the Pyrenees and the Jaysquivel, and up the Landes of Bordeaux, and through Brittany, flitting by night and hiding and feeding as he could by day; and how his mates flew against the lighthouses and were killed by hundreds, and how he essayed the British Channel and was blown back, shrivelled up by bitter blasts; and how he felt, nevertheless, that 'that was water he must cross,' he knew not why; but something told him that his mother had done it before him, and he was flesh of her flesh, life of her life, and had inherited her instinct (as we call hereditary memory in order to avoid the trouble of finding out what it is and how it comes). A duty was laid on him to go back to the place where he was bred, and now it is done, and he is weary and sad and lonely, &c. &c.

This is a very interesting passage, and I am glad to quote it; but it hardly amounts to advancing the theory that instinct is inherited memory. Observing Mr. Romanes' words closely, I see he only says that Canon Kingsley was the first to advance the theory "that many hundred miles of landscape scenery" can "constitute an object of inherited memory;" but as he proceeds to say that "*this*" has since "been independently suggested by several writers," it is plain he intends to convey the idea that Canon Kingsley advanced the theory that instinct generally is inherited memory, which indeed his words do; but it is hardly credible that he should have left them where he did if he had realized their importance.

Mr. Romanes proceeds to inform me personally that the reference to "Nature" in his proof "originally indicated another writer who had independently advanced the same theory as that of Canon Kingsley." After this I have a right to ask him to tell me who the writer is, and where I shall find what he said. I ask this, and at my earliest opportunity will do my best to give this writer, too, the credit he doubtless deserves.

I have never professed to be the originator of the theory connecting heredity with memory. I knew I knew so little that I was in great trepidation when I wrote all the earlier chapters of "Life and Habit." I put them paradoxically, because I did not dare to put them otherwise. As the book went on, I saw I was on firm ground, and the paradox was dropped. When I found what Professor Hering had done, I put him forward as best I could at once. I then learned German, and translated him, giving his words in full in "Unconscious Memory;" since then I have always spoken of the theory as Professor Hering's.

Mr. Romanes says that "the theory in question forms the backbone of all the previous literature on instinct by the above-named writers (not to mention their numerous followers) and is by all of them elaborately stated as clearly as any theory can be stated in words." Few except Mr. Romanes will say this. I grant it ought to have formed the backbone " of all previous literature on instinct by the above-named writers," but when I wrote " Life and Habit" it was not understood to form it. If it had been, I should not have found it necessary to come before the public this fourth time during the last seven years to insist upon it. Of course the theory is not new— it was in the air and bound to come; but when it came, it came through Professor Hering of Prague, and not through those who, great as are the services they have rendered, still did not render this particular one of making memory the keystone of their system. Mr. Romanes now says : " Why, of course, that's what they were meaning all the time." Perhaps they were, but they did not say so, and others—conspicuously Mr. Romanes himself—did not understand them to be meaning what he now discovers that they meant.

When Mr. Romanes attacked me in *Nature*, January 27, 1881, he said I had " been anticipated by Professor Hering," but he evidently did not understand that any one else had anticipated me ; and far from holding, as he now does, that " the theory in question forms the backbone of all the previous" writers on instinct, and " is by all of them elaborately stated as clearly as any theory can be stated in words," he said (in a passage already quoted) that it was " interesting, if advanced merely as an illustration, but to imagine that it maintains any truth of profound significance, or that it can possibly be fraught with any benefit to science, is absurd." Considering how recently Mr.

Romanes wrote the words just quoted, he has soon forgotten them.

I do not, as I have said already, and never did, claim to have originated the theory I put forward in " Life and Habit." I thought it out independently, but I knew it must have occurred to many, and had probably been worked out by many, before myself. My claim is to have brought it perhaps into fuller light, and to have dwelt on its importance, bearings, and developments with some persistence, and to have done so without much recognition or encouragement, till lately. Of men of science, Mr. A. R. Wallace and Professor Mivart gave me encouragement, but no one else has done so. I sometimes saw, as in the Duke of Argyll's case, and in Mr. Romanes' own, that men were writing at me, or borrowing from me, but with the two exceptions already made, and that also of the Bishop of Carlisle, not one of the literary and scientific notables of the day so much as mentioned my name while making use of my work.

A few words more, and I will bring these remarks to a close. Mr. Romanes says I represent " the phenomena of memory as occurring throughout the inorganic world." This implies that I attribute all the phenomena of memory as we see them in animals to such things as stones and gases. Mr. Romanes knows very well that I have never said anything which could warrant his attempting to put the absurdity into my mouth which he here tries to do. The reader who wishes to see what I do maintain upon this subject will find it on pp. 216–218 of the present volume.

EXTRACTS FROM "ALPS AND SANCTUARIES OF PIEDMONT AND THE CANTON TICINO."

DALPE, PRATO, ROSSURA.

(FROM CHAPTER III. OF ALPS AND SANCTUARIES.*)

TALKING of legs, as I went through the main street of Dalpe an old lady of about sixty-five stopped me, and told me that while gathering her winter store of firewood she had had the misfortune to hurt her leg. I was very sorry, but I failed to satisfy her; the more I sympathised in general terms, the more I felt that something further was expected of me. I went on trying to do the civil thing, when the old lady cut me short by saying it would be much better if I were to see the leg at once; so she showed it me in the street, and there, sure enough, close to the groin there was a swelling. Again I said how sorry I was, and added that perhaps she ought to show it to a medical man. "But aren't *you* a medical man?" said she in an alarmed manner. "Certainly not, ma'am," replied I. "Then why did you let me show you my leg?" said she indignantly, and pulling her clothes down, the poor old woman began to hobble off; presently two others joined her, and I heard hearty peals of laughter as she

* The first edition of Alps and Sanctuaries was published Dec. 1882.

recounted her story. A stranger visiting these out-of-the-way villages is almost certain to be mistaken for a doctor. What business, they say to themselves, can any one else have there, and who in his senses would dream of visiting them for pleasure? This old lady had rushed to the usual conclusion, and had been trying to get a little advice gratis.

.   .   .   .   .   .

The little objects looking like sentry-boxes that go all round Prato Church contain rough modern frescoes representing, if I remember rightly, the events attendant upon the crucifixion. These are on a small scale what the chapels on the sacred mountain of Varallo are on a large one. Small single oratories are scattered about all over the Canton Ticino, and indeed everywhere in North Italy, by the road-side, at all halting-places, and especially at the crest of any more marked ascent, where the tired wayfarer, probably heavy laden, might be inclined to say a naughty word or two if not checked. The people like them, and miss them when they come to England. They sometimes do what the lower animals do in confinement when precluded from habits they are accustomed to, and put up with strange makeshifts by way of substitute. I once saw a poor Ticinese woman kneeling in prayer before a dentist's show-case in the Hampstead Road; she doubtless mistook the teeth for the relics of some saint. I am afraid she was a little like a hen sitting upon a chalk egg, but she seemed quite contented.

Which of us, indeed, does not sit contentedly enough upon chalk eggs at times? And what would life be but for the power to do so? We do not sufficiently realise the part which illusion has played in our development. One of the prime requisites for evolution is a certain power for adaptation to varying circumstances, that is to say, of plasticity, bodily and mental. But the power of adaptation is mainly dependent on the power of thinking certain new things sufficiently like certain others to which we have been accustomed for us not to be too much incommoded by the change—upon the power, in fact, of mistaking the new for the old. The power of fusing ideas (and through ideas, structures) depends upon the power of *con*fusing them ; the power to confuse ideas that are not very unlike, and that are presented to us in immediate sequence, is mainly due to the fact of the impetus, so to speak, which the mind has upon it. It is this which bars association from sticking to the letter of its bond ; for we are in a hurry to jump to a conclusion on the first show of plausible pretext, and cut association's statement of claim short by taking it as read before we have got through half of it. We " get it into our notes, in fact," as Mr. Justice Stareleigh did in Pickwick, and having got it once in, we are not going to get it out again. This breeds fusion and confusion, and from this there come new developments.

So powerful is the impetus which the mind has continually upon it that we always, I believe, make an effort to see every new object as a repetition of the object last before us. Objects are so varied and present themselves so rapidly, that as a general rule we renounce this effort too promptly to notice it, but it is always there, and as I have just said, it is because of it that we are able to mistake, and hence to evolve new mental and bodily developments. Where the effort is successful, there is illusion ; where nearly successful but not quite, there is a shock and a sense

R

of being puzzled—more or less, as the case may be; where it so obviously impossible as not to be pursued, there is no perception of the effort at all.

Mr. Locke has been greatly praised for his essay upon human understanding. An essay on human mis-understanding should be no less interesting and impor-tant. Illusion to a small extent is one of the main causes, if indeed it is not the main cause, of progress, but it must be upon a small scale. All abortive speculation, whether commercial or philosophical, is based upon it, and much as we may abuse such specu-lation, we are, all of us, its debtors.

.   .   .   .   .   .

I know few things more touching in their way than the porch of Rossura Church : it is dated early in the last century, and is absolutely without ornament; the flight of steps inside it lead up to the level of the floor of the church. One lovely summer Sunday morning passing the church betimes, I saw the people kneeling upon these steps, the church within being crammed. In the darker light of the porch, they told out against the sky that showed through the open arch beyond them ; far away the eye rested on the mountains—deep blue, save where the snow still lingeréd. I never saw anything more beautiful—and these forsooth are the people whom so many of us think to better by distribut-ing tracts about Protestantism among them !

I liked the porch almost best under an aspect which it no longer presents. One summer an opening was made in the west wall, which was afterwards closed because the wind blew through it too much and made the church too cold. While it was open, one could sit on the church steps and look down through it on to the bottom of the Ticino valley ; and through the windows one could see the slopes about Dalpe and Cornone. Between the two windows there is a picture of austere old S. Carlo Borromeo with his hands joined in prayer.

It was at Rossura that I made the acquaintance of a word which I have since found very largely used throughout North Italy. It is pronounced "chow" pure and simple, but is written, if written at all, "ciau" or "ciao," the "a" being kept very broad. I believe the word is derived from "schiavo," a slave, which became corrupted into "schiao," and "ciao." It is used with two meanings, both of which, however, are deducible from the word slave. In its first and more common use it is simply a salute, either on greeting or taking leave, and means, "I am your very obedient servant." Thus, if one has been talking to a small child, its mother will tell it to say "chow" before it goes away, and will then nod her head and say "chow" herself. The other use is a kind of pious expletive, intending "I must endure it," "I am the slave of a higher power." It was in this sense I first heard it at Rossura. A woman was washing at a fountain while I was eating my lunch. She said she had lost her daughter in Paris a few weeks earlier. "She was a beautiful woman," said the bereaved mother, "but— chow. She had great talents—chow. I had her educated by the nuns of Bellinzona—chow. Her knowledge of geography was consummate—chow, chow," &c. Here "chow" means "pazienza," "I have done and said all that I can, and must now bear it as best I may."

I tried to comfort her, but could do nothing, till at last it occurred to me to say "chow" too. I did so, and was astonished at the soothing effect it had upon her. How subtle are the laws that govern consolation!

I suppose they must ultimately be connected with re-production—the consoling idea being a kind of small cross which *re-generates* or *re-creates* the sufferer. It is important, therefore, that the new ideas with which the old are to be crossed should differ from these last sufficiently to divert the attention, and yet not so much as to cause a painful shock.

There should be a little shock, or there will be no variation in the new ideas that are generated, but they will resemble those that preceded them, and grief will be continued; there must not be too great a shock or there will be no illusion—no confusion and fusion between the new set of ideas and the old, and in consequence there will be no result at all, or, if any, an increase in mental discord. We know very little, however, upon this subject, and are continually shown to be at fault by finding an unexpectedly small cross produce a wide diversion of the mental images, while in other cases a wide one will produce hardly any result. Sometimes again, a cross which we should have said was much too wide will have an excellent effect. I did not anticipate, for example, that my saying "chow" would have done much for the poor woman who had lost her daughter: the cross did not seem wide enough: she was already, as I thought, saturated with "chow." I can only account for the effect my application of it produced by supposing the word to have derived some element of strangeness and novelty as coming from a foreigner—just as land which will give a poor crop, if planted with sets from potatoes that have been grown for three or four years on this same soil, will yet yield excellently if similar sets be brought from twenty miles off. For the potato, so far as I have studied it, is a good-tempered, frivolous plant, easily amused and easily bored, and one, moreover, which if bored, yawns horribly.

I may say in passing that the tempers of plants have not been sufficiently studied; and what little opinion we have formed about their dispositions is for the most part ill formed. The sulkiest tree that I know is the silver beech. It never forgives a scratch. —There is a tree in Kensington gardens a little off the west side of the Serpentine with names cut upon it as long ago as 1717 and 1736, which the tree is as little able to forgive and forget as though the injury had been done not ten years since. And the tree is not an aged tree either.

CALONICO.

(FROM CHAPTER V. OF ALPS AND SANCTUARIES.)

OUR inventions increase in geometrical ratio. They are like living beings, each one of which may become parent of a dozen others—some good and some ne'er-do-weels; but they differ from animals and vegetables inasmuch as they not only increase in a geometrical ratio, but the period of their gestation decreases in geometrical ratio also. Take this matter of Alpine roads for example. For how many millions of years was there no approach to a road over the St. Gothard, save the untutored watercourses of the Ticino and the Reuss, and the track of the bouquetin or the chamois? For how many more ages after this was there not a mere shepherd's or huntsman's path by the river-side—without so much as a log thrown over so as to form a rude bridge? No one would probably have ever thought of making a bridge out of his own unaided imagination, more than any monkey that we know of has done so. But an avalanche or a flood once swept a pine into position and left it there; on this a genius, who was doubtless thought to be doing something very infamous, ventured to make use of it. Another time a pine was found nearly across the stream, but not quite; and not quite, again, in the place where it was wanted. A second genius, to the horror of his fellow-tribesmen—who declared that this

time the world really would come to an end—shifted
the pine a few feet so as to bring it across the stream
and into the place where it was wanted. This man
was the inventor of bridges—his family repudiated
him, and he came to a bad end. From this to cutting
down the pine and bringing it from some distance is
an easy step. To avoid detail, let us come to the old
Roman horse-road over the Alps. The time between
the shepherd's path and the Roman road is probably
short in comparison with that between the mere chamois
track and the first thing that can be called a path of
men. From the Roman we go on to the mediæval
road with more frequent stone bridges, and from the
mediæval to the Napoleonic carriage-road.

The close of the last century and the first quarter
of this present one was the great era for the making
of carriage-roads. Fifty years have hardly passed, and
here we are already in the age of tunnelling and rail-
roads. The first period, from the chamois track to the
foot road, was one of millions of years; the second,
from the first foot road to the Roman military way,
was one of many thousands; the third, from the
Roman to the mediæval, was perhaps a thousand;
from the mediæval to the Napoleonic, five hundred;
from the Napoleonic to the railroad, fifty. What will
come next we know not, but it should come within
twenty years, and will probably have something to do
with electricity.

It follows by an easy process of reasoning that after
another couple of hundred years or so, great sweeping
changes should be made several times in an hour, or
indeed in a second, or fraction of a second, till they
pass unnoticed as the revolutions we undergo in the
embryonic stages, or are felt simply as vibrations.

This would undoubtedly be the case but for the existence of a friction which interferes between theory and practice. This friction is caused partly by the disturbance of vested interests which every invention involves, and which will be found intolerable when men become millionaires and paupers alternately once a fortnight—living one week in a palace and the next in a workhouse, and having perpetually to be sold up, and then to buy a new house and refurnish, &c.—so that artificial means for stopping inventions will be adopted; and partly by the fact that though all inventions breed in geometrical ratio, yet some multiply more rapidly than others, and the backwardness of one art will impede the forwardness of another. At any rate, so far as I can see, the present is about the only comfortable time for a man to live in, that either ever has been or ever will be. The past was too slow, and the future will be much too fast.

The fact is (but it is so obvious that I am ashamed to say anything about it) that science is rapidly reducing time and space to a very undifferentiated condition. Take lamb: we can get lamb all the year round. This is perpetual spring; but perpetual spring is no spring at all; it is not a season; there are no more seasons, and being no seasons, there is no time. Take rhubarb, again. Rhubarb to the philosopher is the beginning of autumn, if indeed the philosopher can see anything as the beginning of anything. If any one asks why, I suppose the philosopher would say that rhubarb is the beginning of the fruit season, which is clearly autumnal, according to our present classification. From rhubarb to the green gooseberry the step is so small as to require no bridging—with one's eyes shut, and plenty of cream and sugar, they are almost indistinguishable—but the gooseberry is quite an autumnal fruit, and only a little earlier than apples and plums, which last are almost winter; clearly, therefore, for scientific purposes rhubarb is autumnal.

As soon as we can find gradations, or a sufficient number of uniting links between two things, they become united or made one thing, and any classification of them must be illusory. Classification is only possible where there is a shock given to the senses by reason of a perceived difference, which, if it is considerable, can be expressed in words. When the world was younger and less experienced, people were shocked at what appeared great differences between living forms; but species, whether of animals or plants, are now seen to be so united, either inferentially or by actual finding of the links, that all classification is felt to be arbitrary. The seasons are like species—they were at one time thought to be clearly marked, and capable of being classified with some approach to satisfaction. It is now seen that they blend either in the present or the past insensibly into one another, much as Mr. Herbert Spencer shows us that geology and astronomy blend into one another,* and cannot be classified except by cutting Gordian knots in a way which none but plain sensible people can tolerate. Strictly speaking, there is only one place, one time, one action, and one individual or thing; of this thing or individual each one of us is a part. It is perplexing, but it is philosophy; and modern philosophy, like modern music, is nothing if it is not perplexing.

A simple verification of the autumnal character of rhubarb may, at first sight, appear to be found in Covent Garden Market, where we can actually see

* Princ. of Psych., ed. 3, Vol. I., p. 136, 1880.

the rhubarb towards the end of October. But this way of looking at the matter argues a fatal ineptitude for the pursuit of true philosophy. It would be "the most serious error" to regard the rhubarb that will appear in Covent Garden Market next October as belonging to the autumn then supposed to be current. Practically, no doubt, it does so, but theoretically it must be considered as the first-fruits of the autumn (if any) of the following year, which begins before the preceding summer (or, perhaps, more strictly, the preceding summer but one—and hence, but any number), has well ended. Whether this, however, is so or no, the rhubarb can be seen in Covent Garden, and I am afraid it must be admitted that to the philosophically minded there lurks within it a theory of evolution, and even Pantheism, as surely as Theism was lurking in Bishop Berkeley's tar-water.

To return, however, to Calonico. The *curato* was very kind to me. We had long talks together. I could see it pained him that I was not a Catholic. He could never quite get over this, but he was very good and tolerant, He was anxious to be assured that I was not one of those English who went about distributing tracts, and trying to convert people. This of course was the last thing I should have wished to do; and when I told him so, he viewed me with sorrow but henceforth without alarm.

All the time I was with him I felt how much I wished I could be a Catholic in Catholic countries, and a Protestant in Protestant ones. Surely there are some things which like politics are too serious to be taken quite seriously. *Surtout point de zèle* is not the saying of a cynic, but the conclusion of a sensible man; and the more deep our feeling is about any

matter, the more occasion have we to be on our guard
against *zèle* in this particular respect. There is but
one step from the "earnest" to the "intense." When
St. Paul told us to be all things to all men he let in
the thin end of the wedge, nor did he mark it to say
how far it was to be driven.

I have Italian friends whom I greatly value, and
who tell me they think I flirt just a trifle too much
with " *il partito nero*," when I am in Italy, for they
know that in the main I think as they do. "These
people," they say, "make themselves very agreeable
to you, and show you their smooth side; we, who see
more of them, know their rough one. Knuckle under
to them, and they will perhaps condescend to patron-
ise you; have any individuality of your own, and they
know neither scruple nor remorse in their attempts
to get you out of their way. ' *Il prete*,' they say, with
a significant look, ' *è sempre prete*.' For the future
let us have professors and men of science instead of
priests."

I smile to myself at this last, and reply, that I am
a foreigner come among them for recreation, and anxious
to keep clear of their internal discords. I do not wish
to cut myself off from one side of their national character—a side which, in some respects, is no less interesting than the one with which I suppose I am on
the whole more sympathetic. If I were an Italian, I
should feel bound to take a side; as it is, I wish to
leave all quarrelling behind me, having as much of
that in England as suffices to keep me in good health
and temper.

In old times people gave their spiritual and intellectual sop to Nemesis. Even when most positive,
they admitted a percentage of doubt. Mr. Tennyson

has said well, "There lives more doubt"—I quote from memory—"in honest faith, believe me, than in half the" systems of philosophy, or words to that effect. The victor had a slave at his ear during his triumph; the slaves during the Roman Saturnalia, dressed in their masters' clothes, sat at meat with them, told them of their faults, and blacked their faces for them. They made their masters wait upon them. In the ages of faith, an ass dressed in sacerdotal robes was gravely conducted to the cathedral choir at a certain season, and mass was said before him, and hymns chanted discordantly. The elder D'Israeli, from whom I am quoting, writes: "On other occasions, they put burnt old shoes to fume in the censors: ran about the church leaping, singing, dancing, and playing at dice upon the altar, while a *boy bishop* or *pope of fools* burlesqued the divine service;" and later on he says: "So late as 1645, a pupil of Gassendi, writing to his master what he himself witnessed at Aix on the Feast of Innocents, says—'I have seen in some monasteries in this province extravagances solemnised which pagans would not have practised. Neither the clergy nor the guardians indeed go to the choir on this day, but all is given up to the lay brethren, the cabbage-cutters, errand-boys, cooks, scullions, and gardeners; in a word, all the menials fill their places in the church, and insist that they perform the offices proper for the day. They dress themselves with all the sacerdotal ornaments, but torn to rags, or wear them inside out: they hold in their hands the books reversed or sideways, which they pretend to read with large spectacles without glasses, and to which they fix the rinds of scooped oranges . . . ! particularly while dangling the censers they keep shaking them in derision, and letting the ashes fly about their heads and faces, one against the other. In this equipage they neither sing hymns nor psalms nor masses, but mumble a certain gibberish as shrill and squeaking as a herd of pigs whipped on to market. The nonsense verses they chant are singularly barbarous :—

"'Hæc est clara dies, clararum clara dierum,
Hæc est festa dies festarum festa dierum.'" *

Faith was far more assured in the times when the spiritual saturnalia were allowed than now. The irreverence which was not dangerous then, is now intolerable. It is a bad sign for a man's peace in his own convictions when he cannot stand turning the canvas of his life occasionally upside down, or reversing it in a mirror, as painters do with their pictures that they may judge the better concerning them. I would persuade all Jews, Mohammedans, Comtists, and free-thinkers to turn high Anglicans, or better still, down-right Catholics for a week in every year, and I would send people like Mr. Gladstone to attend Mr. Brad-laugh's lectures in the forenoon, and the Grecian pantomime in the evening, two or three times every winter. I should perhaps tell them that the Grecian pantomime has nothing to do with Greek plays. They little know how much more keenly they would relish their normal opinions during the rest of the year for the little spiritual outing which I would prescribe for them, which, after all, is but another phase of the wise saying—"*Surtout point de zèle.*" St. Paul attempted an obviously hopeless task (as the Church of Rome very well understands) when he tried to put down seasonarianism. People must and will go to church to

* Curiosities of Literature, Lond. 1866, Routledge & Co., p. 272.

be a little better, to the theatre to be a little naughtier, to the Royal Institution to be a little more scientific, than they are in actual life. It is only by pulsations of goodness, naughtiness, and whatever else we affect that we can get on at all. I grant that when in his office, a man should be exact and precise, but our holidays are our garden, and too much precision here is a mistake.

Surely truces, without even an *arrière pensée* of difference of opinion, between those who are compelled to take widely different sides during the greater part of their lives, must be of infinite service to those who can enter on them. There are few merely spiritual pleasures comparable to that derived from the temporary laying down of a quarrel, even though we may know that it must be renewed shortly. It is a great grief to me that there is no place where I can go among Mr. Darwin, Professors Huxley, Tyndal, and Ray Lankester, Miss Buckley, Mr. Romanes, Mr. Grant Allen and others whom I cannot call to mind at this moment, as I can go among the Italian priests. I remember in one monastery (but this was not in the Canton Ticino) the novice taught me how to make sacramental wafers, and I played him Handel on the organ as well as I could. I told him that Handel was a Catholic; he said he could tell that by his music at once. There is no chance of getting among our scientists in this way.

Some friends say I was telling a lie when I told the novice Handel was a Catholic, and ought not to have done so. I make it a rule to swallow a few gnats a day, lest I should come to strain at them, and so bolt camels; but the whole question of lying is difficult. What *is* "lying"? Turning for moral guidance to my cousins the lower animals, whose unsophisticated nature proclaims what God has taught them with a directness we may sometimes study, I find the plover lying when she lures us from her young ones under the fiction of a broken wing. Is God angry, think you, with this pretty deviation from the letter of strict accuracy? or was it not He who whispered to her to tell the falsehood—to tell it with a circumstance, without conscientious scruple, not once only, but to make a practice of it so as to be a plausible, habitual, and professional liar for some six weeks or so in the year? I imagine so. When I was young I used to read in good books that it was God who taught the bird to make her nest, and if so He probably taught each species the other domestic arrangements best suited to it. Or did the nest-building information come from God, and was there an evil one among the birds also who taught them at any rate to steer clear of priggishness?

Think of the spider again—an ugly creature, but I suppose God likes it. What a mean and odious lie is that web which naturalists extol as such a marvel of ingenuity!

Once on a summer afternoon in a far country I met one of those orchids who make it their business to imitate a fly with their petals. This lie they dispose so cunningly that real flies, thinking the honey is being already plundered, pass them without molesting them. Watching intently and keeping very still, methought I heard this orchid speaking to the offspring which she felt within her, though I saw them not. "My children," she exclaimed, "I must soon leave you; think upon the fly, my loved ones, for this is truth; cling to this great thought in your passage through life, for it is the one thing needful; once lose sight of it and you are lost!" Over and over again she sang this burden in a small still voice, and so I left her. Then straightway I came upon some butterflies whose profession it was to pretend to believe in all manner of vital truths which in their inner practice they rejected; thus, asserting themselves to be certain other and hateful butterflies which no bird will eat by reason of their abominable smell, these cunning ones conceal their own sweetness, and live long in the land and see good days. No: lying is so deeply rooted in nature that we may expel it with a fork, and yet it will always come back again: it is like the poor, we must have it always with us. We must all eat a peck of moral dirt before we die.

All depends upon who it is that is lying. One man may steal a horse when another may not look over 'a hedge. The good man who tells no lies wittingly to himself and is never unkindly, may lie and lie and lie whenever he chooses to other people, and he will not be false to any man: his lies become truths as they pass into the hearers' ear. If a man deceives himself and is unkind, the truth is not in him; it turns to falsehood while yet in his mouth, like the quails in the Wilderness of Sinai. How this is so or why, I know not, but that the Lord hath mercy on whom He will have mercy and whom He willeth He hardeneth.

My Italian friends are doubtless in the main right about the priests, but there are many exceptions, as they themselves gladly admit. For my own part I have found the *curato* in the small subalpine villages of North Italy to be more often than not a kindly excellent man to whom I am attracted by sympathies deeper than any mere superficial differences of opinion can counteract. With monks, however, as a general rule, I am less able to get on: nevertheless I have received much courtesy at the hands of some.

My young friend the novice was delightful—only it was so sad to think of the future that is before him. He wanted to know all about England, and when I told him it was an island, clasped his hands and said, "Oh che Providenza!" He told me how the other young men of his own age plagued him as he trudged his rounds high up among the most distant hamlets begging alms for the poor. "Be a good fellow," they would say to him, "drop all this nonsense and come back to us, and we will never plague you again." Then he would turn upon them and put their words from him. Of course my sympathies were with the other young men rather than with him, but it was impossible not to be sorry for the manner in which he had been humbugged from the day of his birth, till he was now incapable of seeing things from any other standpoint. than that of authority.

What he said to me about knowing that Handel was a Catholic by his music, put me in mind of what another good Catholic once said to me about a picture. He was a Frenchman and very nice, but a *dévot*, and anxious to convert me. He paid a few days' visit to London, so I showed him the National Gallery. While there I pointed out to him Sebastian del Piombo's picture of the raising of Lazarus as one of the supposed masterpieces of our collection. He had the proper orthodox fit of admiration over it, and then we went through the other rooms. After a while we found ourselves before West's picture of "Christ healing the Sick." My French friend did not, I suppose, examine it very carefully, at any rate he believed he was again

s

before the raising of Lazarus by Sebastian del Piombo ; he paused before it, and had his fit of admiration over again : then turning to me he said, " Ah! you would understand this picture better if you were a Catholic." I did not tell him of his mistake.

*PIORA.**

(FROM CHAPTER VI. OF ALPS AND SANCTUARIES.)

AN excursion which may be very well made from Faido is to the Val Piora, which I have already more than once mentioned. There is a large hotel here which has been opened some years, but has not hitherto proved the success which it was hoped it would be. I have stayed there two or three times and found it very comfortable; doubtless, now that Signor Lombardi of the Hotel Prosa has taken it, it will become a more popular place of resort.

I took a trap from Faido to Ambri, and thence walked over to Quinto; here the path begins to ascend, and after an hour Ronco is reached. There is a house at Ronco where refreshments and excellent Faido beer can be had. The old lady who keeps the house would make a perfect Fate; I saw her sitting at her window spinning, and looking down over the Ticino valley as though it were the world and she were spinning its destiny. She had a somewhat stern expression, thin lips, iron-grey eyes, and an aquiline nose; her scanty locks straggled from under the handkerchief which she wore round her head. Her employment and the wistful far-away look she cast upon the expanse below made a very fine *ensemble*. " She would have afforded,"

* See p. 87 of this vol.

as Sir Walter Scott says, "a study for a Rembrandt, had that celebrated painter existed at the period," [*] but she must have been a smart-looking, handsome girl once.

She brightened up in conversation. I talked about Piora, which I already knew, and the *Lago Tom*, the highest of the three lakes. She said she knew the *Lago Tom*. I said laughingly, "Oh, I have no doubt you do. We've had many a good day at the *Lago Tom*, I know." She looked down at once.

In spite of her nearly eighty years she was active as a woman of forty, and altogether she was a very grand old lady. Her house is scrupulously clean. While I watched her spinning, I thought of what must so often occur to summer visitors. I mean what sort of a look-out the old woman must have in winter, when the wind roars and whistles, and the snow drives down the valley with a fury of which we in England can have little conception. What a place to see a snowstorm from! and what a place from which to survey the landscape next morning after the storm is over and the air is calm and brilliant. There are such mornings: I saw one once, but I was at the bottom of the valley and not high up, as at Ronco. Ronco would take a little sun even in midwinter, but at the bottom of the valley there is no sun for weeks and weeks together; all is in deep shadow below, though the upper hill-sides may be seen to have the sun upon them. I walked once on a frosty winter's morning from Airolo to Giornico, and can call to mind nothing in its way more beautiful: everything was locked in frost—there was not a waterwheel but was sheeted and coated with ice: the road was hard as granite—

* Ivanhoe, chap. xxiii., near the beginning.

all was quiet, and seen as through a dark but incredibly transparent medium. Near Piotta I met the whole village dragging a large tree; there were many men and women dragging at it, but they had to pull hard, and they were silent; as I passed them I thought what comely, well-begotten people they were. Then, looking up, there was a sky, cloudless and of the deepest blue, against which the snow-clad mountains stood out splendidly. No one will regret a walk in these valleys during the depth of winter. But I should have liked to have looked down from the sun into the sunlessness, as the old Fate woman at Ronco can do when she sits in winter at her window; or again, I should like to see how things would look from this same window on a leaden morning in midwinter after snow has fallen heavily and the sky is murky and much darker than the earth. When the storm is at its height, the snow must search and search and search even through the double windows with which the houses are protected. It must rest upon the frames of the pictures of saints, and of the sisters " grab," and of the last hours of Count Ugolino, which adorn the walls of the parlour. No wonder there is a *S. Maria della Neve*—a " St. Mary of the Snow ; " but I do wonder that she has not been painted.

I said this to an Italian once, and he said the reason was probably this—that St. Mary of the Snow was not developed till long after Italian art had begun to decline. I suppose in another hundred years or so we shall have a *St. Maria delle Ferrovie*—a St. Mary of the Railways.

From Ronco the path keeps level and then descends a little so as to cross the stream that comes down from Piora. This is near the village of Altanca, the church of which looks remarkably well from here. Then there is an hour and a half's rapid ascent, and at last all on a sudden one finds oneself on the *Lago Ritom*, close to the hotel.

The lake is about a mile, or a mile and a half, long, and half a mile broad. It is 6000 feet above the sea, very deep at the lower end, and does not freeze where the stream issues from it, so that the magnificent trout with which it abounds can get air and live through the winter. In many other lakes, as, for example, the *Lago di Tremorgio*, they cannot do this, and hence perish, though the lakes have been repeatedly stocked. The trout in the *Lago Ritom* are said to be the finest in the world, and certainly I know none so fine myself. They grow to be as large as moderate-sized salmon, and have a deep-red flesh, very firm and full of flavour. I had two cutlets off one for breakfast, and should have said they were salmon unless I had known otherwise. In winter, when the lake is frozen over, the people bring their hay from the farther Lake of Cadagna in sledges across the Lake Ritom. Here, again, winter must be worth seeing, but on a rough snowy day Piora must be an awful place. There are a few stunted pines near the hotel, but the hillsides are for the most part bare and green. Piora in fact is a fine breezy open upland valley of singular beauty, and with a sweet atmosphere of cow about it; it is rich in rhododendrons and all manner of Alpine flowers, just a trifle bleak, but as bracing as the Engadine itself.

The first night I was ever in Piora there was a brilliant moon, and the unruffled surface of the lake took the reflection of the mountains. I could see the cattle a mile off, and hear the tinkling of their bells which danced multitudinously before the ear as fire-flies come and go before the eyes; for all through a fine summer's night the cattle will feed as though it were day. A little above the lake I came upon a man in a cave before a furnace, burning lime, and he sat looking into the fire with his back to the moonlight. He was a quiet moody man, and I am afraid I bored him, for I could get hardly anything out of him but " Oh altro "—polite but not communicative. So after a while I left him with his face burnished as with gold from the fire, and his back silver with the moonbeams ; behind him were the pastures and the reflections in the lake and the mountains and the distant ringing of the cowbells.

Then I wandered on till I came to the chapel of S. Carlo ; and in a few minutes found myself on the *Lago di Cadagna*. Here I heard that there were people, and the people were not so much asleep as the simple peasantry of these upland valleys are expected to be by nine o'clock in the evening. For now was the time when they had moved up from Ronco, Altanca, and other villages in some numbers to cut the hay, and were living for a fortnight or three weeks in the chalets upon the *Lago di Cadagna*. As I have said, there is a chapel, but I doubt whether it is attended during this season with the regularity with which the parish churches of Ronco, Altanca, &c., are attended during the rest of the year. The young people, I am sure, like these annual visits to the high places, and will be hardly weaned from them. Happily the hay will be always there, and will have to be cut by some one, and the old people will send the young ones.

As I was thinking of these things, I found myself going off into a doze, and thought the burnished man from the furnace came up and sat beside me, and laid his hand upon my shoulder. Then I saw the green slopes that rise all round the lake were much higher than I had thought; they went up thousands of feet, and there were pine forests upon them, while two large glaciers came down in streams that ended in a precipice of ice, falling sheer into the lake. The edges of the mountains against the sky were rugged and full of clefts, through which I saw thick clouds of dust being blown by the wind as though from the other side of the mountains.

And as I looked, I saw that this was not dust, but people coming in crowds from the other side, but so small as to be visible at first only as dust. And the people became musicians, and the mountainous amphitheatre a huge orchestra, and the glaciers were two noble armies of women-singers in white robes, ranged tier above tier behind each other, and the pines became orchestral players, while the thick dust-like cloud of chorus-singers kept pouring in through the clefts in the precipices in inconceivable numbers. When I turned my telescope upon them I saw they were crowded up to the extreme edge of the mountains, so that I could see underneath the soles of their boots as their legs dangled in the air. In the midst of all, a precipice that rose from out of the glaciers shaped itself suddenly into an organ, and there was one whose face I well knew sitting at the keyboard, smiling and pluming himself like a bird as he thundered forth a giant fugue by way of overture. I heard the great pedal notes in the bass stalk majestically up and down, as the rays of the Aurora that go about upon the face of the heavens off the coast of Labrador. Then presently the people rose and sang the chorus " Venus Laughing from the Skies;" but ere the sound had well died away, I awoke, and all was changed; a light fleecy cloud had filled the whole basin, but I still thought I heard a sound of music, and a scampering-off of great crowds from the part where the precipices should be. After that I heard no more but a little singing from the chalets, and turned homewards. When I got to the chapel of S. Carlo, I was in the moonlight again, and when near the hotel, I passed the man at the mouth of the furnace with the moon still gleaming upon his back, and the fire upon his face, and he was. very grave and quiet.

S. MICHELE AND MONTE PIRCHIRIANO.

(EXTRACTS FROM CHAPTERS VII. AND X. OF ALPS AND SANCTUARIES.)

THE history of the sanctuary of S. Michele is briefly as follows :——

At the close of the tenth century, when Otho III. was Emperor of Germany, a certain Hugh de Montboissier, a noble of Auvergne, commonly called "Hugh the Unsewn" (*lo sdruscito*), was commanded by the Pope to found a monastery in expiation of some grave offence. He chose for his site the summit of the Monte Pirchiriano in the valley of Susa, being attracted partly by the fame of a church already built there by a recluse of Ravenna, Giovanni Vincenzo by name, and partly by the striking nature of the situation. Hugh de Montboissier, when returning from Rome to France with Isengarde his wife, would, as a matter of course, pass through the valley of Susa. The two—perhaps when stopping to dine at S. Ambrogio—would look up and observe the church founded by Giovannia Vincenzo: they had got to build a monastery somewhere; it would very likely, therefore, occur to them that they could not perpetuate their names better than by choosing this site, which was on a much-travelled road, and on which a fine building would show to advantage. If my view is correct, we have here an illustration of a fact which is continually observable—namely, that all things which come to much, whether they be books, buildings, pictures, music, or living beings, are begotten of others of their own kind. It is always the most successful, like Handel and Shakespeare, who owe most to their forerunners, in spite of the modifications with which their works descend.

Giovanni Vincenzo had built his church about the year 987. It is maintained by some that he had been bishop of Ravenna, but Clareta gives sufficient reason for thinking otherwise. In the "Cronaca Clusina" it is said that he had for some years previously lived as a recluse on the Monte Caprasio, to the north of the present Monte Pirchiriano; but that one night he had a vision, in which he saw the summit of Monte Pirchiriano enveloped in heaven-descended flames, and on this founded a church there, and dedicated it to S. Michael. This is the origin of the name Pirchiriano, which means $\pi\hat{v}\rho$ $\kappa v\rho\acute{\iota}avo\varsigma$, or the Lord's fire.

Avogadro is among those who make Giovanni Bishop, or rather Archbishop, of Ravenna, and gives the following account of the circumstances which led to his resigning his diocese and going to live at the top of the inhospitable Monte Caprasio. It seems there had been a confirmation at Ravenna, during which he had accidentally forgotten to confirm the child of a certain widow. The child, being in weakly health, died before Giovanni could repair his oversight, and this preyed upon his mind. In answer, however, to his earnest prayers, it pleased the Almighty to give him power to raise the dead child to life again; this he did, and having immediately performed the rite of confirmation, restored the boy to his overjoyed mother. He now became so much revered that he began to be alarmed lest pride should obtain dominion over him; he felt, therefore, that his only course was to resign his diocese, and go and live the life of a recluse on the top of some high mountain. It is said that he suffered agonies of doubt as to whether it was not selfish of him to take such care of his own eternal welfare, at the expense of that of his flock, whom no successor could so well guide and guard from evil; but in the end he took a reasonable view of the matter, and concluded that his first duty was to secure his own spiritual position. Nothing short of the top of a very uncomfortable mountain could do this, so he at once resigned his bishopric and chose Monte Caprasio as on the whole the most comfortable uncomfortable mountain he could find.

The latter part of the story will seem strange to Englishmen. We can hardly fancy the Archbishop of Canterbury or York resigning his diocese and settling down quietly on the top of Scafell or Cader Idris to secure his eternal welfare. They would hardly do so even on the top of Primrose Hill. But nine hundred years ago human nature was not the same as now-a-days.

Comparing our own clergy with the best North Italian and Ticinese priests, I should say there was little to choose between them. The latter are in a logically stronger position, and this gives them greater courage in their opinions; the former have the advantage in respect of money, and the more varied knowledge of the world which money will command. When I say Catholics have logically the advantage over Protestants, I mean that starting from premises which both sides admit, a merely logical Protestant will find himself driven to the Church of Rome. Most men as they grow older will, I think, feel this, and they will see in it the explanation of the comparatively narrow area over which the Reformation extended, and of the gain which Catholicism has made of late years here in England. On the other hand, reasonable people will look with distrust upon too much reason. The foundations of action lie deeper than reason can reach. They rest on faith—for there is no absolutely certain incontrovertible premise which can be laid by man, any more than there is any investment for money or security in the daily affairs of life which is absolutely unimpeachable. The Funds are not absolutely safe; a volcano might break out under the Bank of England. A railway journey is not absolutely safe; one person at least in several millions gets killed. We invest our money upon faith, mainly. We choose our doctor upon faith, for how little independent judgment can we form concerning his capacity? We choose schools for our children chiefly upon faith. The most important things a man has are his body, his soul, and his money. It is generally better for him to commit these interests to the care of others of whom he can know little, rather than be his own medical man, or invest his money on his own judgment; and this is nothing else than making a faith which lies deeper than reason can reach, the basis of our action in those respects which touch us most nearly.

On the other hand, as good a case could be made out for placing reason as the foundation, inasmuch as it would be easy to show that a faith, to be worth any-thing, must be a reasonable one—one, that is to say, which is based upon reason. The fact is that faith and reason are like function and organ, desire and power, or demand and supply; it is impossible to say which comes first: they come up hand in hand, and are so small when we can first descry them, that it is impossible to say which we first caught sight of. All we can now see is that each has a tendency continually to outstrip the other by a little, but by a very little only. Strictly they are not two things, but two aspects of one thing; for convenience' sake, however, we classify them separately.

It follows, therefore—but whether it follows or no, it is certainly true—that neither faith alone nor reason alone is a sufficient guide: a man's safety lies neither in faith nor reason, but in temper—in the power of fusing faith and reason, even when they appear most mutually destructive.

That we all feel temper to be the first thing is plain from the fact that when we see two men quarrelling we seldom even try to weigh their arguments—we look instinctively at the tone or spirit or temper which the two display and give our verdict accordingly.

A man of temper will be certain in spite of uncertainty, and at the same time uncertain in spite of certainty; reasonable in spite of his resting mainly upon faith rather than reason, and full of faith even when appealing most strongly to reason. If it is asked, In what should a man have faith? To what faith should he turn when reason has led him to a conclusion which he distrusts? the answer is, To the current feeling among those whom he most looks up to—looking upon himself with suspicion if he is either among the foremost or the laggers. In the rough, homely common sense of the community to which we belong we have as firm ground as can be got. This, though not absolutely infallible, is secure enough for practical purposes.

As I have said, Catholic priests have rather a fascina-

tion for me—when they are not Englishmen. I should
say that the best North Italian priests are more openly
tolerant than our English clergy generally are. I remember picking up one who was walking along a road,
and giving him a lift in my trap. Of course we fell
to talking, and it came out that I was a member of
the Church of England. "Ebbene, Caro Signore," said
he when we shook hands at parting; "mi rincresce
che lei non crede come io, ma in questi tempi non
possiamo avere tutti i medesimi principii."*

.   .   .   .

The one thing, he said, which shocked him with
the English, was the manner in which they went
about distributing tracts upon the Continent. I said
no one could deplore the practice more profoundly
than myself, but that there were stupid and conceited
people in every country, who would insist upon thrust-
ing their opinions upon people who did not want them.
He replied that the Italians travelled not a little in
England, but that he was sure not one of them would
dream of offering Catholic tracts to people, for example,
in the streets of London. Certainly I have never seen
an Italian to be guilty of such rudeness. It seems to
me that it is not only toleration that is a duty; we
ought to go beyond this now; we should conform,
when we are among a sufficient number of those who
would not understand our refusal to do so; any other
course is to attach too much importance at once to our
own opinions and to those of our opponents. By all
means let a man stand by his convictions when the
occasion requires, but let him reserve his strength,
unless it is imperatively called for. Do not let him

---

* "Well, my dear sir, I am sorry you do not think as I do, but in
these days we cannot all of us start with the same principles."

exaggerate trifles, and let him remember that everything is a trifle in comparison with the not giving offence to a large number of kindly, simple-minded people. Evolution, as we all know, is the great doctrine of modern times; the very essence of evolution consists in the not shocking anything too violently, but enabling it to mistake a new action for an old one, without "making believe" too much.

One day when I was eating my lunch near a fountain, there came up a moody, meditative hen, crooning plaintively after her wont. I threw her a crumb of bread while she was still a good way off, and then threw more, getting her to come a little closer and a little closer each time; at last she actually took a piece from my hand. She did not quite like it, but she did it. "A very little at a time," this is the evolution principle; and if we wish those who differ from us to understand us, it is the only method to proceed upon. I have sometimes thought that some of my friends among the priests have been treating me as I treated the meditative hen. But what of that? They will not kill and eat me, nor take my eggs. Whatever, therefore, promotes a more friendly feeling between us must be pure gain.

.   .   .   .

Sometimes priests say things, as a matter of course, which would make any English clergyman's hair stand on end. At one town there is a remarkable fourteenth-century bridge, commonly known as "The Devil's Bridge." I was sketching near this when a jolly old priest with a red nose came up and began a conversation with me. He was evidently a popular character, for every one who passed greeted him. He told me that the devil did not really build the bridge. I said

I presumed not, for he was not in the habit of spending his time so well.

"I wish he had built it," said my friend; "for then perhaps he would build us some more."

"Or we might even get a church out of him," said I, a little slyly.

"Ha, ha, ha! we will convert him, and make a good Christian of him in the end."

When will our Protestantism, or Rationalism, or whatever it may be, sit as lightly upon ourselves?

Another time I had the following dialogue with an old Piedmontese priest who lived in a castle which I asked permission to go over:—

"Vous êtes Anglais, monsieur?" said he in French.

"Oui, monsieur."

"Vous êtes Catholique?"

"Monsieur, je suis de la religion de mes ancêtres."

"Pardon, monsieur, vos ancêtres étaient Catholiques jusqu'au temps de Henri Huit."

"Mais il y a trois cents ans depuis le temps de Henri Huit."

"Eh bien; chacun a ses convictions; vous ne parlez pas contre la religion?"

"Jamais, jamais, monsieur, j'ai un respect enorme pour l'église Catholique."

"Monsieur, faites comme chez vous; allez ou vous voulez; vous trouverez toutes les portes ouvertes. Amusez vous bien."

T

CONSIDERATIONS ON THE DECLINE OF ITALIAN ART.

(FROM CHAPTER XIII. OF ALPS AND SANCTUARIES.)

THOSE who know the Italians will see no sign of
decay about them.   They are the quickest-witted
people in the world, and at the same time have much
more of the old Roman steadiness than they are generally credited with.   Not only is there no sign of
degeneration, but, as regards practical matters, there is
every sign of health and vigorous development.   The
North Italians are more like Englishmen, both in body
and mind, than any other people whom I know; I am
continually meeting Italians whom I should take for
Englishmen if I did not know their nationality.   They
have all our strong points, but they have more grace
and elasticity of mind than we have.

Priggishness is the sin which doth most easily beset
middle-class, and so-called educated Englishmen; we
call it purity and culture, but it does not much matter
what we call it.   It is the almost inevitable outcome
of a university education, and will last as long as Oxford
and Cambridge do, but not much longer.

Lord Beaconsfield sent Lothair to Oxford; it is with
great pleasure that I see he did not send Endymion.
My friend Jones called my attention to this, and we
noted that the growth observable throughout Lord
Beaconsfield's life was continued to the end.   He was

one of those who, no matter how long he lived, would have been always growing : this is what makes his later novels so much better than those of Thackeray or Dickens. There was something of the child about him to the last. Earnestness was his greatest danger, but if he did not quite overcome it (as who indeed can ? It is the last enemy that shall be subdued), he managed to veil it with a fair amount of success. As for Endymion, of course if Lord Beaconsfield had thought Oxford would be good for him, he could, as Jones pointed out to me, just as well have killed Mr. Ferrars a year or two later. We feel satisfied, therefore, that Endymion's exclusion from a university was carefully considered, and are glad.

I will not say that priggishness is absolutely unknown among the North Italians ; sometimes one comes upon a young Italian who wants to learn German, but not often. Priggism, or whatever the substantive is, is as essentially a Teutonic vice as holiness is a Semitic characteristic; and if an Italian happens to be a prig, he will, like Tacitus, invariably show a hankering after German institutions. The idea, however, that the Italians were ever a finer people than they are now, will not pass muster with those who knew them.

At the same time, there can be no doubt that modern Italian art is in many respects as bad as it was once good. I will confine myself to painting only. The modern Italian painters, with very few exceptions, paint as badly as we do, or even worse, and their motives are as poor as is their painting. At an exhibition of modern Italian pictures, I generally feel that there is hardly a picture on the walls but is a sham—that is to say, painted not from love of this particular subject and an irresistible desire to paint it, but from a wish to paint an academy picture, and win money or applause.

The last rays of the sunset of genuine art are to be found in the votive pictures at Locarno or Oropa, and in many a wayside chapel. In these, religious art still lingers as a living language, however rudely spoken. In these alone is the story told, not as in the Latin and Greek verses of the scholar, who thinks he has succeeded best when he has most concealed his natural manner of expressing himself, but by one who knows what he wants to say, and says it in his mother-tongue, shortly, and without caring whether or not his words are in accordance with academic rules. I regret to see photography being introduced for votive purposes, and also to detect in some places a disposition on the part of the authorities to be a little ashamed of these pictures and to place them rather out of sight.

The question is, how has the falling-off in Italian painting been caused? And by doing what may we again get Bellinis and Andrea Mantegnas as in old time? The fault does not lie in any want of raw material: nor yet does it lie in want of taking pains. The modern Italian painter frets himself to the full as much as his predecessor did—if the truth were known, probably a great deal more. I am sure Titian did not take much pains after he was more than about twenty years old. It does not lie in want of schooling or art education. For the last three hundred years, ever since the Caraccis opened their academy at Bologna, there has been no lack of art education in Italy. Curiously enough, the date of the opening of the Bolognese Academy coincides as nearly as may be with the complete decadence of Italian painting. The academic system trains boys to study other people's works rather than nature, and, as Leonardo da Vinci so well says, it makes them nature's grandchildren and not her children. This I believe is at any rate half the secret of the whole matter.

If half-a-dozen young Italians could be got together with a taste for drawing; if they had power to add to their number; if they were allowed to see paintings and drawings done up to the year A.D. 1510, and votive pictures and the comic papers; if they were left with no other assistance than this, absolutely free to please themselves, and could be persuaded not to try and please any one else, I believe that in fifty years we should have all that was ever done repeated with fresh naïveté, and as much more delightfully than even by the best old masters, as these are more delightful than anything we know of in classic painting. The young plants keep growing up abundantly every day—look at Bastianini, dead not ten years since—but they are browsed down by the academies. I remember there came out a book many years ago with the title, "What becomes of all the clever little children?" I never saw the book, but the title is pertinent.

Any man who can write, can draw to a not inconsiderable extent. Look at the Bayeux tapestry; yet Matilda probably never had a drawing lesson in her life. See how well prisoner after prisoner in the Tower of London has cut out this or that in the stone of his prison wall, without, in all probability, having ever tried his hand at drawing before. Look at my friend Jones, who has several illustrations in this book.* The first year he went abroad with me he could hardly draw at all. He was no year away from England more

* For these I must refer the reader to Alps and Sanctuaries itself.

than three weeks. How did he learn? On the old principle, if I am not mistaken. The old principle was for a man to be doing something which he was pretty strongly bent on doing, and to get a much younger one to help him. The younger paid nothing for instruction, but the elder took the work, as long as the relation of master and pupil existed between them. I, then, was making illustrations for this book, and got Jones to help me. I let him see what I was doing, and derive an idea of the sort of thing I wanted, and then left him alone—beyond giving him the same kind of small criticism that I expected from himself—but I appropriated his work. That is the way to teach, and the result was that in an incredibly short time Jones could draw. The taking the work is a *sine quâ non.* If I had not been going to have his work, Jones, in spite of all his quickness, would probably have been rather slower in learning to draw. Being paid in money is nothing like so good.

This is the system of apprenticeship *versus* the academic system. The academic system consists in giving people the rules for doing things. The apprenticeship system consists in letting them do it, with just a trifle of supervision. " For all a rhetorician's rules," says my great namesake, " teach nothing but, to name his tools ; " and academic rules generally are much the same as the rhetorician's. Some men can pass through academies unscathed, but they are very few, and in the main the academic influence is a baleful one, whether exerted in a university or a school. While young men at universities are being prepared for their entry into life, their rivals have already entered it. The most university and examination ridden people in the world are the Chinese, and they are the least progressive.

Men should learn to draw as they learn convey-
ancing: they should go into a painter's studio and
paint on his pictures. I am told that half the conveyances in the country are drawn by pupils; there
is no more mystery about painting than about convey-
ancing—not half in fact, I should think, so much.
One may ask, How can the beginner paint, or draw
conveyances, till he has learnt how to do so? The
answer is, How can he learn, without at any rate
trying to do? It is the old story, organ and function,
power and desire, demand and supply, faith and reason,
etc., the most virtuous action and interaction in the
most vicious circle conceivable. If the beginner likes
his subject, he will try: if he tries, he will soon succeed
in doing something which shall open a door. It does
not matter what a man does; so long as he does it
with the attention which affection engenders, he will
come to see his way to something else. After long
waiting he will certainly find one door open, and go
through it. He will say to himself that he can never
find another. He has found this, more by luck than
cunning, but now he is done. Yet by and by he will
see that there is *one* more small unimportant door
which he had overlooked, and he proceeds through this
too. If he remains now for a long while and sees no
other, do not let him fret; doors are like the kingdom
of heaven, they come not by observation, least of all
do they come by forcing: let him just go on doing
what comes nearest, but doing it attentively, and a
great wide door will one day spring into existence
where there had been no sign of one but a little time
previously. Only let him be always doing something,
and let him cross himself now and again, for belief in
the wondrous efficacy of crosses and crossing is the

corner-stone of the creed of the evolutionists. Then after years—but not probably till after a great many —doors will open up all around, so many and so wide that the difficulty will not be to find a door, but rather to obtain the means of even hurriedly surveying a portion of those that stand invitingly open.

I know that just as good a case can be made out for the other side. It may be said as truly that unless a student is incessantly on the watch for doors he·will never see them, and that unless he is incessantly pressing forward to the kingdom of heaven he will never find it—so that the kingdom does come by observation. It is with this as with everything else—there must be a harmonious fusing of two principles which are in flat contradiction to one another.

The question of whether it is better to abide quiet and take advantage of opportunities that come, or to go farther afield in search of them, is one of the oldest which living beings have had to deal with. It was on this that the first great schism or heresy arose in what was heretofore the catholic faith of protoplasm. The schism still lasts, and has resulted in two great sects —animals and plants. The opinion that it is better to go in search of prey is formulated in animals; the other—that it is better on the whole to stay at home and profit by what comes—in plants. Some intermediate forms still record to us the long struggle during which the schism was not yet complete.

If I may be pardoned for pursuing this digression further, I would say that it is the plants and not we who are the heretics. There can be no question about this; we are perfectly justified, therefore, in devouring them. Ours is the original and orthodox belief, for protoplasm is much more animal than vegetable; it is much more true to say that plants have descended from animals than animals from plants. Nevertheless, like many other heretics, plants have thriven very fairly well. There are a great many of them, and as regards beauty, if not wit—of a limited kind indeed, but still wit—it is hard to say that the animal kingdom has the advantage. The views of plants are sadly narrow; all dissenters are narrow-minded; but within their own bounds they know the details of their business sufficiently well—as well as though they kept the most nicely-balanced system of accounts to show them their position. They are eaten, it is true; to eat them is our intolerant and bigoted way of trying to convert them: eating is only a violent mode of proselytising or converting; and we do convert them—to good animal substance, of our own way of thinking. If we have had no trouble with them, we say they have "agreed" with us; if we have been unable to make them see things from our points of view, we say they "disagree" with us, and avoid being on more than distant terms with them for the future. If we have helped ourselves to too much, we say we have got more than we can "manage." But then, animals are eaten too. They convert one another, almost as much as they convert plants. And an animal is no sooner dead than a plant will convert it back again. It is obvious, however, that no schism could have been so long successful, without having a good deal to say for itself.

Neither party has been quite consistent. Who ever is or can be? Every extreme—every opinion carried to its logical end—will prove to be an absurdity. Plants throw out roots and boughs and leaves: this is a kind of locomotion; and as Dr. Erasmus Darwin long since pointed out, they do sometimes approach nearly to what may be called travelling ; a man of consistent character will never look at a bough, a root, or a tendril without regarding it as a melancholy and unprincipled compromise. On the other hand, many animals are sessile, and some singularly successful genera, as spiders, are in the main liers-in-wait. It may appear, however, on the whole, like reopening a settled question to uphold the principle of being busy and attentive over a small area, rather than going to and fro over a larger one, for a mammal like man, but I think most readers will be with me in thinking that, at any rate as regards art and literature, it is he who does his small immediate work most carefully who will find doors open most certainly to him, that will conduct him into the richest chambers.

Many years ago, in New Zealand, I used sometimes to accompany a dray and team of bullocks who would have to be turned loose at night that they might feed. There were no hedges or fences then, so sometimes I could not find my team in the morning, and had no clue to the direction in which they had gone. At first I used to try and throw my soul into the bullocks' souls, so as to divine if possible what they would be likely to have done, and would then ride off ten miles in the wrong direction. People used in those days to lose their bullocks sometimes for a week or fortnight —when they perhaps were all the time hiding in a gully hard by the place where they were turned out. After some time I changed my tactics. On losing my bullocks I would go to the nearest accommodation house, and stand drinks. Some one would ere long, as a general rule, turn up who had seen the bullocks. This case does not go quite on all fours with what I have been saying above, inasmuch as I was not very industrious in my limited area; but the standing drinks and inquiring was being as industrious as the circumstances would allow.

To return, universities and academies are an obstacle to the finding of doors in later life; partly because they push their young men too fast through doorways that the universities have provided, and so discourage the habit of being on the look-out for others; and partly because they do not take pains enough to make sure that their doors are *bonâ fide* ones. If, to change the metaphor, an academy has taken a bad shilling, it is seldom very scrupulous about trying to pass it on. It will stick to it that the shilling is a good one as long as the police will let it. I was very happy at Cambridge; when I left it I thought I never again could be so happy anywhere else; I shall ever retain a most kindly recollection both of Cambridge and of the school where I passed my boyhood; but I feel, as I think most others must in middle life, that I have spent as much of my maturer years in unlearning as in learning.

The proper course is for a boy to begin the practical business of life many years earlier than he now commonly does. He should begin at the very bottom of a profession; if possible of one which his family has pursued before him—for the professions will assuredly one day become hereditary. The ideal railway director will have begun at fourteen as a railway porter. He need not be a porter for more than a week or ten days, any more than he need have been a tadpole more than a short time; but he should take a turn in practice, though briefly, at each of the lower branches in the profession. The painter should do just the same. He should begin by setting his employer's palette and cleaning his brushes. As for the good side of universities, the proper preservative of this is to be found in the club.

If, then, we are to have a renaissance of art, there must be a complete standing aloof from the academic system. That system has had time enough. Where and who are its men? Can it point to one painter who can hold his own with the men of, say, from 1450 to 1550? Academies will bring out men who can paint hair very like hair, and eyes very like eyes, but this is not enough. This is grammar and deportment; we want wit and a kindly nature, and these cannot be got from academies. As far as mere *technique* is concerned, almost every one now can paint as well as is in the least desirable. The same *mutatis mutandis* holds good with writing as with painting. We want less word-painting and fine phrases, and more observation at first-hand. Let us have a periodical illustrated by people who cannot draw, and written by people who cannot write (perhaps, however, after all, we have some), but who look and think for themselves, and express themselves just as they please,—and this we certainly have not. Every contributor should be at once turned out if he or she is generally believed to have tried to do something which he or she did not care about trying to do, and anything should be admitted which is the outcome of a genuine liking. People are always good company when they are doing what they really enjoy. A cat is good company when it is purring, or a dog when it is wagging its tail.

The sketching-clubs up and down the country might form the nucleus of such a society, provided all professional men were rigorously excluded. As for the old masters, the better plan would be never even to look at one of them, and to consign Raffaelle, along with Plato, Marcus Aurelius Antoninus, Dante, Goethe, and two others, neither of them Englishmen, to limbo, as the Seven Humbugs of Christendom.

While we are about it, let us leave off talking about "art for art's sake." Who is art, that it should have a sake? A work of art should be produced for the pleasure it gives the producer, and the pleasure he thinks it will give to a few of whom he is fond; but neither money nor people whom he does not know personally should be thought of. Of course such a society as I have proposed would not remain incorrupt long. "Everything that grows, holds in perfection but a little moment." The members would try to imitate professional men in spite of their rules, or, if they escaped this and after a while got to paint well, they would become dogmatic, and a rebellion against their authority would be as necessary ere long as it was against that of their predecessors: but the balance on the whole would be to the good.

Professional men should be excluded, if for no other reason yet for this, that they know too much for the beginner to be *en rapport* with them. It is the beginner who can help the beginner, as it is the child who is the most instructive companion for another child. The beginner can understand the beginner, but the cross between him and the proficient performer is too wide for fertility. It savours of impatience, and is in flat contradiction to the first principles of biology. It does a beginner positive harm to look at the master-pieces of the great executionists, such as Rembrandt or Turner.

If one is climbing a very high mountain which will

tax all one's strength, nothing fatigues so much as casting upward glances to the top; nothing encourages so much as casting downward glances. The top seems never to draw nearer; the parts that we have passed retreat rapidly. Let a water-colour student go and see the drawing by Turner in the basement of our National Gallery, dated 1787. This is the sort of thing for him, not to copy, but to look at for a minute or two now and again. It will show him nothing about painting, but it may serve to teach him not to overtax his strength, and will prove to him that the greatest masters in painting, as in everything else, begin by doing work which is no way superior to that of their neighbours. A collection of the earliest known works of the greatest men would be much more useful to the student than any number of their maturer works, for it would show him that he need not worry himself because his work does not look clever, or as silly people say, "show power."

The secrets of success are affection for the pursuit chosen, a flat refusal to be hurried or to pass anything as understood which is not understood, and an obstinacy of character which shall make the student's friends find it less trouble to let him have his own way than to bend him into theirs. Our schools and academies or universities are covertly but essentially radical institutions, and abhorrent to the genius of Conservatism. Their sin is the true radical sin of being in too great a hurry, and the natural result has followed, they waste far more time than they save. But it must be remembered that this proposition like every other wants tempering with a slight infusion of its direct opposite.

I said in an early part of this book that the best

test to know whether or no one likes a picture is to ask oneself whether one would like to look at it if one was quite sure one was alone. The best test for a painter as to whether he likes painting his picture is to ask himself whether he should like to paint it if he was quite sure that no one except himself, and the few of whom he was very fond, would ever see it. If he can answer this question in the affirmative, he is all right; if he cannot, he is all wrong.

I must reserve other remarks upon this subject for another occasion.

SANCTUARIES OF OROPA AND GRAGLIA.

(FROM CHAPTERS XV. AND XVI. OF ALPS AND SANCTUARIES.)

THE morning after our arrival at Biella, we took the daily diligence for Oropa, leaving Biella at eight o'clock. Before we were clear of the town we could see the long line of the hospice, and the chapels dotted about near it, high up in a valley at some distance off; presently we were shown another fine building some eight or nine miles away, which we were told was the sanctuary of Graglia. About this time the pictures and statuettes of the Madonna began to change their hue and to become black—for the sacred image of Oropa being black, all the Madonnas in her immediate neighbourhood are of the same complexion. Underneath some of them is written, "Nigra sum sed sum formosa," which, as a rule, was more true as regards the first epithet than the second.

It was not market-day, but streams of people were coming to the town. Many of them were pilgrims returning from the sanctuary, but more were bringing the produce of their farms or the work of their hands for sale. We had to face a steady stream of chairs, which were coming to town in baskets upon women's heads. Each basket contained twelve chairs, though whether it is correct to say that the basket contained

the chairs—when the chairs were all, so to say, froth
running over the top of the basket—is a point I cannot settle. Certainly we had never seen anything like
so many chairs before, and felt almost as though we
had surprised nature in the laboratory wherefrom she
turns out the chair-supply of the world. The road
continued through a succession of villages almost running into one another for a long way after Biella was
passed, but everywhere we noticed the same air of
busy thriving industry which we had seen in Biella
itself. We noted also that a preponderance of the
people had light hair, while that of the children was
frequently nearly white, as though the infusion of
German blood was here stronger even than usual.
Though so thickly peopled, the country was of great
beauty. Near at hand were the most exquisite pastures
close shaven after their second mowing, gay with
autumnal crocuses, and shaded with stately chestnuts;
beyond were rugged mountains, in a combe on one of
which we saw Oropa itself now gradually nearing;
behind, and below, many villages, with vineyards and
terraces cultivated to the highest perfection; farther
on, Biella already distant, and beyond this a "big
stare," as an American might say, over the plains of
Lombardy from Turin to Milan, with the Apennines
from Genoa to Bologna hemming the horizon. On the
road immediately before us, we still faced the same
steady stream of chairs flowing ever Biella-ward.

After a couple of hours the houses became more
rare; we got above the sources of the chair-stream;
bits of rough rock began to jut out from the pasture;
here and there the rhododendron began to shew itself
by the roadside; the chestnuts left off along a line as
level as though cut with a knife; stone-roofed *cascine*

U

began to abound, with goats and cattle feeding near them; the booths of the religious trinket-mongers increased; the blind, halt, and maimed became more importunate, and the foot-passengers were more entirely composed of those whose object was, or had been, a visit to the sanctuary itself. The numbers of these pilgrims—generally in their Sunday's best, and often comprising the greater part of a family—were so great, though there was no special festa, as to testify to the popularity of the institution. They generally walked barefoot, and carried their shoes and stockings; their baggage consisted of a few spare clothes, a little food, and a pot or pan or two to cook with. Many of them looked very tired, and had evidently tramped from long distances—indeed, we saw costumes belonging to valleys which could not be less than two or three days distant. They were almost invariably quiet, respectable, and decently clad, sometimes a little merry, but never noisy, and none of them tipsy. As we travelled along the road, we must have fallen in with several hundreds of these pilgrims coming and going; nor is this likely to be an extravagant estimate, seeing that the hospice can make up more than five thousand beds. By eleven we were at the sanctuary itself.

Fancy a quiet upland valley, the floor of which is about the same height as the top of Snowdon, shut in by lofty mountains upon three sides, while on the fourth the eye wanders at will over the plains below. Fancy finding a level space in such a valley watered by a beautiful mountain stream, and nearly filled by a pile of collegiate buildings, not less important than those, we will say, of Trinity College, Cambridge. True, Oropa is not in the least like Trinity, except that one of its courts is large, grassy, has a chapel and a foun-

tain in it, and rooms all round it; but I do not know
how better to give a rough description of Oropa than
by comparing it with one of our largest English colleges.

The buildings consist of two main courts. The first
comprises a couple of modern wings, connected by the
magnificent façade of what is now the second or inner
court. This façade dates from about the middle of the
seventeenth century; its lowest storey is formed by an
open colonnade, and the whole stands upon a raised
terrace from which a noble flight of steps descends
into the outer court.

Ascending the steps and passing under the colonnade, we find ourselves in the second or inner court,
which is a complete quadrangle, and is, so at least we
were told, of rather older date than the façade. This is
the quadrangle which gives its collegiate character to
Oropa. It is surrounded by cloisters on three sides,
on to which the rooms in which the pilgrims are
lodged open—those at least that are on the ground-
floor, but there are three storeys. The chapel, which
was dedicated in the year 1600, juts out into the court
upon the north-east side. On the north-west and
south-west sides are entrances through which one may
pass to the open country. The grass at the time of
our visit was for the most part covered with sheets
spread out to dry. They looked very nice, and, dried
on such grass, and in such an air, they must be de-
licious to sleep on. There is, indeed, rather an appearance as though it were a perpetual washing-day at
Oropa, but this is not to be wondered at considering
the numbers of comers and goers; besides, people in
Italy do not make so much fuss about trifles as we do.
If they want to wash their sheets and dry them, they
do not send them to Ealing, but lay them out in the

first place that comes handy, and nobody's bones are broken.

On the east side of the main block of buildings there is a grassy slope adorned with chapels that contain figures illustrating scenes in the history of the Virgin. These figures are of terra-cotta, for the most part life-size, and painted up to nature. In some cases, if I remember rightly, they have hemp or flax for hair, as at Varallo, and throughout realism is aimed at as far as possible, not only in the figures, but in the accessories. We have very little of the same kind in England. In the Tower of London there is an effigy of Queen Elizabeth going to the city to give thanks for the defeat of the Spanish Armada. This looks as if it might have been the work of some one of the Valsesian sculptors. There are also the figures that strike the quarters of Sir John Bennett's city clock in Cheapside. The automatic movements of these last-named figures would have struck the originators of the Varallo chapels with envy. They aimed at realism so closely that they would assuredly have had recourse to clockwork in some one or two of their chapels; I cannot doubt, for example, that they would have eagerly welcomed the idea of making the cock crow to Peter by a cuckoo-clock arrangement, if it had been presented to them. This opens up the whole question of realism *versus* conventionalism in art—a subject much too large to be treated here.

As I have said, the founders of these Italian chapels aimed at realism. Each chapel was intended as an illustration, and the desire was to bring the whole scene more vividly before the faithful by combining the picture, the statue, and the effect of a scene upon the stage in a single work of art. The attempt would

be an ambitious one though made once only in a
neighbourhood, but in most of the places in North
Italy where anything of the kind has been done, the
people have not been content with a single illustration ;
it has been their scheme to take a mountain as though
it had been a book or wall and cover it with illustrations. In some cases—as at Orta, whose Sacro Monte
is perhaps the most beautiful of all as regards the site
itself—the failure is complete, but in some of the
chapels at Varese and in many of those at Varallo,
great works have been produced which have not yet
attracted as much attention as they deserve. It may
be doubted, indeed, whether there is a more remarkable
work of art in North Italy than the crucifixion chapel
at Varallo, where the twenty-five statues, as well as
the frescoes behind them, are (with the exception of
the figure of Christ, which has been removed) by
Gaudenzio Ferrari. It is to be wished that some one
of these chapels—both chapel and sculptures—were
reproduced at South Kensington.

Varallo, which is undoubtedly the most interesting
sanctuary in North Italy, has forty-four of these illus-
trative chapels ; Varese, fifteen ; Orta, eighteen ; and
Oropa, seventeen. No one is allowed to enter them,
except when repairs are needed ; but when these are
going on, as is constantly the case, it is curious to
look through the grating into the somewhat darkened
interior, and to see a living figure or two among the
statues ; a little motion on the part of a single figure
seems to communicate itself to the rest and make them
all more animated. If the living figure does not move
much, it is easy at first to mistake it for a terra-cotta
one. At Orta, some years since, looking one evening
into a chapel when the light was fading, I was suprised

to see a saint whom I had not seen before; he had no glory except what shone from a very red nose; he was smoking a short pipe, and was painting the Virgin Mary's face. The touch was a finishing one, put on with deliberation, slowly, so that it was two or three seconds before I discovered that the interloper was no saint.

The figures in the chapels at Oropa are not as good as the best of those at Varallo, but some of them are very nice notwithstanding. We liked the seventh chapel the best—the one which illustrates the sojourn of the Virgin Mary in the Temple. It contains forty-four figures, and represents the Virgin on the point of completing her education as head girl at a high-toned academy for young gentlewomen. All the young ladies are at work making mitres for the bishop, or working slippers in Berlin wool for the new curate, but the Virgin sits on a dais above the others on the same platform with the venerable lady-principal, who is having passages read out to her from some standard Hebrew writer. The statues are the work of a local sculptor, named Aureggio, who lived at the end of the seventeenth and beginning of the eighteenth century.

The highest chapel must be a couple of hundred feet above the main buildings, and from near it there is an excellent bird's-eye view of the sanctuary and the small plain behind; descending on to this last, we entered the quadrangle from the north-west side, and visited the chapel in which the sacred image of the Madonna is contained. We did not see the image itself, which is only exposed to public view on great occasions. It is believed to have been carved by St. Luke the Evangelist. It is said that at one time there was actually an inscription on the image in Greek characters, of which the translation is, "Eusebius. A token of respect and affection from his sincere friend, Luke;" but this being written in chalk or pencil only, has been worn off, and is known by tradition only. I must ask the reader to content himself with the following account of it which I take from Marocco's work upon Oropa :—

"That this statue of the Virgin is indeed by St. Luke is attested by St. Eusebius, a man of eminent piety; and no less enlightened than truthful, and the store which he set by it is proved by his shrinking from no discomforts in his carriage of it from a distant country, and by his anxiety to put it in a place of great security. His desire, indeed, was to keep it in the spot which was most near and dear to him, so that he might extract from it the higher incitement to devotion, and more sensible comfort in the midst of his austerities and apostolic labours.

"This truth is further confirmed by the quality of the wood from which the statue is carved, which is commonly believed to be cedar; by the Eastern character of the work; by the resemblance both of the lineament and the colour to those of other statues by St. Luke; by the tradition of the neighbourhood, which extends in an unbroken and well-assured line to the time of St. Eusebius himself; by the miracles that have been worked here by its presence, and elsewhere by its invocation, or even by indirect contact with it; by the miracles, lastly, which are inherent in the image itself,[*] and which endure to this day, such as is its immunity from all worm and from the decay which would

---

* "Dalle meraviglie finalmente che sono inerenti al simulacro stesso." —Cenni storico artistici intorno al santuario di Oropa. (Prof. Maurizio, Marocco. Turin, Milan, 1866, p. 329.)

naturally have occurred in it through time and damp —more especially in the feet, through the rubbing of religious objects against them.

.   .   .   .   .

"The authenticity of this image is so certainly and clearly established, that all supposition to the contrary becomes inexplicable and absurd. Such, for example, is a hypothesis that it should not be attributed to the Evangelist, but to another Luke, also called 'Saint,' and a Florentine by birth. This painter lived in the eleventh century—that is to say, about seven centuries after the image of Oropa had been known and venerated! This is indeed an anachronism.

"Other difficulties drawn either from the ancient discipline of the Church or from St. Luke the Evangelist's profession, which was that of a physician, vanish at once when it is borne in mind—firstly, that the cult of holy images, and especially of that of the most blessed Virgin, is of extreme antiquity in the Church, and of apostolic origin, as is proved by ecclesiastical writers and monuments found in the catacombs which date as far back as the first century (see among other authorities, Nicolas, La Vergine vivente nella Chiesa, lib. iii. cap. iii. § 2); secondly, that as the medical profession does not exclude that of artists, St. Luke may have been both artist and physician; that he did actually handle both the brush and the scalpel is established by respectable and very old traditions, to say nothing of other arguments which can be found in impartial and learned writers upon such matters."

I will only give one more extract. It runs:—

"In 1855 a celebrated Roman portrait-painter, after having carefully inspected the image of the Virgin

Mary at Oropa, declared it to be certainly a work of the first century of our era." *

I once saw a common cheap china copy of this Madonna announced as to be given away with two pounds of tea, in a shop near Hatton Garden.

The church in which the sacred image is kept is interesting from the pilgrims who at all times frequent it, and from the collection of votive pictures which adorn its walls. Except the votive pictures and the pilgrims the church contains little of interest, and I will pass on to the constitution and objects of the establishment.

The objects are—1. Gratuitous lodging to all comers for a space of from three to nine days as the rector may think fit. 2. A school. 3. Help to the sick and poor. It is governed by a president and six members, who form a committee. Four members are chosen by the communal council, and two by the cathedral chapter of Biella. At the hospice itself there reside a director, with his assistant, a surveyor to keep the fabric in repair, a rector or dean with six priests, called *cappellani*, and a medical man. "The government of the laundry," so runs the statute on this head, "and analogous domestic services are entrusted to a competent number of ladies of sound constitution and good conduct, who live together in the hospice under the direction of an inspectress, and are called daughters of Oropa."

The bye-laws of the establishment are conceived in a kindly, genial spirit, which in great measure accounts for its unmistakable popularity. We understood that the poorer visitors, as a general rule, avail themselves of the gratuitous lodging, without making any present when they leave, but in spite of this it is quite clear

* Marocco, p. 331.

that they are wanted to come, and come they accordingly do. It is sometimes difficult to lay one's hands upon the exact passages which convey an impression, but as we read the bye-laws which are posted up in the cloisters, we found ourselves continually smiling at the manner in which almost anything that looked like a prohibition could be removed with the consent of the director. There is no rule whatever about visitors attending the church; all that is required of them is that they do not interfere with those who do. They must not play games of chance, or noisy games; they must not make much noise of any sort after ten o'clock at night (which corresponds about with midnight in England). They should not draw upon the walls of their rooms, nor cut the furniture. They should also keep their rooms clean, and not cook in those that are more expensively furnished. This is about all that they must not do, except fee the servants, which is most especially and particularly forbidden. If any one infringes these rules, he is to be admonished, and in case of grave infraction or continued misdemeanor he may be expelled and not readmitted.

Visitors who are lodged in the better-furnished apartments can be waited upon if they apply at the office; the charge is twopence for cleaning a room, making the bed, bringing water, &c. If there is more than one bed in a room, a penny must be paid for every bed over the first. Boots can be cleaned for a penny, shoes for a halfpenny. For carrying wood, &c., either a halfpenny or a penny will be exacted according to the time taken. Payment for these services must not be made to the servant, but at the office.

The gates close at ten o'clock at night, and open at sunrise, " but if any visitor wishes to make Alpine excursions, or has any other sufficient reason, he should let the director know." Families occupying many rooms must—when the hospice is very crowded, and when they have had due notice—manage to pack themselves into a smaller compass. No one can have rooms kept for him. It is to be strictly " first come, first served." No one must sublet his room. Visitors must not go away without giving up the key of their room. Candles and wood may be bought at a fixed price.

Any one wishing to give anything to the support of the hospice must do so only to the director, the official who appoints the apartments, the dean or the cappellani, or to the inspectress of the daughters of Oropa, but they must have a receipt for even the smallest sum; alms-boxes, however, are placed here and there into which the smaller offerings may be dropped (we imagine this means anything under a franc).

The poor will be fed as well as housed for three days gratuitously—provided their health does not require a longer stay; but they must not beg on the premises of the hospice; professional beggars will be at once handed over to the mendicity society in Biella, or even perhaps to prison. The poor for whom a hydropathic course is recommended, can have it under the regulations made by the committee—that is to say, if there is a vacant place.

There are *trattorie* and cafés at the hospice, where refreshments may be obtained both good and cheap. Meat is to be sold there at the prices current in Biella; bread at two centimes the chilogramma more, to pay for the cost of carriage.

Such are the bye-laws of this remarkable institution.

Few except the very rich are so under-worked that

two or three days of change and rest are not at times a boon to them, while the mere knowledge that there is a place where repose can be had cheaply and pleasantly is itself a source of strength. Here, so long as the visitor wishes to be merely housed, no questions are asked; no one is refused admittance, except for some obviously sufficient reason; it is like getting a reading ticket for the British Museum, there is practically but one test—that is to say, desire on the part of the visitor—the coming proves the desire, and this suffices. A family, we will say, has just gathered its first harvest; the heat on the plains is intense, and the malaria from the rice-grounds little less than pestilential; what, then, can be nicer than to lock up the house and go for three days to the bracing mountain air of Oropa? So at daybreak off they all start trudging, it may be, their thirty or forty miles, and reaching Oropa by nightfall. If there is a weakly one among them, some arrangement is sure to be practicable whereby he or she can be helped to follow more leisurely, and can remain longer at the hospice. Once arrived, they generally, it is true, go the round of the chapels, and make some slight show of pilgrimage, but the main part of their time is spent in doing absolutely nothing. It is sufficient amusement to them to sit on the steps, or lie about under the shadow of the trees, and neither say anything nor do anything, but simply breathe, and look at the sky and at each other. We saw scores of such people just resting instinctively in a kind of blissful waking dream. Others saunter along the walks which have been cut in the woods that surround the hospice, or if they have been pent up in a town and have a fancy for climbing, there are mountain excursions, for the making of which the hospice affords excellent headquarters, and which are looked upon with every favour by the authorities.

It must be remembered also that the accommodation provided at Oropa is much better than what the people are, for the most part, accustomed to in their own homes, and the beds are softer, more often beaten up, and cleaner than those they have left behind them. Besides, they have sheets—and beautifully clean sheets. Those who know the sort of place in which an Italian peasant is commonly content to sleep, will understand how much he must enjoy a really clean and comfortable bed, especially when he has not got to pay for it. Sleep, in the circumstances of comfort which most readers will be accustomed to, is a more expensive thing than is commonly supposed. If we sleep eight hours in a London hotel we shall have to pay from 4d. to 6d. an hour, or from 1d. to $1\frac{1}{2}$d. for every fifteen minutes we lie in bed; nor is it reasonable to believe that the charge is excessive when we consider the vast amount of competition which exists. There is many a man the expenses of whose daily meat, drink, and clothing are less than what an accountant would show us we, many of us, lay out nightly upon our sleep. The cost of really comfortable sleep-necessaries cannot, of course, be nearly so great at Oropa as in a London hotel, but they are enough to put them beyond the reach of the peasant under ordinary circumstances, and he relishes them all the more when he can get them.

But why, it may be asked, should the peasant have these things if he cannot afford to pay for them; and why should he not pay for them if he can afford to do so? If such places as Oropa were common, would not lazy vagabonds spend their lives in going the rounds of them, &c., &c.? Doubtless if there were many Oropas, they would do more harm than good, but there are some things which answer perfectly well as rarities or on a small scale, out of which all the virtue would depart if they were common or on a larger one; and certainly the impression left upon our minds by Oropa was that its effects were excellent.

Granted the sound rule to be that a man should pay for what he has, or go without it; in practice, however, it is found impossible to carry this rule out strictly. Why does the nation give A. B., for instance, and all comers a large, comfortable, well-ventilated, warm room to sit in, with chair, table, reading-desk, &c., all more commodious than what he may have at home, without making him pay a sixpence for it directly from year's end to year's end? The three or nine days' visit to Oropa is a trifle in comparison with what we can all of us obtain in London if we care about it enough to take a very small amount of trouble. True, one cannot sleep in the reading-room of the British Museum—not all night, at least—but by day one can make a home of it for years together except during cleaning times, and then it is hard if one cannot get into the National Gallery or South Kensington, and be warm, quiet, and entertained without paying for it.

It will be said that it is for the national interest that people should have access to treasuries of art or knowledge, and therefore it is worth the nation's while to pay for placing the means of doing so at their disposal; granted, but is not a good bed one of the great ends of knowledge, whereto it must work, if it is to be accounted knowledge at all? and it is not worth a nation's while that her children should now and again have practical experience of a higher state of things than the one

they are accustomed to, and a few days' rest and change
of scene and air, even though she may from time to
time have to pay something in order to enable them to
do so? There can be few books which do an averagely-
educated Englishman so much good, as the glimpse of
comfort which he gets by sleeping in a good bed in a
well-appointed room does to an Italian peasant; such
a glimpse gives him an idea of higher potentialities in
connection with himself, and nerves him to exertions
which he would not otherwise make. On the whole,
therefore, we concluded that if the British Museum
reading-room was in good economy, Oropa was so also;
at any rate, it seemed to be making a large number of
very nice people quietly happy—and it is hard to say
more than this in favour of any place or institution.

The idea of any sudden change is as repulsive to
us as it will be to the greater number of my readers;
but if asked whether we thought our English universities would do most good in their present condition
as places of so-called education, or if they were turned
into Oropas, and all the educational part of the story
totally suppressed, we inclined to think they would be
more popular and more useful in this latter capacity.
We thought also that Oxford and Cambridge were
just the places, and contained all the appliances and
endowments almost ready made for constituting two
splendid and truly imperial cities of recreation—universities in deed as well as in name. Nevertheless
we should not venture to propose any further actual
reform during the present generation than to carry the
principle which is already admitted as regards the
M.A. a degree a trifle further, and to make the B.A.
degree a mere matter of lapse of time and fees—leaving
the little go, and whatever corresponds to it at Oxford,

as the final examination. This would be enough for the present.

There is another sanctuary about three hours' walk over the mountain behind Oropa, at Andorno, and dedicated to St. John. We were prevented by the weather from visiting it, but understand that its objects are much the same as those of the institution I have just described. I will now proceed to the third sanctuary for which the neighbourhood of Biella is renowned.

.   .   .   .

At Graglia I was shown all over the rooms in which strangers are lodged, and found them not only comfortable but luxurious—decidedly more so than those of Oropa; there was the same cleanliness everywhere which I had noticed in the restaurant. As one stands at the windows or on the balconies and looks down to the tops of the chestnuts, and over these to the plains, one feels almost as if one could fly out of the window like a bird; for the slope of the hills is so rapid that one has a sense of being already suspended in mid-air.

I thought I observed a desire to attract English visitors in the pictures which I saw in the bedrooms. Thus there was "A view of the Black-lead Mine in Cumberland," a coloured English print of the end of the last century or the beginning of this, after, I think, Loutherbourg, and in several rooms there were English engravings after Martin. The English will not, I thing, regret if they yield to these attractions. They will find the air cool, shady walks, good food, and reasonable prices. Their rooms will not be charged for, but they will do well to give the same as they would have paid at a hotel. I saw in one room one of those flippant, frivolous, Lorenzo de' Medici matchboxes on which there was a gaudily-coloured nymph in high-heeled boots and tights, smoking a cigarette. Feeling that I was in a sanctuary, I was a little surprised that such a matchbox should have been tolerated. I suppose it had been left behind by some guest. I should myself select a matchbox with the Nativity or the Flight into Egypt upon it, if I were going to stay a week or so at Graglia. I do not think I can have looked surprised or scandalised, but the worthy official who was with me could just see that there was something on my mind. "Do you want a match?" said he, immediately reaching me the box. I helped myself, and the matter dropped.

There were many fewer people at Graglia than at Oropa, and they were richer. I did not see any poor about, but I may have been there during a slack time. An impression was left upon me, though I cannot say whether it was well or ill founded, as though there were a tacit understanding between the establishments at Oropa and Graglia that the one was to adapt itself to the poorer, and the other to the richer classes of society; and this not from any sordid motive, but from a recognition of the fact that any great amount of intermixture between the poor and the rich is not found satisfactory to either one or the other. Any wide difference in fortune does practically amount to a specific difference, which renders the members of either species more or less suspicious of those of the other, and seldom fertile *inter se*. The well-to-do working-man can help his poorer friends better than we can. If an educated man has money to spare, he will apply it better in helping poor educated people than those who are more strictly called the poor. As long as the world is progressing, wide class distinctions are inevitable;

their discontinuance will be a sign that equilibrium has been reached. Then human civilisation will become as stationary as that of ants and bees. Some may say it will be very sad when this is so; others, that it will be a good thing; in truth, it is good either way, for progress and equilibrium have each of them advantages and disadvantages which make it impossible to assign superiority to either; but in both cases the good greatly overbalances the evil; for in both the great majority will be fairly well contented, and would hate to live under any other system.

Equilibrium, if it is ever reached, will be attained very slowly, and the importance of any change in a system depends entirely upon the rate at which it is made. No amount of change shocks—or, in other words, is important—if it is made sufficiently slowly, while hardly any change is too small to shock if it is made suddenly. We may go down a ladder of ten thousand feet in height if we do so step by step, while a sudden fall of six or seven feet may kill us. The importance, therefore, does not lie in the change, but in the abruptness of its introduction. Nothing is absolutely important or absolutely unimportant; absolutely good, or absolutely bad.

This is not what we like to contemplate. The instinct of those whose religion and culture are on the surface only is to conceive that they have found, or can find, an absolute and eternal standard, about which they can be as earnest as they choose. They would have even the pains of hell eternal if they could. If there had been any means discoverable by which they could torment themselves beyond endurance, we may be sure they would long since have found it out; but fortunately there is a stronger power which bars them inexorably from their desire, and which has ensured that intolerable pain shall last only for a very little while. For either the circumstances or the sufferer will change after no long time. If the circumstances are intolerable, the sufferer dies: if they are not intolerable, he becomes accustomed to them, and will cease to feel them grievously. No matter what the burden, there always has been, and always must be, a way for us also to escape.

A PSALM OF MONTREAL.

[The City of Montreal is one of the most rising and, in many respects, most agreeable on the American continent, but its inhabitants are as yet too busy with commerce to care greatly about the masterpieces of old Greek Art. A cast of one of these masterpieces—the finest of the several statues of Discoboli, or Quoit-throwers—was found by the present writer in the Montreal Museum of Natural History; it was, however, banished from public view, to a room where were all manner of skins, plants, snakes, insects, &c., and in the middle of these, an old man, stuffing an owl. The dialogue—perhaps true, perhaps imaginary, perhaps a little of one and a little of the other—between the writer and this old man gave rise to the lines that follow.]

STOWED away in a Montreal lumber-room,
The Discobolus standeth, and turneth his face to the wall;
Dusty, cobweb-covered, maimed, and set at naught,
Beauty crieth in an attic, and no man regardeth.
　　　　　　　　　O God! O Montreal!

Beautiful by night and day, beautiful in summer and winter,
Whole or maimed, always and alike beautiful,—
He preacheth gospel of grace to the skins of owls,
And to one who seasoneth the skins of Canadian owls.
　　　　　　　　　O God! O Montreal!

When I saw him, I was wroth, and I said, "O Discobolus!
Beautiful Discobolus, a Prince both among gods and men,
What doest thou here, how camest thou here, Discobolus,
Preaching gospel in vain to the skins of owls?"
　　　　　　　　　O God! O Montreal!

And I turned to the man of skins, and said unto him, "Oh!
    thou man of skins,
Wherefore hast thou done thus, to shame the beauty of the
    Discobolus?"
But the Lord had hardened the heart of the man of skins,
And he answered, "My brother-in-law is haberdasher to Mr.
    Spurgeon."   O God! O Montreal!

"The Discobolus is put here because he is vulgar,—
He hath neither vest nor pants with which to cover his
    limbs;
I, sir, am a person of most respectable connections,—
My brother-in-law is haberdasher to Mr. Spurgeon."
                       O God! O Montreal!

Then I said, "O brother-in law to Mr. Spurgeon's haber-
    dasher!
Who seasonest also the skins of Canadian owls,
Thou callest 'trousers' 'pants,' whereas I call them
    'trousers,'
Therefore thou art in hell-fire, and may the Lord pity thee!
                       O God! O Montreal!

"Preferrest thou the gospel of Montreal to the gospel of
    Hellas,
The gospel of thy connection with Mr. Spurgeon's haber-
    dashery to the gospel of the Discobolus?"
Yet none the less blasphemed he beauty, saying, "The
    Discobolus hath no gospel,—
But my brother-in-law is haberdasher to Mr. Spurgeon."
                       O God! O Montreal!

PRINTED BY BALLANTYNE, HANSON AND CO.
EDINBURGH AND LONDON.

BRITISH
1 2 MA 84
MUSEUM

Works by the same Author.

——o——

Sixth Edition. Crown 8vo, Cloth, 6s.
EREWHON ; or, OVER THE RANGE. Op. 1.
A WORK OF SATIRE AND IMAGINATION.

Second Edition. Demy 8vo, Cloth, 7s. 6d.
THE FAIR HAVEN. Op. 2.

A work in Defence of the Miraculous Element in our Lord's
Ministry on earth, both as against Rationalistic Impugners and
certain Orthodox Defenders. Written under the pseudonym
of JOHN PICKARD OWEN, with a Memoir by his supposed
brother, WILLIAM BICKERSTETH OWEN.

Second Edition. Crown 8vo, Cloth, 7s. 6d.
LIFE AND HABIT. Op. 3.

AN ESSAY AFTER A COMPLETER VIEW OF EVOLUTION.

Second Edition, with Appendix and Index. Crown 8vo, Cloth, 10s. 6d.
EVOLUTION, OLD AND NEW. Op. 4.

A Comparison of the theories of Buffon, Dr. Erasmus Darwin, and
Lamarck, with that of the late Mr. Charles Darwin, with copious
extracts from the works of the three first-named writers.

Crown 8vo, Cloth, 7s. 6d.
UNCONSCIOUS MEMORY. Op. 5.

A Comparison between the theory of Dr. Ewald Hering, Professor
of Physiology at the University of Prague, and the "Philosophy
of the Unconscious" of Dr. Edward Von Hartmann, with
translations from both these authors, and preliminary chapters
bearing on "Life and Habit," "Evolution, Old and New,"
and Mr. Charles Darwin's edition of Dr. Krause's "Erasmus
Darwin."

Pott Quarto, Cloth, 21s.
ALPS AND SANCTUARIES OF PIEDMONT AND THE CANTON TICINO. Op. 6.

Profusely Illustrated by Charles Gogin, H. F. Jones,
and the Author.

CPSIA information can be obtained at www.ICGtesting.com
Printed in the USA
LVOW071742030612

284456LV00012B/87/P